D0983458

City-Systems
in Advanced Economies

City-Systems in Advanced Economies

Past Growth, Present Processes
and Future Development Options

Allan Pred

Professor of Geography
University of California,
Berkeley

A Halsted Press Book

John Wiley & Sons, New York

Published in the U.S.A. by Halsted Press,
a Division of John Wiley & Sons, Inc.
New York.

Library of Congress Cataloging in Publication Data.
Pred, Allan Richard, 1936 –
    City-Systems in Advanced Economies.

    "A Halsted Press book."
    Bibliography.
    1. Urban economics.   2. Cities and towns – Growth.
I. Title
HT321.P73 1977   330.9′173′2   76-58376
ISBN 0-470-99073-2

Printed in Great Britain

Contents

A note to the reader

In large measure this book combines key elements from my previous writings with completely new materials to present what is, I hope, a well-integrated heuristic view of the past and ongoing growth and development processes of city-systems in advanced economies. Certain elementary concepts are spelled out because it is assumed that many readers will be students with little or no previous training in geography. In order to meet the needs of more advanced students and interested scholars, new materials are formulated at length, numerous references are provided, and clarifying footnotes and table notes are included. It is hoped that sufficient insights are provided in the initial portions of this book to enable readers of all levels to consider the final chapter's discussion of future development options with a highly critical eye. For, if adequate, the insights supplied should permit the readers of any advanced economy to reach independent conclusions concerning regional development and national settlement policy choices in their own country.

1 Basic problems and basic concepts

Introduction

To much of the population in the economically advanced nations of Western Europe, North America, Japan and the southwest Pacific this is an age of bewilderment, powerlessness and alienation. Problem-causing changes in the political, economic and social environment follow one another at a rapid pace. Particular changes – whether they occur on a local, regional, national or international scale – are generally fleetingly perceived and dimly comprehended because so much is occurring simultaneously, because there is often so little in the way of repetitive or redundant information, and because the individual normally is so far removed from the source(s) of trans-formation. Many individuals and groups find that the overall flurry of change-related problems associated with economic in-stability, periodic resource shortages, environmental pollution and the increasing concentration of power in large business organiza-tions is not readily sorted into simply diagnosed groups. In the face of all this it is perhaps not unwarranted for the geographer to attempt to provide some interpretative and planning-relevant insights into a small but significant subset of these basic problems by, among other things, identifying the processes by which interdependent cities and regions – or systems of cities – grow and develop in economically advanced societies.

One of the most widespread basic problems stemming from to-day's quickly changing economic, technological and political en-vironment is unemployment. While unemployment of both the short-term and long-term varieties is a pervasive problem in the United States, the United Kingdom, and just about every other highly in-dustrialized capitalist country, it is more acute and persistent in some regions than in others (Robinson, 1969; EFTA, 1974; Hansen, 1974). Because of this fact, regional and national policy-makers and planners have become increasingly concerned with creating interregionally equitable labour-market conditions (Sundqvist, 1975). In the minds of some, an interregional equality of labour-market conditions does not only require a short-run sizable reduction of unemployment in those regions where it is most severe. It also implies an interregionally comparable spectrum of differentiated job opportunity types to insure that people dwelling in regions which are currently 'backward', 'lagging' or 'depressed' will be able to withstand future business-cycle fluctuations and structural changes in the economy. (An interregionally comparable spectrum of employment alternatives can also be equated with a levelling out of interregional discrepancies in *per capita* income). In order fully to appreciate the difficulties entailed in reducing or eliminating interregional inequalities of employment opportunity, it is necessary to gain at least some preliminary comprehension of the processes by which systems of cities grow and develop. This is so because the processes that alter the spatial distribution of job opportunities in advanced economies – or 'post-industrial' societies – are essentially synonymous with the processes affecting the growth and development of systems of cities.

Interregional inequalities of employment opportunity are but one symptom of interregional variations in the 'quality of life'. The growing public concern with preservation of the natural environment, social justice and the welfare of the individual called forth by the multitude of recent problem-inducing changes has been translated by planners, politicians and others into a concern with the 'quality of life'. This phrase has been used loosely and ambiguously to symbolize collectively both people's living conditions and the goals of urban and regional planning. One common denominator is to be found among the various definitions given to this term. At the very least the 'quality of life' in a city or region refers to the accessibility of its inhabitants to employment alternatives, educational and medical facilities, essential public social services, a representative range of commercial and cultural services, and 'nature', or extensive recreational open spaces. For all but the last-named criterion, accessibility is normally greatest in the largest metropolitan complexes, or conurbations, of a nation. Despite the decline of central cities and many 'inner suburbs' much recent population and employment growth in the United States, France, Great Britain, Canada, Australia and other advanced economies has been concentrated in *or* around large metropolitan complexes. As a result of rising property costs, the extension of freeway systems and new communications technology, population and employment growth has been especially noticeable in the peripheral areas of the 'urban fields' within 50–120 miles of the traditional cores of large metropolitan complexes, where small- and medium-size 'metropolitan areas' with populations of 50000 to 500000 or more are found (e.g. Alonso and Medrich, 1972; Beaujeu-Garnier, 1974; Berry, 1973; Burnley, 1974; Richardson, 1973b; Simmons, 1974a).[1]* That is, the polarization of much growth around certain already large metropolitan complexes has perpetuated interregional inequalities in most aspects of the 'quality of life' (cf. Wingo, 1973). At the same time, the negative features of population concentration in large metropolitan complexes – lengthy commuting journeys, congestion, unnecessarily large and impersonal public service units, stress, individual and group alienation, and pollution – are widely regarded with increasing uneasiness by residents, potential migrants and planners alike. This combination of forces has led to efforts in most advanced economies to develop policies capable of simultaneously dampening the future growth of large metropolitan complexes – even if that is already occurring – and enhancing the growth and 'quality of life' of presently disadvantaged regions. In order clearly to realize the difficulties of greatly or completely reversing the growth of large metropolitan complexes – and their expanding peripheries – so as to improve conditions elsewhere, it is once again necessary to acquire some grasp on the processes by which entire systems of cities grow and develop. This is so because the growth of individual metropolitan complexes does not occur in an isolated vacuum, but is instead greatly influenced by events both in other metropolitan centres and in lesser cities and towns.

The primary objective of this book is to provide at least provisional answers to two interrelated questions. What are the processes underlying the past and present growth and development of large 'post-industrial' metropolitan complexes and the economically advanced systems of cities to which they belong? What are the implications of the ongoing processes of city-system growth and development for efforts to reduce or largely eliminate interregional inequalities of employment opportunity? Examination of the latter question will permit brief consideration of an overlapping third question. What are the implications of the ongoing processes of city-system growth and development for efforts to stimulate long-

---

* Superior figures refer to notes on pages 219–30.

term 'quality-of-life' improvements in 'backward', 'lagging' or 'depressed' regions?

The answers to these questions to be provided on the following pages are far from definitive or exhaustive. At present the state of knowledge relating to the processes that generate metropolitan concentration and interregional economic and social inequalities must be regarded as little more than primitive. Moreover, the factors influencing the growth and development of economically advanced city-systems are so numerous and complex that in all likelihood they prohibit a complete and definitive modelling of their operation (cf. Simmons, 1974b). Hence only heuristic models are presently possible. In this context it must be confessed that the concepts, perspectives and interpretations that subsequently appear here are not necessarily those that would be presented by other geographers seeking to answer the same or related questions.

The strategy to be used in dealing with the three above-mentioned questions is as follows. First, some concepts basic to the discussion of city-system growth are introduced in the remainder of this chapter. These include the fundamental properties of systems of cities; 'spatial biases' in the circulation and availability of specialized information and their impact on locational decision-making; and the relationship between the matching of 'population' and 'activity' systems on the one hand, and migration and local and non-local employment multiplier effects on the other hand. In the next chapter the growth and development of systems of cities during the nineteenth and early twentieth centuries are given a summary interpretation. This step is undertaken both because of repeated evidence concerning the very long-term stability in the national or regional population rank of today's leading metropolitan complexes, and because of the means by which early established channels of interurban growth transmission apparently become deeply ingrained and thereby influence subsequent channels of interurban growth transmission. In the third chapter the processes of contemporary city-system growth in economically advanced countries are interpreted. Here the emphasis is on the role played by 'multilocational organizations', or those large business and government organizations that comprise a number of functionally differentiated and spatially separated units. These organizations are objects of focus because they dominate highly industrialized economies and because they directly or indirectly account for most of the employment and interurban growth transmission that occurs in such economies. Finally, future regional development and national settlement policy alternatives are considered in the light of what has been learned about large multilocational organizations and the growth and development processes of systems of cities. Future planning alternatives are placed in this context since experience has shown that – in the absence of any understanding of the processes of interurban growth transmission – regional planning policies in advanced economies have for the most part yielded quite modest results, especially in terms of creating interregionally comparable labour-market conditions. In accord with continuing structural shifts in the occupational composition of the work force in advanced economies, in this final chapter particular stress is placed on the future locational alternatives for administrative functions, related business services and office activities in general.

Selected basic concepts

Fundamental properties of systems of cities

The term 'system of cities', as used here, encompasses all those individual urban units – however defined – in a country or large region which are economically linked to one or more other individual urban units in the same country or large region. More precisely, a system of cities is defined as a national or regional set of cities which are interdependent in such a way that any significant change in the economic activities, occupational structure, total income or population of one member city will directly or indirectly bring about some modification in the economic activities, occupational structure, total income, or population of one or more other set members (cf. Berry, 1964; Wärneryd, 1968; Bourne, 1974, 1975).[2] A system of cities may be regarded as a particular example of a 'complex social system'. As such it is an open system, i.e. some of the units belonging to the system interact directly with units outside the system (cities in other countries or regions) and the system as a whole may be affected by events occurring elsewhere. As a 'complex social system' a system of cities can be expected also to have a structural pattern of interdependencies and information linkages between its units that becomes increasingly intricate with the passage of time (Buckley, 1967).

In so far as growth and development processes are concerned, perhaps the two most important attributes of any national or regional set of cities are the extent and structural composition of its internal interdependencies and its degree of openness or closure. The economic interdependence of cities always has an interactional counterpart. That is, in order for economic change in one city to call forth economic change in another urban centre there must be some form of interaction between the two places. Such interaction may take the form of goods shipments, service provision, capital movements, or the flow of specialized information. (Flows of specialized information are always involved when cities are interdependent, for the movement of goods, services and capital between places cannot occur without some exchange of information (Pred, 1973a).) When the internal interaction, or interdependence, and closure characteristics of a national or regional set of cities are jointly considered, the principal growth determinants of individual urban units within the set can be grossly generalized. For illustrative purposes, a wide spectrum of combined internal interdependence and closure conditions can be collapsed into four categories (cf. Vapnarsky, 1969).

Low internal interaction, or interdependence, and high closure   In these circumstances the cities of a given territory participate in little or no economic exchange either among themselves or with cities located elsewhere. Without any significant internal or external interdependence, the urban settlements in question by definition do not belong to any system of cities. Such conditions are virtually nonexistent today, but were sometimes characteristic of small feudally organized states in, for example, medieval Europe and precolonial Africa. The growth of a city which did not belong to a system of cities (as here defined) normally depended upon its exploitation of a surrounding agricultural hinterland, especially through the appropriation of surplus production (cf. Harvey, 1973, pp. 238–40).[3]

Low internal interaction, or interdependence, and low closure   In this instance the cities of a country or extensive region are not bound together by economic flows of any magnitude but are intensely connected by economic linkages to cities located in the 'outside world'. In the absence of any important internal interaction, such sets of cities cannot in themselves constitute a true national or regional system of cities. Instead they function as outliers of city-systems situated elsewhere. The port cities of colonies – whether in eighteenth-century North America or nineteenth- and twentieth-century Africa, Asia and Latin America – best exemplified this category in the past (e.g. Vance, 1970). Even now, the port cities of former colonies frequently continue to exhibit the features of this category. Particularly in West Africa there are large port cities that function basically as economic couplings between their interior hinterlands and one or a few foreign powers, but have little interaction with major sister ports (Logan, 1970). Significantly, the principal cities and metropolitan areas of the 'backward' and 'depressed' regions of advanced economies usually do not interact enough to form well-integrated growth-transmitting regional city-systems, but instead stand in a 'colonial' relationship to other parts of the national city-system. Thus, the major urban centres of Appalachia are not closely linked economically to one another, but are well tied to various large metropolitan complexes elsewhere in the United States (Hale, 1972). Likewise, the largest urban centres in Sweden's comparatively 'lagging' northern region of Norrland – Sundsvall, Luleå and Umeå – have few linkages with each other. Instead they interact primarily with Stockholm and secondarily with Göteborg, Malmö, and other urban units in south-central and southern Sweden. Whatever the particular national or regional case, the growth and development of individual cities belonging to sets in this category is largely determined by external economic decisions and actions.

High internal interaction, or interdependence, and low closure   Under this pair of conditions most of the urban units of a country or large region possess strong economic linkages with other set members, while several cities simultaneously exchange a considerable volume of goods, services and specialized information with foreign (or extraregional) centres via overland, sea or air transportation. These twin circumstances typify the national systems of cities of most industrialized economies. The city-systems of Japan, Australia, New Zealand and individual Western European countries, for example, fall into this category because a relatively large share of the gross national product is tied up in international trade, and because domestically headquartered business organizations have sizable operations overseas at the same time that foreign headquartered business organizations have extensive domestic holdings. Similarly, the city-systems of certain broadly defined regions, such as the Northeastern US or the US Pacific Coast, can be placed in this category because of the scope of their interregional goods and service trade and the nature of their corporate ownership relationships. By definition, the growth or decline of individual urban units belonging to sets in this category is highly influenced by the growth or decline of other city-system members and, in many instances, external economic decisions and actions.

High internal interaction, or interdependence, and high closure   Here most of the members of a set of cities have important economic ties with several other urban units in the same set, while the system as a whole has relatively weak relationships with places located beyond its borders. The occurrence of this unusual combination of circumstances is confined to a very few cases, and even then can be perceived only by some stretching of the imagination. The national city-systems of the USSR and the United States can be assigned to this category because, despite great absolute import and export volumes, a relatively small fraction (6 per cent or less) of the gross national product is involved in international trade. (Actually, in this and other contexts it is more accurate to speak of a single US–Canadian system of cities – in spite of the somewhat retarding effect the border between the two countries has on urban–economic interaction (Simmons, 1974a). The unification of the US and Canadian city-systems is largely justified by the fact that US-based corporations own a larger share of the assets of all Canadian manufacturing, petroleum and natural gas, and mining and smelting activities than do business organizations based in Canada itself.)[4] It is also possible to regard the metropolitan areas of the advanced economies of Western Europe as constituting a single system of cities that belongs in this category. Such a gesture is not unreasonable given, first, the growing reliance of manufacturers in different Western European countries on one another for component inputs; secondly, the fact that most of the leading foreign trade partners of any specific Western European country are other Western European countries; and, finally, the specific multinational characteristics of so many of the largest business organizations based in Western Europe. With few exceptions, the growth and development of individual urban units belonging to this type of city-system are influenced primarily by the growth and development of other city-system members, and only secondarily – if at all – by external economic decisions and actions.

The properties of systems of cities are frequently discussed in terms of Zipf's (1941) rank-size rule (e.g. Berry, 1961; Berry and Horton, 1970; Robson, 1973). In its simplest form the rank-size rule states that the population of any city n (expressed as P_n) is equal to the population of the country's or region's largest city (P_1) divided by the national or regional population rank of the city in question (r_n); i.e. $P_n = P_1/r_n$. Or, the second largest city should have a population one-half that of the largest national or regional city, the tenth largest city should have a population one-tenth of the largest national or regional city, and so on. In many countries and regions the rank-size rule does not hold unless r_n is weighted by a constant. In yet other instances, the rule does not hold at all because of the existence of a 'primate' city which is many times the size of the next ranking cities. It has been hypothesized at times that a clear rank-size distribution of city sizes reflects a well-integrated and economically advanced regional or national city-system, while a primate-city distribution of city sizes reflects a poorly integrated and economically underdeveloped city-system. However, this hypothesis does not hold: e.g. the rank-size rule is inapplicable to economically advanced countries such as Denmark and Australia (cf. von Böventer, 1973). Moreover, the just completed discussion of combined internal interdependence and closure categories indicated that the cities of a country or region occasionally belong to a larger city-system to which rank-size analysis could perhaps be more meaningfully applied. In addition, the rank-size rule at present is no more than an empirical regularity with no agreed theoretical foundation. For these reasons the rank-size rule is not further employed here for either descriptive or interpretative purposes.

In the conventional geographic and planning literature on systems of cities excessive emphasis is placed on the hierarchical structure of interdependencies. This often uncritical and unjustified emphasis is derived from the central-place theories of Christaller (1966) and, to a lesser degree, Lösch (1954).[5] According to Christallerian central-place theory the variety of consumer goods and services offered by establishments in cities of a class, or order, of given size is dependent upon the number of 'thresholds' the combined population of the city and its hinterland can fulfil. (A 'threshold' is the minimum volume of sales or demand necessary to sustain economically a given type of establishment, e.g. a gas station, bank or department store.) That is, the greater the population of a city and its hinterland, the greater the array of retail goods and services it can offer. Moreover, whenever a city cannot fulfil a given threshold level, it must obtain that class of goods and services from the nearest more populous city which does meet the threshold requirement in question. Thus the market areas of cities of each size class are 'nested' into the market areas of higher-order centres until – with respect to the very highest threshold goods and services – the entire country or region falls within the market area of the single largest urban unit. As should become evident from the next two chapters, the resulting hierarchical pattern of relationships (Figure 1.1) is highly unrealistic as a

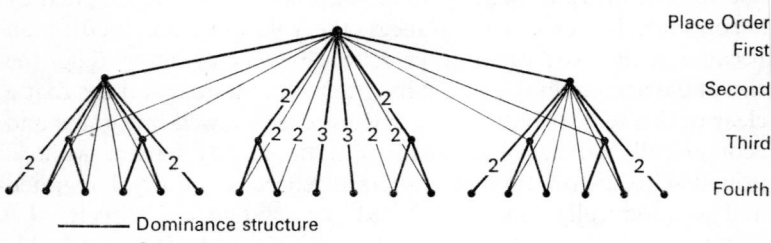

Place Order
First
Second
Third
Fourth

———— Dominance structure
———— Other dyads

Figure 1.1: *The structure of interdependencies, or growth transmission channels, in a Christallerian central-place system organized according to the 'marketing principle', according to which all parts of a region 'are supplied from the minimum possible number of functioning central places'. (Christaller also arrived at strictly hierarchically structured central-place systems according to a 'transportation principle' and an 'administrative principle'. However, his empirical work led him to conclude that 'the marketing principle is the primary and chief law of the distribution of central places'.) The only undiagrammed interdependencies stem from the importation of first-order goods and services from the single first-order place by the six left-most and six right-most fourth-order places. Numbers indicate the number of orders of goods and services procured by smaller cities from larger cities. Unnumbered interdependencies involve only one order of goods and services.*

depiction of the *total* structural composition of city-system inter-dependencies in advanced economies. This is so because the largest urban unit is required to be completely self-reliant, because there can be no large-city interdependence (i.e. no lateral exchange of goods and services between the second- and third-order cities of Figure 1.1), because there can be no larger-city acquisition of goods or services from smaller cities, and because each 'nesting' arrangement culminating at the single first-order place is in effect a fully *closed* regional subsystem of cities.

The structure of interdependencies, or growth-transmission channels, permitted by Löschian central-place theory is somewhat more in conformity with the conditions prevailing in economically advanced systems of cities. Because of the market-area determination principles used in Lösch's less rigid central-place theory, urban size does not automatically define which goods and services are locally available. Consequently, while strictly hierarchical relationships still predominate, interdependence can also occasionally express itself either in the form of comparably-sized places providing some functions for one another, or in the form of larger centres obtaining some goods and services from smaller places. None the less, the Löschian framework is also unrealistic in so far as it requires a city-system's largest unit to be entirely self-supporting and prohibits any large-city interdependencies whatsoever. Lösch's framework is also far removed from real-world conditions in so far as it limits interaction to places located in the same or adjacent 60° sectors, or pie-wedges, of the 'economic landscape' extending outward from the largest centre (Pred, 1971a, 1973a, 1973b).[6]

That the central-place theories of Christaller and Lösch should account for a subset, rather than the complete set, of the interdependence properties in economically advanced systems of cities is understandable. These theories are basically concerned with optimizing the convergence of consumers at points of supply, or with market area and city–hinterland relationships. In contrast, the most critical growth-generating city-system interdependencies in economically advanced countries are largely the product either of input–output relationships, or of job-control and decision-making relationships within multilocational business and government organizations (cf. Parr, 1973a).

'Spatial biases' in the circulation and availability of specialized information and their impact on locational decision-making

Given our definition of a system of cities, the growth and development process of such a system can be seen largely as an accumulation of decisions directly and indirectly affecting the location and size of job-providing activities in the private and public sectors. All the specific locational choices and related economic decisions affecting the evolution of a city-system are to some extent dependent on the decision-making unit's stock of specialized or pertinent information, whether intentionally or unintentionally obtained.[7] This is because all economic and locational actors – whether individual entrepreneurs, business firms and corporations, or government organizations – can choose only from alternatives of which they have become aware either through information search or accidentally acquired information.

The specialized information pertaining to costs, prices, supply, demand, and technological and other matters which influences the decisions underlying city-system growth and development is virtually never universally available. On the contrary, the circulation of specialized information is 'spatially biased'. That is, because of the means by which different forms of specialized information circulate through contact networks, the probability of a particular bundle of specialized information being known or acquired varies from place to place at any given time. And, conversely, any actor possessing specialized information at a given location is more likely to have sought or unintentionally obtained it from some contacts or places rather than others.

Specialized information becomes available and circulates in three different forms: private information, public information, and visual information.

Private information encompasses all information conveyed by person-to-person contacts, including face-to-face meetings, written exchanges via the mails, and telegraph (or 'telex') and telephone encounters. Spatial biases in the circulation of private information have traditionally arisen because of the time and monetary costs associated with acquisition. Nearby private information has always been more cheaply obtained than distant private information. Thus the uniquely detailed total array of contacts – or 'information field' – surrounding an individual's or group's place of work or residence has always been inclined to decrease in density with increasing distance (Hägerstrand, 1965, 1967; Morrill and Pitts, 1967). Constant improvements in transportation and communications technology have tended to diminish – but by no means eliminate – the 'distance decay', or density fall-off, of private information contact networks or fields. High-level business and government decision-makers in contemporary advanced economies frequently devote a great deal of time and money to establishing and maintaining long-distance specialized private information contacts. All the same, their specialized private information fields are usually spatially biased by the existing set of intraorganizational and interorganizational relationships of the corporation or government agency employing them.

Public information consists of all those messages circulated via the printed media, the electronic mass media (radio, television and films), live spoken communication to an audience, and government sources. Information in this category, by definition, reaches its initial recipients without any alteration of its content by one or more third parties. However, in its subsequent circulation, public information is frequently converted into private information of somewhat modified content, through a 'two-step' or 'multi-step' flow. That is, bundles of information often apparently flow from the mass media or a public source to 'influentials' or 'opinion leaders' and from them to 'less active sections of the population' in the form of private information (e.g. Katz, 1957; Rogers and Shoemaker, 1971). Specialized public information of the type under discussion here is usually spatially biased in part because, in modern circumstances, it normally does not appear in the nationwide mass media, but in special-audience newspapers (e.g. the *Wall Street Journal* and the *Financial Times*) and in limited-circulation trade, technical and scientific journals. Publications of this type normally are more quickly and readily available in some places than in others. Furthermore, the circulation of such specialized public information may become spatially biased in so far as it is transformed into private information whose further movement in space and time is apt to be highly influenced by the channels which existing economic relationships follow.

Specialized visual information, or individual visual observations and perceptions, circulates in the sense that individuals bear it from place to place. The availability of specialized visual information (e.g. observation of the operation of some new technology) commonly declines with distance from the point of origin due to the 'distance decay' of human travel patterns. More importantly, visual information, if of any significance, is almost without exception converted into private or public information. Once this happens, visually acquired specialized information is subject to the same spatial biases of availability and circulation as specialized information otherwise obtained.

Most of the decisions that directly and indirectly determine the size and location of job-providing activities, and thereby city-system growth, are especially sensitive to spatial biases in the circulation and availability of specialized information since such decisions are usually made from a small range of alternatives, or after limited search. A variety of inquiries into the decision-making behaviour of individual entrepreneurs and organizations indicate that in the great majority of instances a very limited scanning of the environment is undertaken to eliminate obviously inappropriate alternatives, and that what is deemed to be a 'satisfactory alternative' is selected before the search for information has proceeded very far (e.g. Cyert and March, 1963; Aguilar, 1967; Williams and Scott, 1970; Dicken, 1971; North, 1973). Limited search behaviour often may be economically rational in so far as the marginal cost of search may quickly begin to exceed the marginal improvement in alternatives identified. To the extent that decisions are based upon limited search they are likely to be based upon the most readily accessible specialized information. And the most readily accessible specialized information is almost certain to be spatially biased in one way or another, most typically in the sense that it is obtained from or near the decision-making unit's already existing contacts of both a direct and intermediary character.

The types of decision that are fundamental to the growth and development of systems of cities fall into two broad categories: explicit locational decisions and implicit locational decisions.

Explicit locational decisions occur whenever an entrepreneur, corporation or government agency decides to establish or physically expand a factory, retailing unit, service outlet, office or some other kind of job-providing facility. The impact of spatial biases in the availability and circulation of specialized information on this class of decisions can be seen from at least two perspectives. One possibility is to focus on specific decisions individually – as has been the practice in so much of the literature on industrial-location theory and the geography of manufacturing (Smith, 1971) – and to consider the influence of informational spatial biases on the ultimate location chosen. Another option is to view particular types of job-providing facilities and production processes as innovations and to examine the role of spatial biases in the availability and circulation of specialized information in the diffusion of those growth-inducing innovations. Information circulation is central to such diffusion processes for several reasons. Obviously, the patterns of specialized-information circulation influence the spatial dissemination of knowledge regarding either the existence of any given economic innovation, or the market justification necessary for an organization internally to develop or perfect an innovation. Furthermore, because of the technical, cost or marketing uncertainty to be overcome, and the risk-taking frequently involved (Schon, 1967; Zaltman, Duncan and Holbek, 1973) adoption or rejection of a growth-inducing innovation usually requires that a considerable quantity of redundant and new information be searched for or otherwise acquired. At this point spatially biased information concerning the reactions and experience of previous adopters is frequently crucial. Finally, once a decision to adopt is reached, spatially biased specialized information – especially the existing contacts of the adopting entrepreneur or organization – is likely to affect the selection of a location at which to implement the growth-inducing innovation in question (Pred, 1973a; Lasuen, 1971, 1973). (This need not be necessarily so if the innovation is a technological one that can be appended to an already functioning facility.)

Implicit locational decisions occur every time a business or government unit decides to purchase goods or services, to award a contract or subcontract, or to make some miscellaneous allocation of capital. These decisions – which have been given all too scant attention by geographers and planners – may be relatively insignificant individually, but they are of tremendous aggregate importance to city-system growth and development. These decisions are not usually conceived as being locational in nature by their perpetrators. However, such decisions are locational, and contribute to growth in a spatially discriminating way, in so far as they inevitably must involve some place(s) rather than others.

Implicit locational decisions may be of a routine (programmed) or nonroutine (nonprogrammed) character. Routine implicit locational decision-making normally rests on the direct feedback of information from ongoing organizational activities. Such feedback may indicate, for example, that stocks of a given item have decreased to a level where additional purchases from *an already identified source* are necessary. Such routine decisions require no search for alternatives since the search and spatially biased information employed previously where similar decisions have been made has, via experience feedback, resulted in a learning process and the identification of what is judged to be a satisfactory standard solution (Dicken, 1971; Steed, 1971). In contrast, nonroutine locational decisions have few or no precedents and, by definition, demand the use of search and spatially biased specialized information to identify and select alternatives. In particular, those who make nonroutine locational decisions frequently attempt to reduce uncertainty and avoid perceived risks by choosing alternatives that are 'similar' to those opted for in the recent past either by themselves, or by other firms or organizations of which they have become aware through their spatially biased array of direct and intermediary contacts.

It is to be further recognized that both implicit and explicit locational decisions contribute to further spatial biases in the availability and circulation of specialized information. This is because, when implemented, they always create or expand goods, service, capital or administrative linkages whose existence and maintenance are dependent upon information flows.

So far spatially biased specialized information circulation has been treated solely in terms of its influence on the range of opportunities and alternatives which explicit and implicit locational decision-makers become aware of and choose among. With increasing frequency informational spatial biases are also affecting explicit locational decisions in the sense that place-to-place variations in the availability and accessibility – or *cost* – of information are deliberately considered as a factor of location for administrative headquarters, advertising agencies, banks, other financial intermediaries, law firms, public relations firms, management consultants, data-processing service centres, and office and business-service activities in general. Metropolitan locations where activities of this type are already clustered are generally perceived to offer new or relocating sister units the advantages of, first, easily arranged short-notice group meetings and face-to-face contacts between client and customer; secondly, a greater choice of opportunities; and, thirdly, risk-reducing 'knowledge in a hurry' about changes in the economic or technological environment (e.g. Deutsch, 1961; Goddard, 1973b, 1975; Wilmoth, 1974). The costs of not having a location in a large metropolitan complex favoured by spatial biases in the availability and accessibility of information are ordinarily regarded as prohibitive, especially since numerous office and business-service personnel spend twenty hours or more per week exchanging information (Stewart, 1967; Törnqvist, 1970).

When compared with smaller metropolitan areas and cities, large metropolitan complexes provide superior air-transport connections as well as informational cost savings and spatial biases. In other words, in the age of jet transportation, when the cruising speed of planes precludes many stops, it is inefficient in time and cost terms for a private- or public-sector activity to maintain a wide array of non-local personal contacts from a centre which does not have numerous daily non-stop flights to the leading metropolitan complexes within its given system of cities (Engström and Sahlberg, 1973; Törnqvist, 1973; Pred, 1973c). The air-transport based information advantages of large metropolitan complexes are well illustrated by the Greater London metropolitan complex. There, in recent years, numerous British organizations with operations or business serving the Western European system of cities have placed high-level administrative office units in Croydon and other places within the southern and western portions of the complex so as to have easy access to Gatwick and Heathrow airports.

The cost-factor locational influence of spatial biases in the circulation and availability of specialized information has been mounting over the past two decades in advanced economies because of ongoing structural shifts in the occupational composition of the work force. The work force of any advanced economy which has crossed the threshold of the 'post-industrial' era is generally characterized by a stable or declining number of jobs associated with the processing and transportation of natural resources and already manufactured goods, and an increasing number of jobs associated with the processing and exchange of specialized information. Even before the onset of the recession which became so pronounced in 1974–5, production-line manufacturing jobs in advanced economies had either essentially ceased to grow, as in the case of the United States, or had experienced absolute decreases, as in the case of the United Kingdom and Sweden. At present roughly 50 per cent of all US employment falls within the so-called 'white-collar' occupations, or positions held by administrators, managers, clerical workers, sales personnel and professionals. In addition, 'office workers', or all white-collar workers other than salespersons, now answer for approximately 42 per cent of all US employment – as opposed to 17 per cent in 1900. This group is expected to account for 50 per cent of total US employment some time during the 1980s. Even more significantly, highly salaried office employment has been growing more rapidly than clerical employment. This is largely due to the computerization of routine functions, and the corporate planning activities made necessary by fast technological change and swift alterations in the structure of demand. (In Great Britain, for example, clerical occupations grew by a mere 5 per cent between 1966 and 1971, while administrative and professional employment simultaneously expanded 23 per cent.) Perhaps most importantly, during the 1960s and early 1970s explicit and implicit locational decisions in the US, Great Britain, Sweden and other advanced economies led to a growing concentration of the most information-sensitive office employment in major metropolitan complexes at the same time as those places experienced absolute losses in manufacturing production-line employment (e.g. Armstrong, 1972; Berry, 1973; Cameron and Evans, 1973; Daniels, 1975; Engström, 1974).

The matching of 'population' and 'activity' systems

Migration and local and non-local employment multiplier effects, two of the most elemental event classes involved in the past and present growth and development of city-systems, can be approached through an elaboration of the 'population-' and 'activity'-system concepts used by Hägerstrand and his associates in their effort to design a 'time-geography' model of society (Hägerstrand, 1970a, 1970b, 1972, 1975; Hägerstrand, Mårtensson, Lenntorp, Jenstav and Wallin, 1974; Hägerstrand, Ellegård and Lenntorp, 1975; Pred, 1973c).

The 'population system' of an urban unit (including its surrounding commuting field) or any other geographically defined area embraces all the individuals resident in that area. For illustrative purposes these individuals, who are bound together in households, can be represented by vertical lines arranged in age order from the youngest to the oldest (upper right, Figure 1.2). On a daily basis the population system possesses total time resources equal to 24 hours × the number of its inhabitants (upper left, Figure 1.2). Each day these time resources are completely consumed in different activities that arise from individual and institutional needs, wants and obligations (lower right, Figure 1.2). The activities in which individuals participate occur in daily time packages. Activities can be grouped according to many different criteria, depending on the purpose of analysis. Here it is most appropriate to restrict the discussion to three crude categories (lower left, Figure 1.2): physiological activities (sleeping, eating, and personal care – activities which cannot be delegated from one person to another); employment activities; and miscellaneous activities (interactivity travel, recreation, household chores and errands, service consumption,

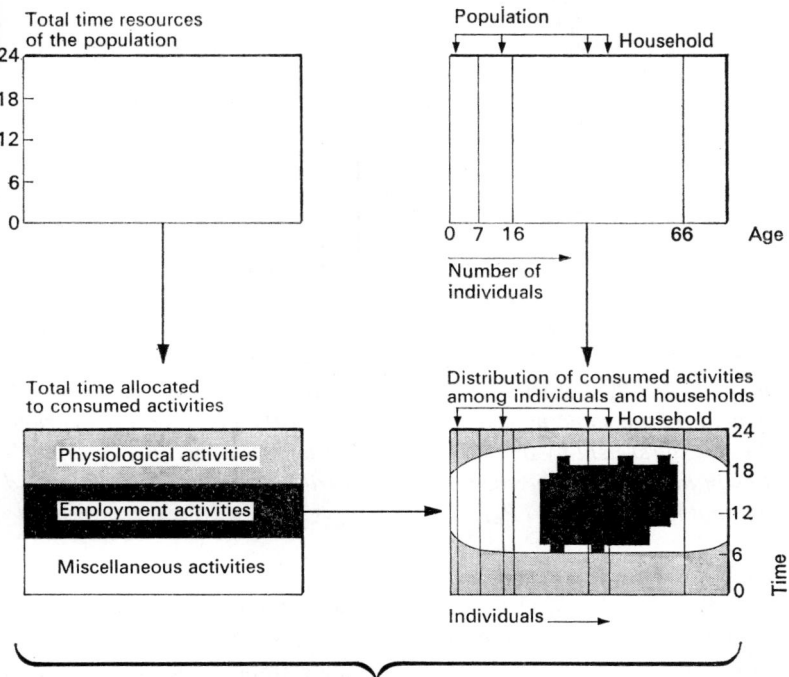

Figure 1.2: *The matching of a population system and an activity system as seen from a daily perspective. Temporarily vacant roles in the activity system are not represented. Modified from Hägerstrand (1972), and Hägerstrand, Ellegård and Lenntorp (1975).*

care of children and the aged, and schooling). Each employment activity, or job, and certain miscellaneous activities can be thought of as a role whose life stretches over months or years and whose existence is independent in the sense that when it is not filled by one person it sooner of later must be filled by another person (Figure 1.3a). Thus the 'activity system' of a given place or area consists of all those time-consuming activities locally carried out – regardless of their necessity or value – *plus* any independently existing employment or miscellaneous activity roles that are temporarily vacant.

Each time-consuming component of the activity system can be

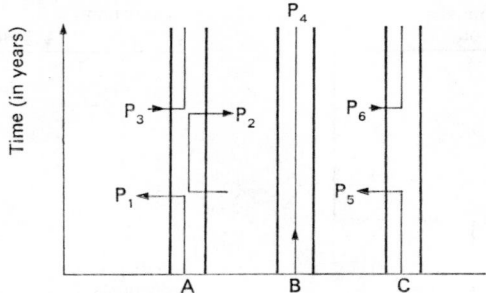

Figure 1.3a: *Jobs, or other activities, as roles independently existing over longer periods of time. Job A is successively occupied by several individuals (P₁–P₃) without being vacant for any extensive time. Job B is held by the same person (P₄) throughout the observed time-period. Job C is first held by one individual (P₅) and then, because of difficulties in finding a replacement, is temporarily vacant before being filled by another individual (P₆).*

thought of as 'seeking a bearer' in the population system. Or, oppositely, each individual picks his way to a series of activity bundles in the available activity system. This superimposition of individuals upon employment and miscellaneous activities, or the matching of population and activity systems is seldom free of conflict. One of the reasons why matching difficulties occur is the fact that individuals are indivisible units. Once an individual participates in a specified activity bundle at a given time and place, she cannot simultaneously be somewhere else doing something else, i.e. she cannot choose any pair of activities which have overlapping time requirements. (For example, an unmarried mother cannot take a job beginning at 8 a.m. if she is unable to arrange for the care of her pre-school child before 8.30 a.m. (Palm and Pred, 1974).) The matching problems caused by simultaneity conflicts are often compounded by the fact that once an activity bundle is fully staffed, it becomes closed to other candidates. Such capacity conflicts are encountered, for example, by individuals wishing to be employed at a specific work-place where all the jobs are already filled, or by individuals wishing to see a cultural or sports event for which no tickets remain available. The matching of population and activity systems is also troublesome because movement from one local activity bundle to another is time-consuming. Thus individuals frequently cannot partake in two activities which are free of any simultaneity conflict because the time difference between the end-time of one and the start-time of the other is greater than the travel-time between the two. In addition, matching difficulties may arise from insufficient information or as a result of differences between the capabilities of individuals and the education or other competency requirements set up for activity participation.

Migration – which along with natural increase and decrease contributes to the population growth or decline of city-system units – is often attributable to incompatible population and activity systems. For example, out-migration from urban units in 'depressed' or 'lagging' regions customarily results from an inability of the local activity system's supply of jobs to meet the local population system's demand for employment activities in general and high-competency employment activities for the young in particular. Or, if the employment opportunities of an urban unit's activity system cannot be matched by the time resources or competencies of individuals belonging to its corresponding population system, then interurban or rural-to-urban migration to that place is likely to be generated (Wallin, 1974).[8]

The creation of a new employment facility or the expansion of an existing employment facility in and of itself may or may not call forth migration to the urban unit at which it occurs. Slack in the daily time resources of the local population system may permit the direct filling of employment-role additions to the activity system; e.g. through the labour-market entry of persons who are either partly or entirely unemployed, or newly graduated. Or locally contained 'chains of opportunity' may be called into being whereby new employment roles are filled by already locally employed individuals who switch jobs, only to have their newly abandoned roles filled by other already locally employed individuals, who in turn have their newly abandoned roles filled by yet other locally employed individuals, and so on until a population-system member who is not currently employed assumes an abandoned role (Figure 1.3b; cf. White, 1970). (Single local 'chains of opportunity' also may be set in motion when retiring or out-migrating individuals leave employment role vacancies behind them.) However, in-migration is likely to follow the creation or expansion of employment activities either if unemployed local individuals cannot hop directly into the new roles in question, or if 'chains of opportunity' cannot be locally broken. In smaller centres the probabilities of in-migration are

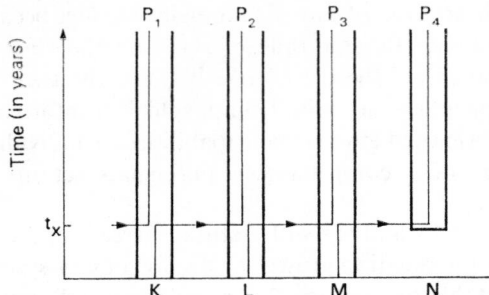

Figure 1.3b: *A locally contained 'chain of opportunity'. Column N represents a newly created job, or employment role, at date t_x. Columns K, L and M indicate previously existing jobs. P_1–P_4 are individuals belonging to the local population system.*

especially great when newly created employment roles have rather high or particularized competency requirements – even if overall local unemployment is extensive. Thus, when the multilocational business or government organizations of an advanced economy commence or expand operations in a small- or medium-sized city they commonly move in administrators, technicians or factory managers from organizational units located elsewhere.

Despite the examples given thus far, it should be emphasized that the migration of individuals and households does not always occur specifically because of inadequately matched activity and population systems. Migration patterns in advanced economies may be ascribed to a number of other factors, including life-cycle stage, climatic and life-style preferences, interurban distances, and ease of travel and communication (e.g. Olsson, 1965; Zelinsky, 1971). However, whatever the causes and motivations for migration, whenever it adds to the population system of an urban unit it has ramifications for the population system-activity system matching of that place.

Additional relationships between migration and the matching of population and activity systems stem from the generation of multiplier effects. Any time a new employment facility is born or an existing job-providing facility experiences a significant increase in the scale of its operations, it will sooner or later propagate some employment multiplier effects. Employment multiplier effects may be of the *backward linkage* variety (the new or expanded facility demands goods or services at a scale which eventually justifies job additions at the supplying units), the *forward linkage* variety (the output of goods or services achieved by the new or expanded facility eventually induces other facilities to increase their level of consumption and employment), or the *employee expenditure* variety (the aggregate income spending behaviour of employees at the new or expanded facility is sufficient to cause the expansion or birth of certain consumer-serving facilities). Employment multiplier effects may occur locally or non-locally; i.e. cause local growth or interurban growth transmission. When they occur locally they are synonymous with an increased number of employment roles in the local activity system. Consequently, if the urban unit's population system lacks individuals with the required time resources or competencies some in-migration will be necessary above and beyond that directly stimulated by the initial facility birth or expansion. When employment multiplier effects transpire non-locally, or are a manifestation of new or intensified interdependence with other urban units, they definitionally shape additional employment roles in the activity system of each of those units. If the population system of any affected urban centre cannot meet the time-resource or competency demands of new employment positions then some in-migration will once again be necessary. In short, whenever an employment facility comes into being or is significantly expanded, it may possibly produce both local in-migration and non-local in-migration (Figure 1.3c).

The employment multiplier effects so far discussed are initial, or first-round, effects. Each of the facilities expanding as a result of first-round effects may in turn generate additional, or second-round, backward-linkage, forward-linkage and employee-expenditure multipliers of their own. Some of the possible complexities of city-system growth and development begin to appear from the different ways in which second-round employment multipliers can express themselves. The second-round employment multipliers following an initial *local* multiplier effect may also occur locally or non-locally. Moreover, the second-round employment multipliers triggered by a specific first-round *non-local* multiplier effect may be confined to the same non-local urban centre, may involve still other non-local urban units, or be reflexive, i.e. feed back through increased goods or service consumption to the urban unit at which the multiplier sequence commenced. Therefore, depending on the compatibility of particular population and activity systems, it is also possible for second-round employment multipliers to stimulate both local in-migration and non-local in-migration.

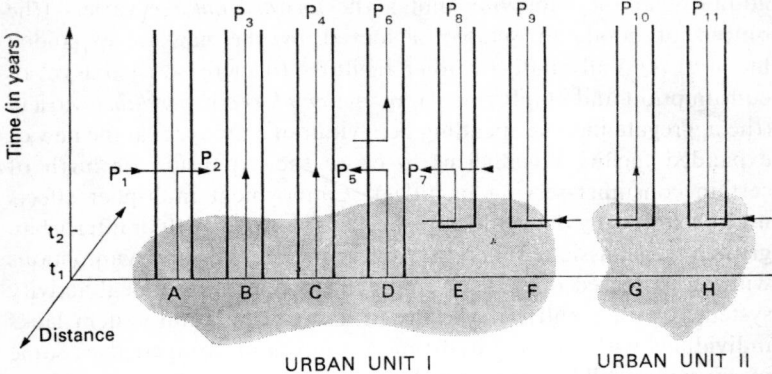

Figure 1.3c: *New or expanded job-providing facilities, multiplier effects and migration. Jobs A–D represent a sample from the total array of employment roles directly associated with the birth or expansion of a facility at urban unit I at date t_1. By date t_2 the new or expanded facility precipitates both local employment multipliers (represented by the job sample E–F) and non-local employment multipliers at urban unit II (represented by the job sample G–H). P_2–P_8 are 'native' members of the population system at urban unit I, while P_1 and P_9 are in-migrants to that centre. P_{10} is a 'native' member of the population system at urban unit II, while P_{11} is an in-migrant to that place.*

2 Past growth: information circulation and channels of interdependence

The long-term rank stability of leading metropolitan complexes

One of the most striking features of the historical growth and development of city-systems in those countries which can currently be classified as economically advanced is the long-term stability in the national or regional population rank of their leading metropolitan complexes. Typically, over very long periods of time, the presently most important metropolitan complexes of the city-systems of broadly defined regions and entire 'post-industrial' countries have experienced either no shift in population rank at all, or an upward or downward shift of one or two ranks. However, in some instances significant adjustments to their population ratios have occurred. (Whatever the details in any specific region or country, it must be emphasized that the phenomenon of long-term *rank stability* among leading metropolitan complexes *is not to be confused with* the earlier discussed *rank-size* rule (pp. 16–17). (In both 1801 and 1911 the four largest urban centres in England and Wales were, in size order, London, Manchester, Liverpool and Birmingham (Robson, 1973). Today the four most populous metropolitan complexes – or Metropolitan Economic Labour Areas (Hall, 1971) – of England and Wales are the same, their size order now being London, Birmingham, Manchester and Liverpool.[1] Newcastle and Leeds, currently the fifth- and sixth-ranking metropolitan complexes of England and Wales, were respectively ranked sixth and eighth in 1801. In Sweden the contemporary system of cities is much dominated by the three highest-ranked metropolitan complexes, Stockholm, Göteborg (Gothenburg) and Malmö. In 1855 the functionally defined antecedents of these complexes were respectively ranked first, second and fourth (ERU, 1974). Data for Ontario, Quebec and Canada as a whole also clearly demonstrate the long-term rank stability of large metropolitan centres (Bourne and Gad, 1972; Davies, 1972; Simmons, 1974b; Bannister, 1975).

There are numerous other pieces of evidence indicating that once a few urban centres rise to the highest population ranks of a national or regional city-system they are highly unlikely to be displaced from those positions of dominance. However, perhaps the most impressive examples involve regional city-systems within the US. Madden (1956), Lukermann (1966) and others have pointed to the stability of rank-size relationships within the US system of cities as a whole since 1790. All the same such analyses tend to mask the degree of rank or dominance stability, since as population spread westward during the nineteenth century new – and often subsequently prominent – urban units were constantly added to the national city-system. (Chicago, the third-ranking US metropolitan complex in 1970, did not become part of the US system of cities until the 1830s, while the system debut of Los Angeles, now the second most populous US metropolitan complex, occurred about twenty-five years later.) If the US is decomposed into broadly defined economic-geographic regions, it is usually found that the metropolitan units today occupying the highest regional city-system size ranks were identified as regional leaders long before their populations had reached more than a very small fraction of their present totals. For example, in the Northeast (the entire area due north of the Potomac River except for western Pennsylvania, westernmost New York, and Washington DC) the four largest metropolitan complexes of the 1970s were already singled out in 1790. At that time New York, Philadelphia, Boston and Baltimore had populations ranging between 0·20 and 0·83 per cent of their corresponding 1970 metropolitan complex totals. In addition, by 1810 Providence and Albany had obtained regional city-system rankings very similar to the fifth and sixth positions held by their 1970 metropolitan-complex descendants (Table 2.1).[2]

Rank and population percentage figures for the now dominant centres of the eastern Great Lakes (Detroit, Cleveland and Buffalo) and the Ohio and Upper Mississippi valleys (St Louis, Pittsburgh, Cincinnati and Louisville) provide equally clear illustrations of the long-term regional rank stability phenomenon in the US (Pred, 1973b). As another case in point, Chicago had risen to first rank in the regional city-system focusing on the western Great Lakes by 1840, when its population (4470) represented a mere 0·06 per cent of that found within its corresponding 1970 metropolitan complex (7612314). In fact, it is only in the Southeast that rank stability did not set in at a very early stage of regional population growth.

Table 2.1: Population and regional city-system rank of leading Northeastern urban complexes, 1810 and 1970

Urban complex	1810 Population[a]	Rank	1970 Population	Rank	1810 population as percentage of 1970 population
New York	100 775	1	16 894 371[b]	1	0·60[c]
Philadelphia	87 303	2	5 317 407[d]	2	1·64[e]
Boston	38 746	4	3 388 795[f]	3	1·13[g]
Baltimore	46 555	3	2 700 670[h]	4	2·25[i]
Providence	10 071	7	905 558[j]	5	1·11
Albany	10 672	6	777 793[k]	6[l]	1·38

(a) 'Suburbs' are included in the 1810 populations of New York (Brooklyn), Philadelphia (Northern Liberties and Southwark) and Boston (Charlestown). These adjacent 'suburbs', although not yet legally annexed, were physically and functionally integrated with their respective component central cities.

(b) New York–New Jersey SCA (Standard Consolidated Area) + Stamford SMSA (Standard Metropolitan Statistical Area) + Bridgeport SMSA + Norwalk SMSA. This combination of metropolitan areas into a larger metropolitan complex is based on highly overlapping commuting patterns and the sharing of major airport facilities. Cf. chapter note 1.

(c) In 1790 New York had a population (33 131) that was 0·20 per cent of its 1970 metropolitan total. At the former date New York ranked second in size both regionally and nationally.

(d) Philadelphia SMSA + Wilmington (Delaware) SMSA. Cf. note (b), above.

(e) In 1790, when Philadelphia was the nation's largest urban

unit, its population (44 096) was 0·83 per cent of that contained within its 1970 metropolitan counterpart.

(f) Boston SMSA + Brockton SMSA + Lawrence–Haverhill SMSA + Lowell SMSA. Cf. note (b), above.

(g) In 1790, when Boston's regional city-system rank was identical with that of 1970, its population (18 320) was 0·54 per cent of its 1970 metropolitan total.

(h) Baltimore SMSA.

(i) In 1790, when Baltimore's regional city-system rank was identical with that of 1970, its population (13 503) was 0·65 per cent of its 1970 metropolitan total.

(j) Providence–Warwick–Pawtucket SMSA.

(k) Albany–Schenectady–Troy SMSA.

(l) Albany's 1970 regional city-system rank is seventh rather than sixth if the Hartford metropolitan complex is given a more liberal definition than the one assigned to it by US census authorities.

(Charleston, South Carolina, the largest city in the Southeast in 1810, has since fallen fifteen to twenty ranks, depending on how one chooses to define the Southeastern regional city-system.) However, the Southeast does not constitute an exception in so far as its leading cities of the early nineteenth century were not significantly interdependent. That is, rather than belonging to a well-articulated regional city-system of their own, these centres were – as a result of their economic linkages and informational ties – 'colonial' outliers of the Northeastern regional city-system. Significantly, once the railroad network of the Southeast became well developed after the Civil War, and once a Southeastern city-system thereby began to emerge, with Atlanta at its centre, rank-stability among today's leading Southeastern metropolitan complexes also began to be apparent.

While long-term rank stability characterizes the largest metropolitan complexes of economically advanced national and regional city-systems, this is generally not true for either intermediate- and small-size metropolitan areas or lesser towns and cities. Instead, data for a number of advanced economies (e.g. Pedersen, 1971; Alonso and Medrich, 1972; Robson, 1973; Simmons, 1974b; Bourne, 1975) consistently indicate that the probability of size-rank change for urban units is inversely proportional to population. In other words, the smaller the population of a group of similarly sized urban units at the end of one time period, the greater its variance in growth rates is likely to be during the ensuing time period.

Various avenues of approach can be used to try to 'explain' the long-term rank stability of leading metropolitan complexes on the one hand, and the more variable rank stability of less populous urban units on the other hand. Most of these are purely statistical. The sole use of either elementary statistical theory or various probabilistic growth models – as opposed to the complementary use of inferential statistics and probability concepts – leaves something to be desired, however, since such approaches have no explicit economic or decision-making components. Therefore, they are not at all revealing as to *how* individual urban units grow and how the *processes* underlying the growth and development of entire systems of cities function (cf. Robson, 1973).

As an alternative, it is here contended that the long-term rank stability of large metropolitan complexes in particular, and the growth and development of city-systems in general, can be most plausibly explained by the tendency of early established major channels of interdependence, or interurban growth transmission, to be self-reinforcing, thereby becoming increasingly deeply entrenched and influencing subsequent channels of interurban growth transmission. In this context, and in the context of earlier observations on spatial biases in the circulation and availability of specialized information and their impact on implicit and explicit locational decision-making, it is instructive to examine some of the conditions of city-system development in the US during the period 1790–1840. There are at least two good reasons for this.

First, the technology of information transmission over long distances at that time – it was not until 1844 that the first electromagnetic telegraph line was opened between Baltimore and Washington – makes it in some respects easier than it is at present to specify the nature and consequences of spatial biases in the circulation and availability of specialized information. Secondly, and more importantly, during the 1790–1840 period the mechanization and far-flung extension of transportation networks helped domestic commerce to replace foreign commerce as the primary source of US economic growth. That is, during that pivotal period of initial westward expansion the major cities of the former colonies ceased functioning merely as outliers of the British system of cities and instead became increasingly interdependent among themselves, thereby creating the initial skeleton of both the national city-system and several regional city-systems.

While a summary examination of 1790–1840 US conditions presumably casts some light on the *general* feedback mechanisms by which the rank stability of leading metropolitan complexes sets in, *it should be kept in mind that the growth and development of no pair of advanced-economy city-systems have been identical in terms of specific historical, institutional and political influences.*

Thus, for example, while the same general feedback mechanisms apparently have been at work in all currently advanced economies, city-system growth and development in France and Australia have been far from identical to one another. In the former case the characteristics of the national city-system have been greatly influenced by the very early centralization of political and economic power in Paris. In the latter case the relatively recent political integration of British-oriented colonial states has deeply affected the attributes of the national city-system and its regional subsystems.

Interurban information circulation and trade in the US before the telegraph[3]

Before the initial application and diffusion of the electromagnetic telegraph, interurban and long-distance specialized information circulation was inseparable from human spatial interaction. Until modern telecommunications technology became available, specialized information of the type that affects the evolution of city-systems could only be moved from place to place via business travel, the mails (if a postal service existed, as it did in the US in 1790), and the printed media. Obviously, business travel was synonymous with human spatial interaction. And even the information contained in letters or newspapers and other printed matter could circulate from place to place only if borne by foot or horse, or carried in vehicles or vessels under human guidance.

Before looking more closely at the different modes of pretelegraphic specialized information circulation, three interrelated observations are necessary.

First, because pretelegraphic specialized information circulation required human spatial interaction it was extremely time-consuming, with the speed of transmission at any date being a function of the existing transportation technology. Thus, although private and public information crawled over distances by modern standards throughout the 1790–1840 period, the construction of turnpikes, the adoption of the steamboat for passenger and freight purposes, and the initial diffusion of the railroads in the 1830s meant that specialized knowledge could be disseminated with increasing rapidity.

Secondly, since pretelegraphic specialized information circulation was highly time-consuming, its availability was spatially biased by time lags as well as the composition of contact networks, or 'information fields'. That is, at a given point in time (t_x) after the occurrence of an event at an earlier date (t_y), public or private word of it was potentially available only to individuals dwelling within the irregularly shaped area around the source node over which it was feasible to travel (or ship mail and newspapers) during the interval t_x minus t_y.

Lastly, there was an intimate connection between spatial biases in the interurban circulation and availability of specialized information and patterns of interregional (or international) and interurban trade. In particular, when trade was undertaken at the initiative of the demand sector (a purchasing retailer, wholesaler, industrial unit or importer), the actual goods shipment had to be preceded by some knowledge of and information exchange with the supply source. Likewise, when trade was initiated by the supply sector (a middleman exporter of agricultural or industrial items, or an urban manufacturing unit) the actual movement of goods had to be preceded by some knowledge of and information exchange with the marketing outlet. In short, spatially biased specialized knowledge bred trade and trade-related information exchange, which in turn led to further spatially biased specialized knowledge. Put otherwise, knowledge of supply sources and marketing outlets was affected by existing spatial biases in the availability of specialized information (largely the outcome of existing interurban trade patterns); and the information exchange necessary to the implementation of trade created or compounded spatial biases in the availability of specialized information. This cycle of events presumably was in some measure influenced by limited-search and uncertainty-reducing behaviour.

The interurban circulation of specialized information through newspapers

In pretelegraphic days newspapers provided the only regular means by which news of distant origin could be made locally available in the form of public information. At the same time they were the only means by which locally originating news could be spread non-locally as public information. Despite their mounting number and total circulation, newspapers had a very limited number of subscribers and purchasers throughout the pretelegraphic age. As late as 1840 the number of newspaper copies encountered *per capita* in the course of a year for the entire US was probably less than nine (Table 2.2). In the US and elsewhere the low circulation of pretelegraphic newspapers was attributable to the improving but still limited production capacity of printing-press technology, to high purchase costs which were beyond the reach of those with low or average incomes, and to widespread illiteracy.

In terms of their impact on implicit and explicit locational decision-making, and thereby on city-system growth, three characteristics of pretelegraphic US newspapers were especially noteworthy. These were their advertising function, their inclusion of shipping intelligence and their listing of wholesale prices. By 1800, twenty of the twenty-four dailies in existence bore the term *Advertiser* somewhere in their title; and three-quarters or more of the typical paper was

Table 2.2: The growth of United States newspaper circulation, 1790–1840[a]

Data category	1790	1810	1820	1840	1840/1790
US population (thousands)	3 929	7 224	9 618	17 120	4·4
Newspapers published	92	371	512	1 404	15·3
Newspaper editions per week[b]	147	549	759	2 281	15·5
Daily newspapers	8	26	42	138	17·3
Estimated annual circulation (thousands)	3 975	24 577	50 000	147 500	37·1
Annual newspaper copies *per capita*	1·0	3·4	5·2	8·6	8·6

(a)   For sources, additional data, and estimate bases see Pred (1973b), p. 21.
(b)   In addition to the dailies, which appeared six times per week, there were papers which appeared thrice weekly, twice weekly and once weekly.

devoted to importers' announcements, cargo-space notices, the offerings of commodity brokers, and other advertisements. The publication of shipping intelligence, or lists indicating the shipping arrivals and clearances of non-local coastal, river and lake ports, received much emphasis from 1790 onward, and especially after the War of 1812. Competing newspapers in the larger cities, and especially New York, made considerable efforts to outdo one another with respect to both shipping intelligence and the listing of local and non-local wholesale prices and other commercial statistics of potential use to the business community.

Before the appearance of wire services and the use of non-locally based correspondents, the individual newspaper's main source of domestic and foreign news and specialized information was the columns of other journals. Whether reporting major events or specialized economic information, most newspapers relied directly or indirectly on the coverage of the paper nearest to the source. Indirect exploitation, which was common, occurred when the reportage was lifted from the pages of a New York daily or some other large-city paper, which in turn had gained its information from the paper nearest the source. The practice of mutual journalistic plagiarism had been institutionalized by the Postal Act of 1792, which

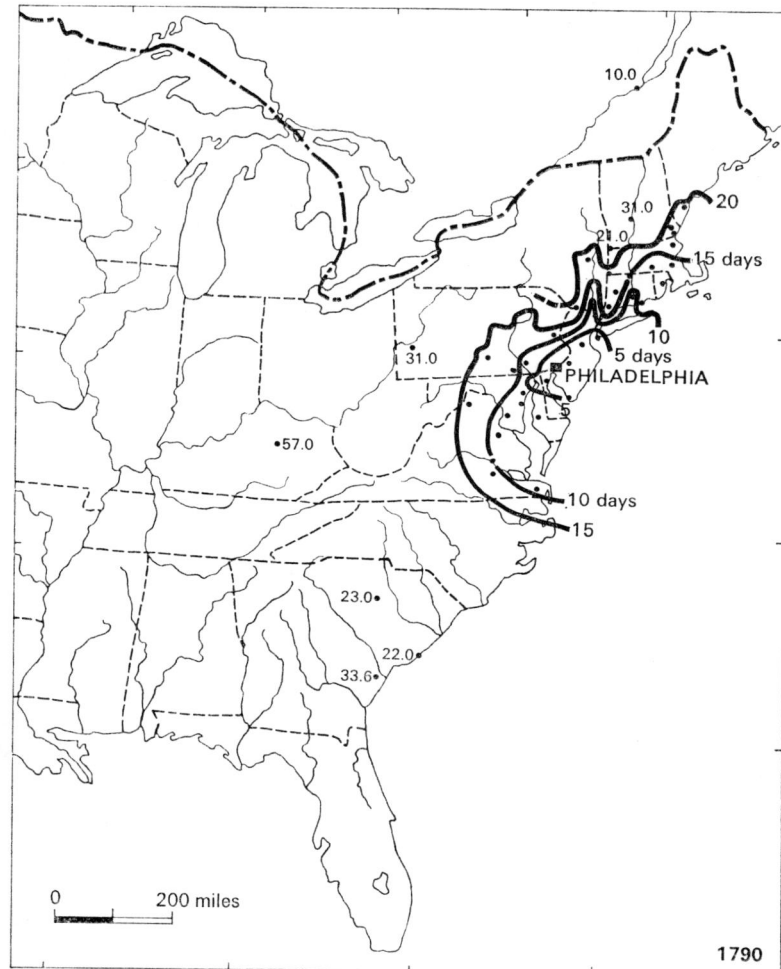

Figure 2.1: *Mean public-information time lags for Philadelphia in 1790 (*Figure 2.1a *above*), *1794, 1817 and 1841. For sources see Pred (1973b), pp 37, 40, 45, 53.*

granted newspaper publishers and editors exemption from postage when mailing copies to each other. One way of describing the resulting spatial biases in the availability of *domestic* information is to construct time-lag surface maps for individual cities at selected dates.

Time-lag surface maps are presented here for New York, Philadelphia, Boston and Charleston (South Carolina) at various dates

Figure 2.1b: *Mean public-information time lag for Philadelphia in 1794.*

between 1790 and 1841 (Figures 2.1–2.4). Each map is based on the news content of a seasonally stratified sample of forty-eight issues of a local paper for the city and date in question. Whenever the date and location of a non-local event was indicated, the discrepancy in days was computed. This allowed, for each yearly sample, the deriva-tion of a mean event-to-publication time lag for every recorded location. The maps contain a wealth of information, only a small part of which is summarized below on a chronological basis.

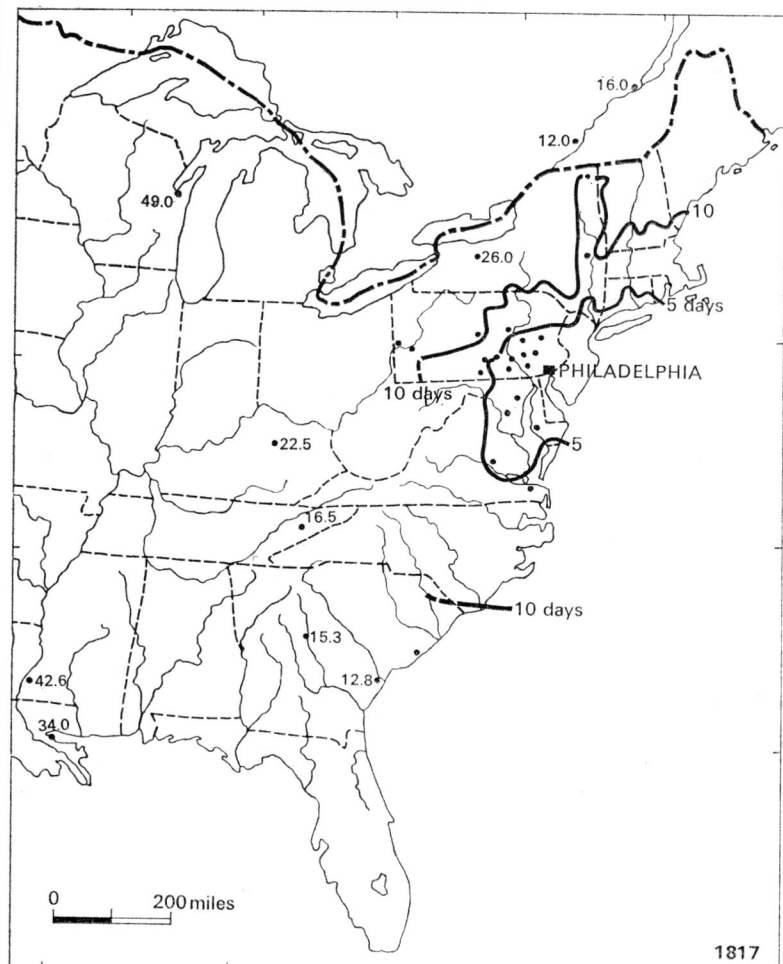

Figure 2.1c: *Mean public-information time lag for Philadelphia in 1817.*

Time-lag surface maps for 1790 and 1794 In absolute terms, the entire nation was in a pronounced state of public-information isolation during the 1790s. However, some places were clearly more informationally remote than others. The most extreme informational isolation existed in the sparsely populated wilderness to the west of the Alleghenies (note the time lag from Lexington (Kentucky) to Philadelphia) and the area south of Richmond (note the Charleston-to-Boston time lag). In general public information flowed most

Figure 2.1d: *Mean public-information time lag for Philadelphia in 1841.*

rapidly along an axis passing diagonally through Boston, New York, Philadelphia and Baltimore – the four largest centres in the emerging city-systems of both the nation as a whole and the Northeast. By 1794 the speediest intelligence currents within this corridor ran between Philadelphia and New York, partly due to the introduction of superior stagecoach and postal services between the two, and partly because two cities with daily papers were nowhere more closely spaced. At the same time the inland, or westward, gradient

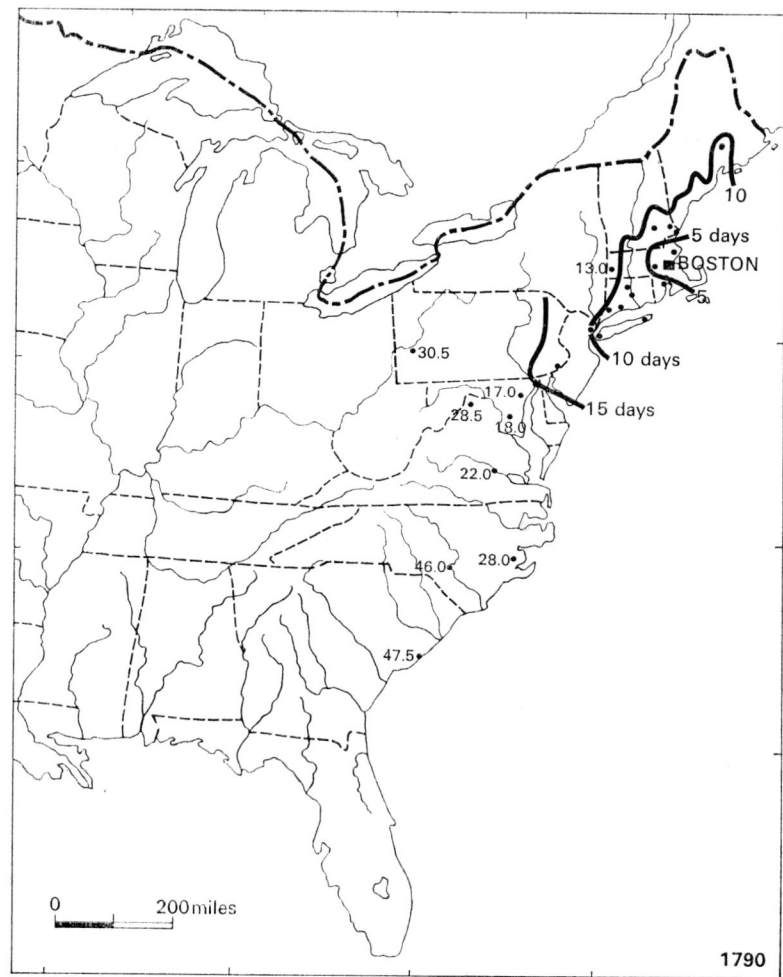

Figure 2.2: *Mean public-information time lags for Boston in 1790 (*figure 2.2a *above) and 1841. For sources see Pred (1973b), pp. 38, 52.*

from isoline to isoline was so steep that the time lag between New York and Philadelphia was smaller than that between each of the cities and many more physically proximate areas normally considered to be part of their hinterlands. Furthermore, New York was already beginning to show signs of having the greatest overall access to

Figure 2.2b: *Mean public-information time lag for Boston in 1841.*

specialized public information. For example, in 1794 the time lag between New York and Charleston was less than that between Philadelphia and Charleston – which are somewhat closer to one another – presumably because of the greater frequency of shipping interaction between the first pair of cities.

Time-lag surface maps for 1817   By 1817 New York had clearly outdistanced Philadelphia and all other competitors and had

Figure 2.3: *Mean public-information time lags for New York in 1794 (*Figure 2.3a *above), 1817 and 1841. For sources see Pred (1973b), pp. 41, 44, 51.*

established a specialized information hegemony. The area enclosed by New York's five-day isoline exceeded that engulfed by Philadelphia's, because its five-day information reach stretched farther southward as well as northward. Because of its more frequent coastal exchanges with the leading Southeastern ports (New Orleans,

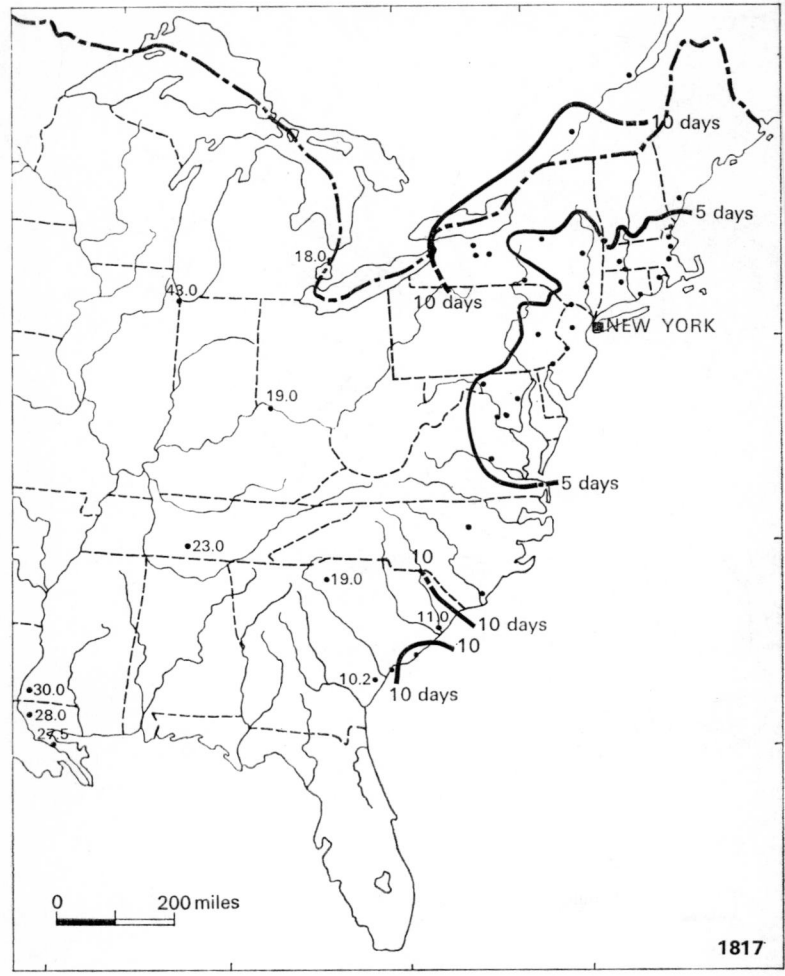

Figure 2.3b: *Mean public-information time lag for New York in 1817.*

Charleston, Savannah and Norfolk) New York was usually the first Northeastern centre to obtain economic information from those places. Thus, the wholesale prices and other specialized information appearing in the Philadelphia and Baltimore press was often acquired from New York papers. As a result of the introduction of integrated stage and steamboat schedules on Long Island Sound and the New York–Philadelphia route, public information still flowed most swiftly along the Boston-to-Baltimore axis, which

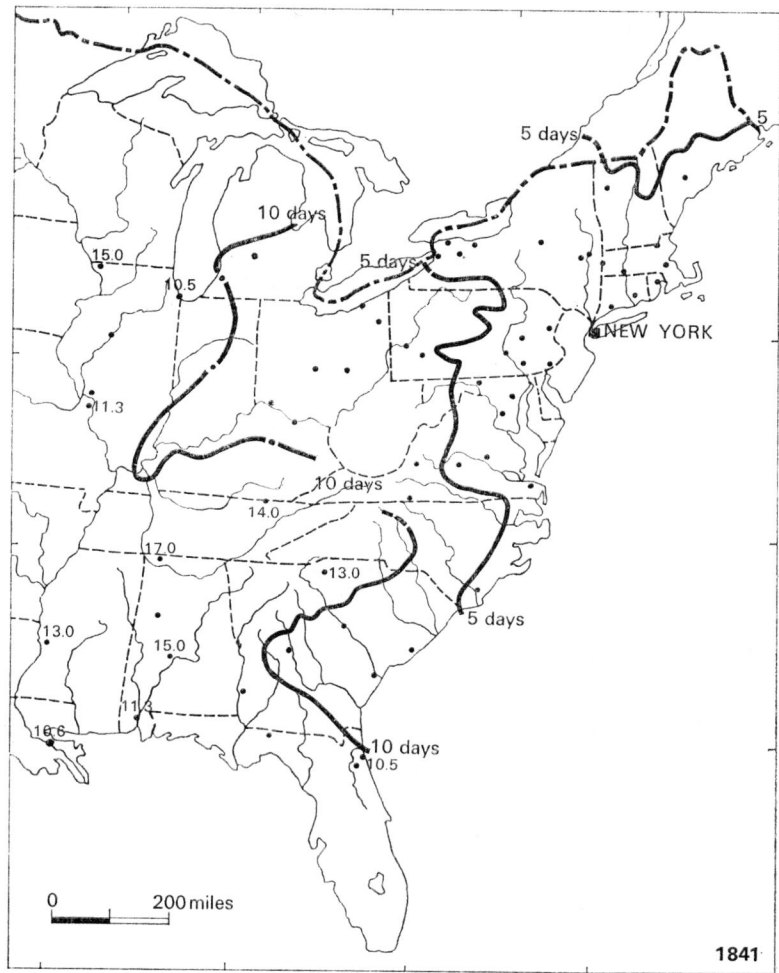

Figure 2.3c: *Mean public-information time lag for New York in 1841.*

actually now extended to Washington DC. News flows were forced to be noticeably slower elsewhere by the very limited extent of similarly integrated transport schedules, and by the absence of daily newspapers in all but a few other places. The relatively extreme spatial biases in domestic information availability yet prevailing in the Southeast are reflected by the 1817 conditions of Charleston, one of the few places outside the Northeast where daily journalism flourished. There the five-day isoline covered a much smaller area

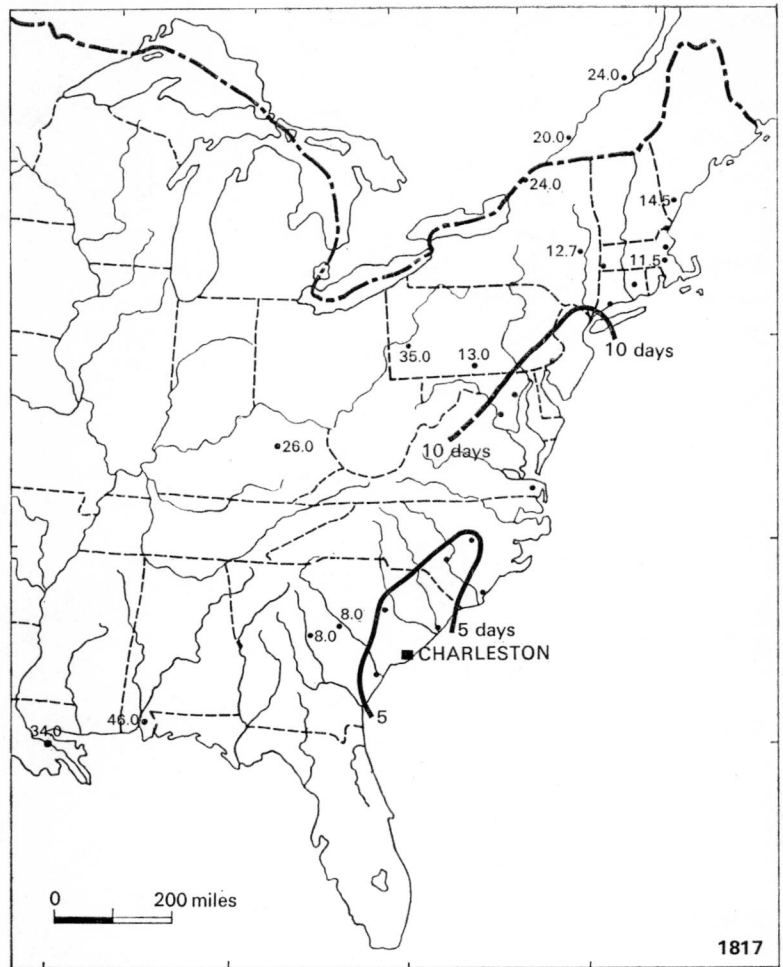

Figure 2.4: *Mean public-information time lags for Charleston in 1817. For source see Pred (1973b), p. 47.*

than that for Philadelphia and especially that for New York. Moreover, because of a small volume of shipping interaction, Charleston newspaper reader scould expect their New Orleans economic information to be four to nine weeks old. Although some improvements were unmistakably evident, the area west of the Alleghenies remained at a great informational distance from the more densely populated Northeast. For example, Detroit-to-New York and Cincinnati-to-New York public-information time lags now stood at eighteen and nineteen days respectively.

Time-lag surface maps for 1841 At the start of the 1840s New York's five-day isoline encompassed an area resembling its 1817 ten-day isoline. New York now dominated domestic public information flows to an even greater extent than previously. This was because of the express relays founded by some New York papers (but later taken over by the Post Office), because of the city's fleet of regularly scheduled packets to major Southeastern ports, and because of the city's volume of business with the West and Southeast as well as the general aggressiveness of its editors. In 1841 news quite often moved between pairs of cities over roundabout paths that passed through New York. News from Washington, for example, sometimes moved to Charleston via New York. And the similar southern extent of Boston's and Philadelphia's ten-day isolines reflected the dependence of papers in those cities on the New York press for information originating in the Southeast. Owing largely to the substitution of integrated railroad and steamboat schedules for stagecoach–steamboat connections, the Baltimore-to-Boston axis remained the scene of the country's most rapid news transmission. In the Southeast the major ports were no longer as informationally isolated from the Northeast as before, due to the inception of regularly scheduled sailing services and other transport improvements. However, with the exception of a few places on the overland post route to New Orleans, inland Southeastern towns were still relatively inaccessible to public information in 1841. In most instances public informational remoteness could be traced to either the complete absence of a local paper, or low accessibility to non-local papers. By 1841 the tide of east–west trade, the multiplication of steamboat traffic, and postal reforms had greatly altered the mean time lags of Cincinnati and other young cities of the Western interior. In 1817 Western cities had been much further removed informationally from New York than were Charleston and Savannah, despite the fact that most of them were physically closer to New York. But by 1841 Cincinnati and Detroit were on a more equal footing with Charleston and Savannah.

Since there is considerable evidence indicating a great amount of postage-free editorial exchange, a mapped measure of place-to-place variations in access to all US newspapers can serve as an additional indicator of spatial biases in the availability of specialized public information.

Geographical patterns of accessibility to population, demand, or any other unequally distributed phenomenon frequently are shown on isarithmic maps based on 'potential' values for selected points in the area under consideration. The potential for any particular point, designated $_iV_1$, is equal to

$$\sum_{j=1}^{n} \frac{P_j}{d_{ij}}$$

where P_j is the population or value of the phenomenon at every other point and d_{ij} is the distance separating the particular point and every other point (cf. Harris, 1954; Isard, 1960). In the public-information accessibility maps for 1790, 1820 and 1840 shown here (Figure 2.5), P_j was assessed for all counties having newspapers, with the value being set by the number of editions published locally per week. Intercounty distances were based on the population centroid of each county in 1960[4] and a measure of average intracounty distances was used to derive self-potential, or intracounty, accessibility. For comparative purposes, all potentials for 1790, 1820 and 1840 were converted to a base, with New York's value in 1790 set at 100. For the most part, the maps speak for themselves. Therefore, only a few remarks are necessary.

Public-information accessibility map for 1790   Not surprisingly, the highest levels of newspaper accessibility in 1790 occurred along the Baltimore-to-Boston axis. Within this area, accessibility declined so rapidly from the New York–Philadelphia core that values at the northern and southern extremes were only one-quarter of those at the New York summit. The previously indicated public-informational remoteness of the Southeast and Western interior is vividly illustrated by the very low potential values obtaining throughout both of those regions. The extreme character of locational differences in accessibility to specialized public information is further underlined by comparing 1790 public information accessibility with 1790 population accessibility (Figure 2.6). Clearly, public-information accessibility fell off much more quickly from New York than would be expected from the pattern of population accessibility. For example, in heavily settled eastern Virginia, where newspaper publication was inhibited by the illiteracy of slaves and others as well as conservative attitudes

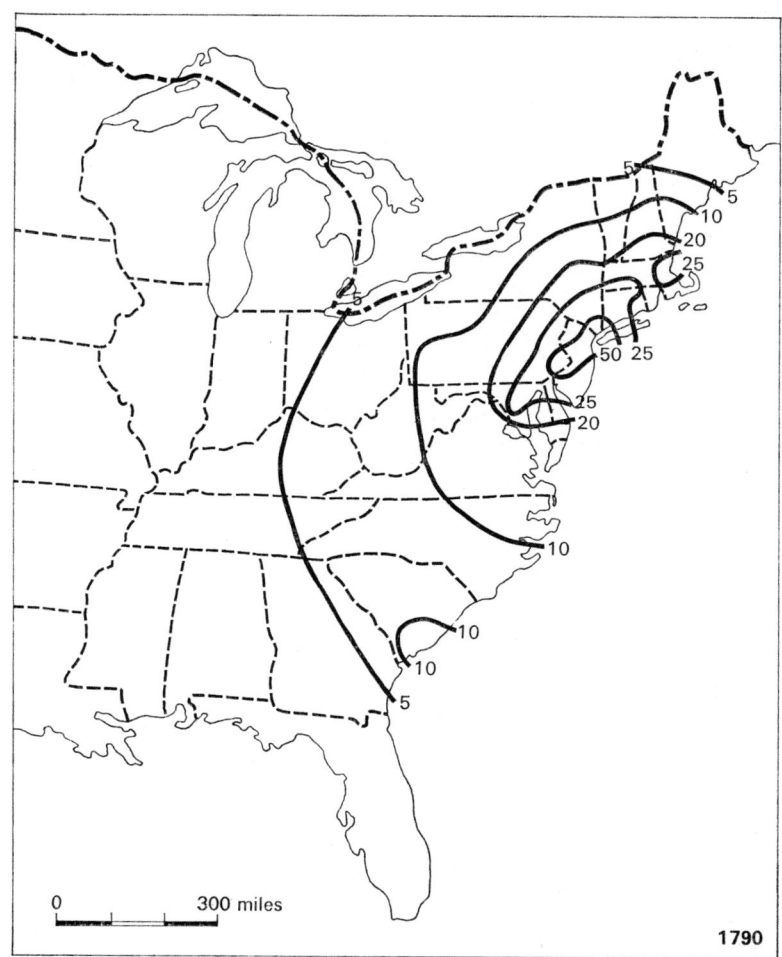

Figure 2.5: *Public information accessibility in 1790* (Figure 2.5a *above*), *1820 and 1840. Value for New York in 1790=100.*

toward printing, population accessibility stood at 80 per cent or more of the New York standard, but public-information accessibility was only 10 to 23 per cent of that registered in New York.

Public-information accessibility map for 1820 Although levels of news accessibility had advanced considerably over thirty years,

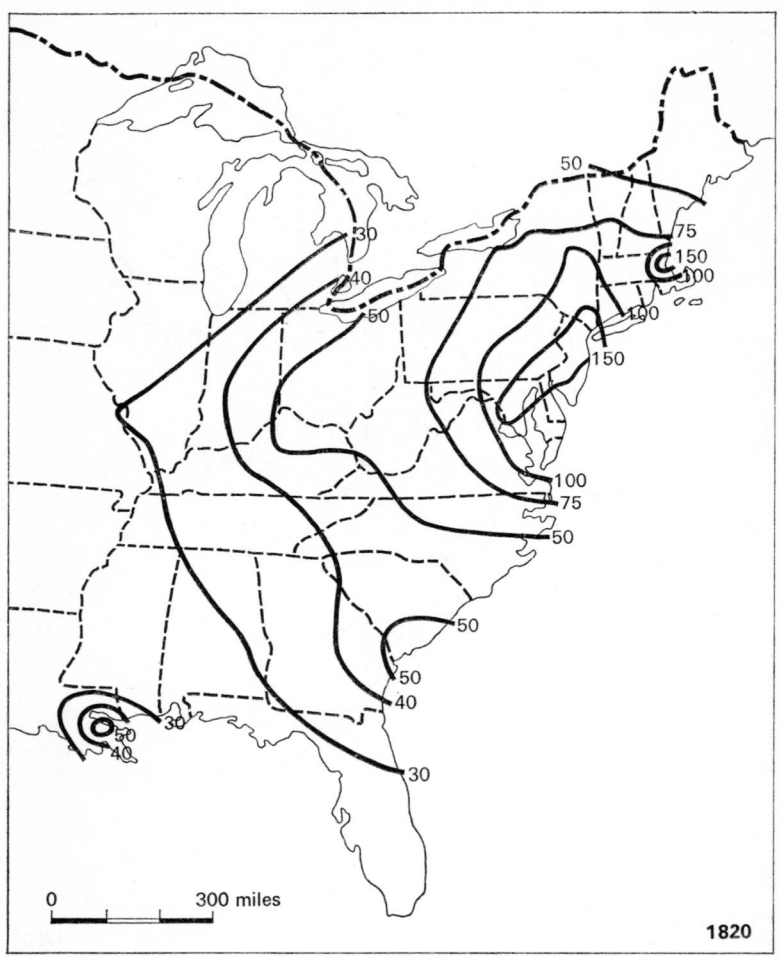

Figure 2.5b: *Public information accessibility in 1820.*

mainly due to the increased diffusion of newspaper publication
(Table 2.2, p. 40), marked spatial differences in accessibility to non-
local economic information were still plainly observable in 1820. The
perpetuation of pronounced spatial biases in the availability of
specialized public information is best summarized by the fact that
most of the country in 1820 had failed to attain public-information
accessibility measures comparable to that of New York in 1790. In
contrast, by 1820 substantial portions of the West and Southeast had
achieved population accessibility values that equalled or surpassed

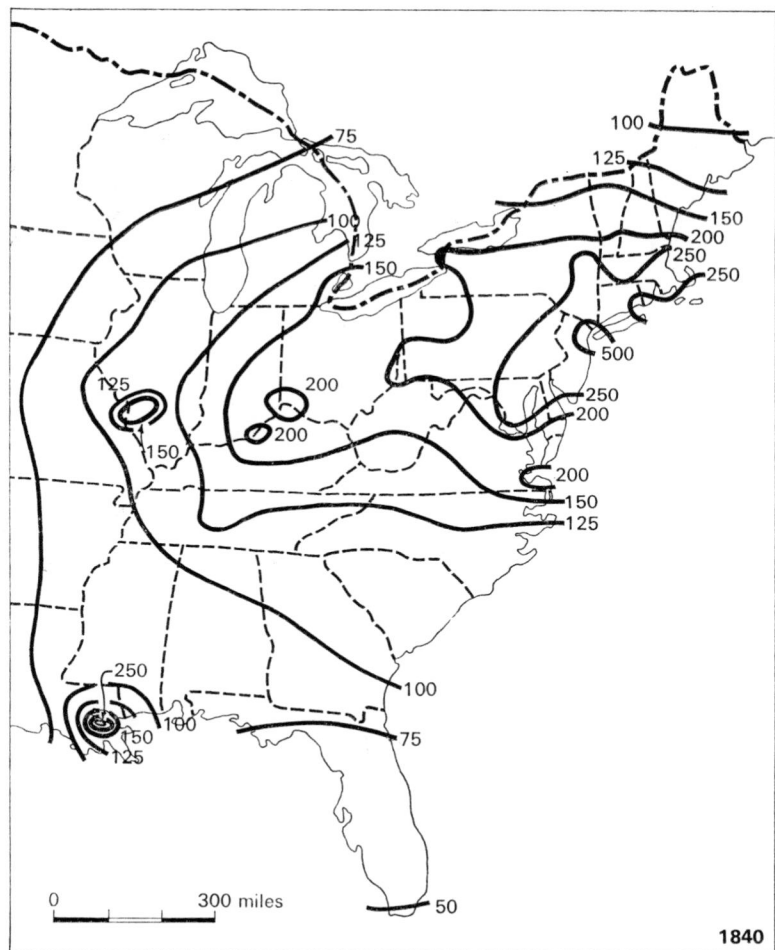

Figure 2.5c: *Public information accessibility in 1840.*

that of New York in 1790, while the public-information potential of New York itself (unmapped value 302) had more than tripled during the same interlude.

Public-information accessibility map for 1840 In 1840 the belt of greatest public-information potential, with values now over 280, still paralleled the Baltimore–Boston axis. The dominance of New York over the US news circulation system was now complete. The discrepancy between the public-information potential of New York

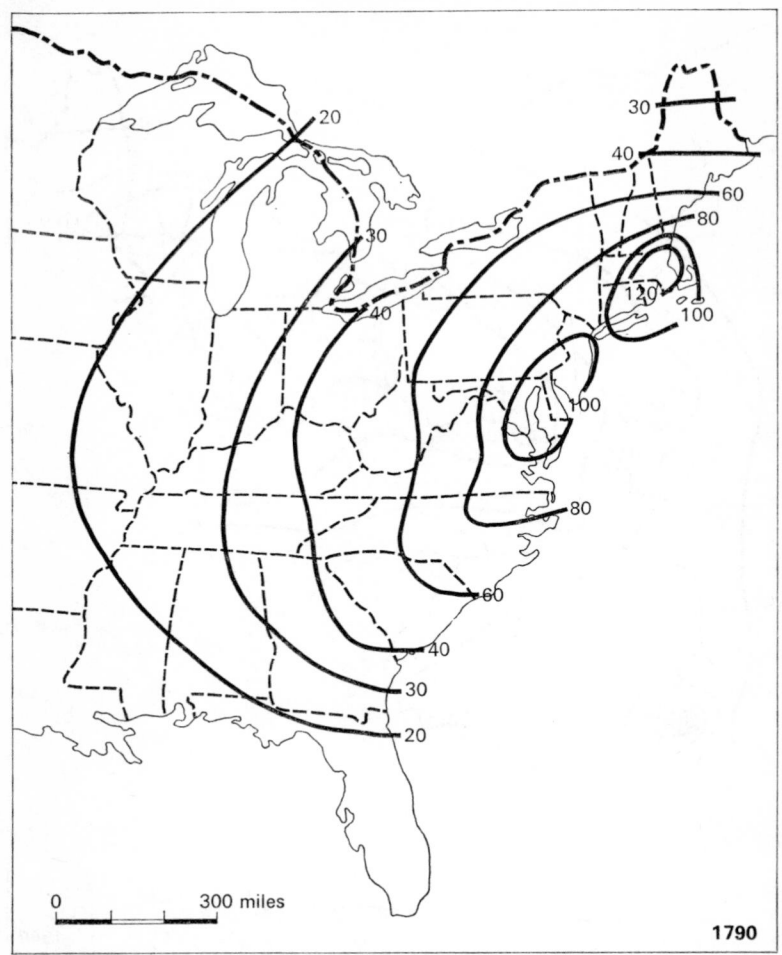

Figure 2.6: *Population accessibility in 1790 (Figure 2.6a above), 1820 and 1840. Value for New York in 1790=100. Adapted from Berry (1968).*

(unmapped value 825) and that of other places was much greater than the discrepancy between corresponding population potentials. However, nearly all the well-settled area west of the Appalachians, plus large parts of the Southeast, had finally attained a level of public-information accessibility that topped New York's 1790 value. Quite significantly, zones of moderately high accessibility had grown up around Cincinnati, Louisville, St Louis and Pittsburgh – the

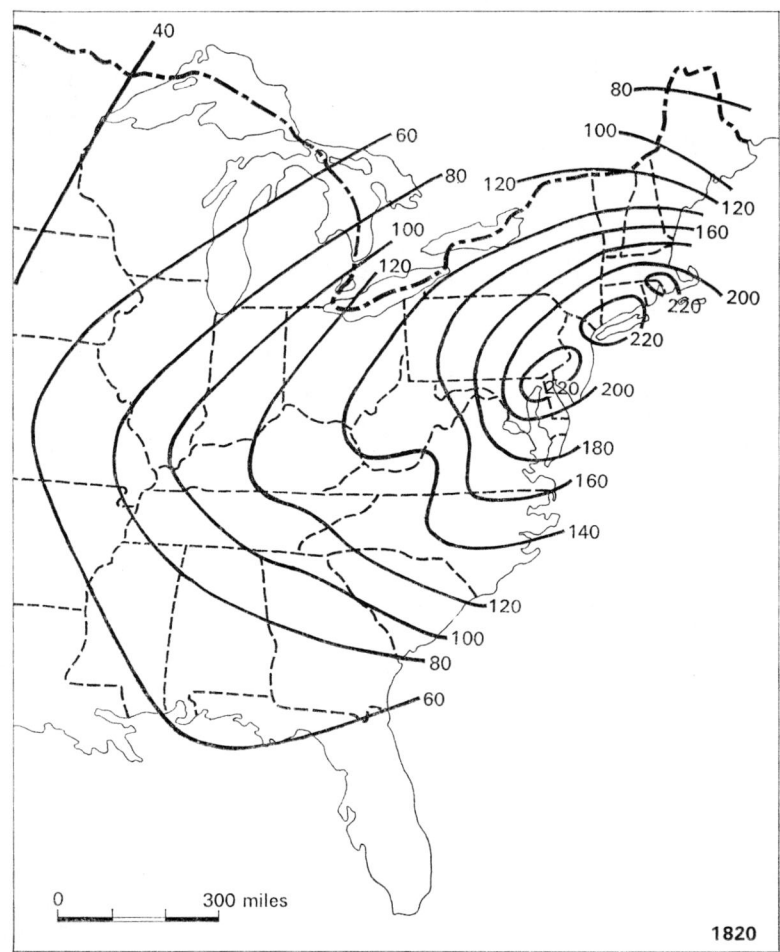

Figure 2.6b: *Population accessibility in 1820.*

quartet of cities that were already dominating the regional system of cities of the Ohio and Upper Mississippi valleys.

New York's public-information potential values for 1820 and 1840 are undervalued in so far as they are not weighted with the foreign newspaper editions that entered the country via that port. In short, the availability of *foreign* specialized public information was also extremely spatially biased between 1790 and 1840. Prior to 1818 the probability of British and European papers – as well as news in general – being first received at an Atlantic port was a func-

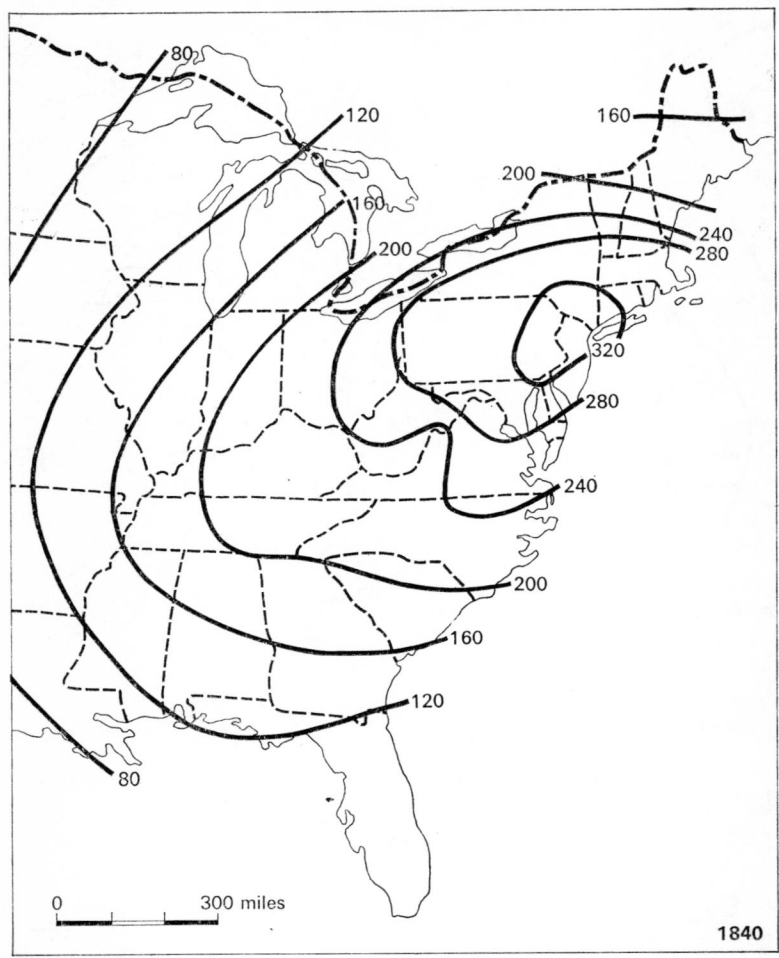

Figure 2.6c: *Population accessibility in 1840.*

tion of that place's total volume of foreign shipping arrivals or imports. Because of its early developed import pre-eminence, until 1818
New York was therefore the most likely place for foreign economic
news to appear first. Thereafter, and until 1840, a growing array of
regularly scheduled packet services to Liverpool, London and Le
Havre provided the city's press with a near monopoly of first access
to British and continental European newspapers and economic
information. Once published in New York, specialized information
of foreign origin circulated to the rest of the country in a manner

which was indistinguishable from the flow patterns associated with information of local origin or receipt. The ideal-typical, but by no means invariable, pattern of foreign news dissemination from New York is portrayed in Figure 2.7. Weeklies and other newspapers in the immediate hinterlands of the larger cities shown in Figure 2.7 plagiarized their European information either from papers in those larger places or, where the mails allowed, directly from a New York journal.

Postal services and the interurban circulation of specialized information

During the fifty years between 1790 and 1840, the services of the US Post Office were considerably fleshed out. The number of post offices, the mileage of postal routes, and total annual postage receipts all climbed rapidly (Table 2.3), while the daily movement of newspapers to non-local editors and subscribers over some postal routes reached a level where it could be measured in tons. Despite these spectacular developments, at the end of the period use of the mails for transmitting private information over long distances was still confined to a relatively small minority of the total population. As late as 1837 the total volume of mail carried annually did not total more than 2·05 letters *per capita*, and in earlier years the figure was much lower. The major share of private correspondence was accounted for by shipping and commission merchants, brokers, factors,

Table 2.3: The growth of United States postal services, 1790–1840[a]

Data category	1790	1810	1820	1840	1840/1790
US population (thousands)	3 929	7 224	9 618	17 120	4·4
Post offices	75	2 300	4 500	13 468	179·6
Population per post office (thousands)	52·4	3·1	2·1	1·3	—
Miles of post routes	1 875	36 406	73 492	155 739	83·1
Postage revenues (thousands of dollars)	37·9	551·7	1 111·9	4 543·0	119·9
Postage revenues *per capita* (dollars)	0·01	0·08	0·12	0·27	27·0

(a) For sources and additional data see Pred (1973b), p. 80.

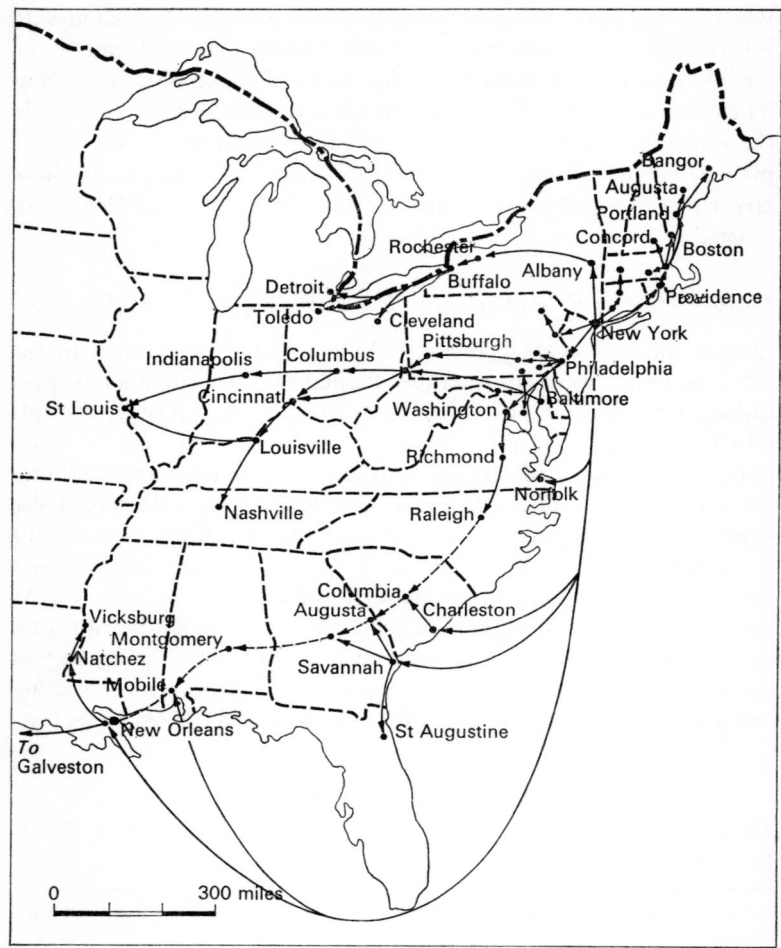

Figure 2.7: *Ideal-typical flow of foreign and other pretelegraphic information from New York newspapers to papers in the rest of the country. Path directions do not necessarily represent actual routes. The pattern for the West is for the 1820s and after. The dashed line from Raleigh to New Orleans represents the principal Southeastern postal route, which gained in importance as a purveyor of New York newspaper information toward the close of the pretelegraphic era.*

retailers and other commercial agents. For most other segments of the population the more or less stable postage rates prevailing after 1792 must have appeared quite high, or even prohibitive. Rates were graduated by distance zones and charged by the sheet or page. Thus, for example, during most of the 1790–1840 period the cost of sending a three-page letter over 400 miles was roughly equivalent to the average daily wage rate for non-farm labour.

The tremendous expansion of postal operations from 1790 to 1840 was not spatially uniform, but characterized by regional variations in the extent of route developments and the frequency and speed of services. This was so despite government policies insuring that the reach of the developing postal network would not lag far behind the westward spread of settlement. In the early nineteenth century, service was faster on some routes because the roads were less treacherous than was normally the case. Thereafter, service discrepancies between the best and poorest routes became reinforced and accentuated. This was owing to the spread of turnpike construction, the authorization granted to the Postmaster General in 1815 to contract steamboat lines to carry the mails, the modest inception of railroad usage by the Post Office in 1834, and the appearance of express services two years later.

Typically, an increased volume of mail and improved service went side by side. Thus, the New York–Philadelphia mail route was virtually always the first postal linkage to be given new unmatched levels of service frequency. That route was also the pace-setter with respect to the introduction of new transportation technology for mail-carrying purposes. The remainder of the Washington–Boston axis was rarely far behind in experiencing postal-service innovations. In short, the sequence of four routes directly connecting Boston, New York, Philadelphia, Baltimore and Washington consistently had the quickest and most frequent services. Even the postal services from each of these cities to the leading centres in their respective hinterlands was generally inferior to that along the Boston–Washington axis itself. Deliveries elsewhere in the country were frequently made under primitive conditions, and many places had to be satisfied with weekly or fortnightly services. However, it is significant that the postal route from Buffalo to Cleveland to Detroit (the long-term dominants of the eastern Great Lakes regional city-system), as well as the routes connecting Pittsburgh, Cincinnati, Louisville and St Louis (the long-term dominants of the regional city-system of the Ohio and Upper Mississippi valleys), quite early came to be *intra-*

regionally superior in terms of the frequency and speed of their services. The poor quality of roads was particularly limiting to the postal services of the Southeast. Moreover, the alignment of the major chain of postal routes in the Southeast was such that the major centres of New Orleans and Mobile on the one hand, and Charleston and Savannah on the other hand, had no direct mailing connections (Figure 2.7).

Whatever regional variations may have existed in the speed, frequency, and reliability of postal services, the most telling aspect of spatial biases in the availability of postally conveyed private information throughout the entire 1790–1840 period was the extremely disproportionate urban concentration of mail origins and destinations. From 1826 to 1841 New York was consistently responsible for 10 or more per cent of the country's postal receipts. In both the early 1820s and the early 1840s, as well as at every intervening date for which figures have been found, New York, Philadelphia, Boston and Baltimore took in close to one-quarter or more of all US postal receipts, although the four cities had only 3·92 per cent of the nation's population in 1820, and 4·94 per cent in 1840. Major cities in other parts of the country apparently dominated the flow of specialized private information through the mails at the regional level to a degree at least equal to the four leading Northeastern ports. For example, St Louis was responsible for 42·5 per cent of Missouri's postal receipts in 1840–1, but for only 4·3 per cent of its 1840 population.

Finally, for the period from 1820 to 1840 there was an extremely close relationship between absolute urban population growth and absolute increases in postal receipts, or specialized private information transactions. When 1822–40 receipt increases for twenty-nine cities were tested against 1820–40 population increments for the same selected centres, a correlation of 0·9921 was obtained.[5] In the extreme case this meant that the city with the largest population growth – New York – had far and away the largest postal increases, while the city with the smallest absolute population expansion – Portsmouth, New Hampshire – actually had an absolute decline in postal receipts. Since wholesaling-trading activities were the major source of urban-size growth during these years, the high correlation is consistent with the part ascribed to the commercial population in generating mail.

Business travel and the interurban circulation of specialized information

Between 1790 and 1840 high fares, the expense of overnight stops, and other travel costs usually made long-distance interurban travel by common carrier out of the question for all but businessmen and the economic elite. For example, the cost of fares alone would have required that the average urban worker sacrifice ten days' wages to travel one-way from Boston to New York in 1802, twenty days' wages to move one-way from Philadelphia to Pittsburgh in 1812, and nine days' pay to make the short Baltimore–Philadelphia round-trip journey in 1840. If interurban travel was generally expensive, the cost per passenger-mile was particularly so between those South Atlantic cities (Norfolk, Charleston and Savannah) and Gulf Coast cities (New Orleans and Mobile) that were isolated informationally and economically from one another.

For the country as a whole, migrants were the only significant group to use interurban common carriers in addition to various types of businessmen (e.g. retailers making purchase trips, wholesaling merchants, and manufacturers' selling agents). Migrants were able to constitute an exception, especially after the breakthrough of the steamboat, because they could travel – usually under jammed conditions – on a few major routes at special low fares. However, while normally passing through several cities, the contribution of westward migrants to interurban specialized information circulation must have been small in proportion to their numbers; for most of them had rural destinations, many were moving from rural surroundings, others of European origin did not speak English, and virtually all were one-way passengers.

The pretelegraphic intercity business traveller was a vital cog in the long-distance spread of specialized information. He could verbally communicate economic information from his city of residence, or from other points along his route to individuals in the places to which he journeyed. He could likewise bring back private economic information to his home city. Upon his return, he could also convert newly acquired visual information or perceptions into either verbal or published form. In addition, specialized information acquired while he was away could influence the returning traveller to adopt an economic innovation, thereby creating new specialized visual information for fellow urban residents.

Because of the variety of ways in which interurban business travel contributed to pretelegraphic information circulation, estimated figures on the volume of common-carrier travel between specific urban pairs should provide yet another indication of spatial biases in the availability of specialized information. Such figures for New York and Philadelphia are presented in Table 2.4. Although there may be a

Table 2.4 Estimated common-carrier travel volumes between New York and Philadelphia, 1790–1840[a]

Year	Estimated one-way trips from New York to Philadelphia and from Philadelphia to New York	Combined population of New York and Philadelphia[b]	One-way trips *per* thousand New York and Philadelphia *capita*
1790	10 000 (9 000–11 250)[c]	77 227	130 (116–146)
1804	22 500 (21 000–25 250)[c]	148 475[d]	151 (135–170)
1816	33 900 (29 800–36 100)[c]	219 045[d]	155 (136–165)
1828	80 000	348 950[d]	229
1833	120 000	434 196[d]	276
1840	200 000	569 366	351

(a) For sources and estimate bases see Pred (1973b), p. 158.
(b) Including 'suburbs'. Cf. note (a), Table 2.1.
(c) Range given in parentheses due to imprecision of source data.
(d) Interpolated from nearest census-date populations.

wide margin of error in several of the estimates contained in that table, it is nevertheless clear that the amount of specialized information exchange via business travel between the two fledgling metropolises became relatively more intense between 1790 and 1840. Since the number of one-way trips *per* thousand New York and Philadelphia *capita* grew from between 116 and 146 to roughly 351, travel volumes between the two cities expanded 2·4 to 3·0 times faster than would be expected from their combined population growth, and travel-generated information between them probably grew to at least the same degree.[6] Estimates for common-carrier travel between New York and Boston and between Philadelphia and Baltimore indicate that the other major cities of the Northeast were also experiencing a multiplication of business travel (and specialized information) exchange with each other that was several times greater than could be anticipated from their population increases. Although interurban travel figures for the regional city-system of the Ohio and Upper Mississippi valleys from 1820 onward are much bloated by migrants paying low steamboat fares, it is again apparent that the volume of business travel and related economic information flows among the young dominants of that system – Pittsburgh, Cincinnati, Louisville and St Louis – grew from 1820 to 1840 at a pace that much exceeded their rates of population growth. The same is evidently true for the volume of commercial travel and associated specialized information moving back and forth among Buffalo, Cleveland and Detroit, the already identified dominants of the eastern Great Lakes regional city-system.

While rapidly burgeoning business traffic between specific urban pairs contributed to rather pronounced intraregional contact-array spatial biases in the availability of specialized information elsewhere in the country, this was not the case in the Southeast. In the mid-1830s business travellers still marvelled at the limited amount of traffic south of Richmond, Virginia. A few regularly scheduled steamboats operated over the short routes between Richmond and Norfolk, Charleston and Savannah, and Mobile and New Orleans. But even such limited services did not exist between any other major Southeastern urban pair, partly due to the lengthy detour around Florida that is necessary to reach New Orleans and Mobile by sea. In contrast to the dearth of passengers between the leading Southeastern cities themselves, a well-established travel network existed between those centres and, primarily, New York, and, secondarily, Boston, Philadelphia and Baltimore. Here too there are signs that the growth rate of travel-generated specialized information circulation much surpassed the tempo of population expansion for the involved Northeastern–Southeastern urban pairs.

The solidification of New York's position atop the size hierarchy of the national city-system was paralleled by its emergence as the national hub of specialized private information circulation via business travel. In terms of absolute passenger numbers, the most important interurban travel links in the US near the end of the pretelegraphic period were those between New York and Philadelphia; New York and Boston; New York and Albany (and on to Buffalo); Philadelphia and Baltimore; Cincinnati and Louisville; Pittsburgh and Cincinnati; Buffalo, Cleveland and Detroit; and New York and the Southeastern 'Cotton Ports'. In four of the eight instances New York was directly involved. In two other instances (Philadelphia–Baltimore and Buffalo–Cleveland–Detroit), there was a sizable component that had New York as its ultimate origin or destination. Even in the remaining two cases (Cincinnati–Louisville and Pittsburgh–Cincinnati), there were more than a few who were coming from or going to New York. An avowedly conservative claim made in 1828 put New York's arrivals and departures by steamboat alone at a minimum of 320000 passengers. By the late 1830s the number of one-way trips originating and terminating in the city probably surpassed 1300000 – *exclusive* of those made by the city's own resident businessmen.

Interurban trade and the circulation of specialized information

The full significance of the mutual relationships between interurban trade patterns and interurban information flows[7] can be more fully appreciated if it is realized that most long-distance trade in the pretelegraphic US was in some sense interurban. That is, at some point in their journey from ultimate origin to ultimate destination, agricultural products, raw materials and manufactured goods usually moved either from one port city to another, or from an urban collection centre to an urban distribution centre.

While expanding during the first two decades after 1790, interurban trade in the US was overshadowed by the trade links between US port-cities and British and continental European ports. Thereafter, and especially as a consequence of the War of 1812 and the spread of settlement, domestic interregionally and intraregionally oriented trade between cities acquired an increasing primacy over foreign-oriented interurban trade. Despite some railroad construction during the 1830s and some improvement in the quality of the most important roads, the vast bulk of interurban trade within the US up to 1840 occurred via coastal shipping, the rapidly expanding network of canals, and other inland waterways. (The limited role of overland transportation in domestic interurban trade was a result of its costliness. Bulk commodities could not move overland for any appreciable distance without raising their prices to unmarketable levels. In 1816 the charge for carting corn 136 miles to Philadelphia was alone equal to its selling price. In 1839 canal rates, which were considerably higher than those imposed by coasting vessels, were on the average about 1·5 cents per ton-mile, or less than one-tenth the overland cost absorbed in most instances.) Therefore, coastal and inland-waterway shipping data for individual cities should serve as a good indicator of the overall pattern of interurban trade and trade-generated information flows of those same cities.

Through the repeated emphasis economic historians have given to the growth of economic exchange between the Southeast and Northeast during the first four decades of the nineteenth century, the fact that there was a considerable volume of goods movement between the four largest cities of the national (and Northeastern) city-system has been generally obscured. Data for 1820 and 1840 display that the extent of coastal shipping interaction between New York, Philadelphia, Boston and Baltimore was great in relative as well as absolute terms (Table 2.5). The coastal commodity flows crisscrossing between these places were of three basic types: agricultural or raw-material production from the hinterland of the port of origin; manufactures produced in the port of origin or its hinterland urban dependants; and redistributive shipments.[8]

As might be expected, each of the four major cities additionally had an important commerce with smaller cities in its own interior and coastal hinterland. However, in city-system development terms, it is the degree of *large-city interdependence* existing even at these early dates that is most impressive. In 1820 and 1840 New York and Boston each provided more arrivals for Philadelphia than any other port inside or outside the Northeast. In those same two years New York and Boston each accounted for more arrivals in Baltimore than any other port in the country. Likewise, in 1820 and 1840 New York, Philadelphia and Baltimore were among Boston's four most important shipping-arrival origins (in both years the outsider was New Orleans, the country's fifth largest city). In 1840 Baltimore was less important than Boston and Philadelphia in New York's coastal trade. However, it still ranked fifth among New York's domestic arrival origins (both New Orleans and Mobile surpassed it in that respect, owing to the scale of the cotton trade). Only between Philadelphia and Baltimore, separated by an extremely roundabout route to the south of Cape Charles, was the volume of through coastal shipping interaction relatively small.[9] There is a strong contrast between this complex picture of large-city interdependence, with coastal interaction occurring in both directions between every possible pair of ports, and what is permissible according to a central-place view of hierarchically structured city-system interdependencies. As far as the four leading cities of the Northeast are concerned, the latter would only allow a one-way flow of goods from New York to each of the three centres immediately below it in the urban-size hierarchy, and from the larger Philadelphia to the smaller Baltimore.

Table 2.5: Coastal shipping arrival matrices for major Northeastern cities, 1820 and 1840[a]

Place of arrival[b]	1820 Place of departure			
	New York	Philadelphia	Boston	Baltimore
New York	—	100	101	54
Philadelphia	68	—	72	12[c]
Boston	91	43	—	72
Baltimore	38	13[c]	56	—

Place of arrival[d]	1840 Place of departure			
	New York	Philadelphia	Boston	Baltimore
New York	—	210 (333)[e]	335 (577)	175 (290)
Philadelphia	233 (370)	—	90 (172)	5 (9)[f]
Boston	245 (388)	191 (320)	—	107 (178)
Baltimore	144 (250)	4 (6)[f]	67 (124)	—

(a) For sources and further details on weighting of 1840 data (note (d), below) see Pred (1973b), pp. 115–16.

(b) The 1820 arrival totals are somewhat more crude than those for 1840 because the data source made no distinction between ships, brigs, schooners and sloops. The differences in carrying capacity between these different types of vessel were considerable.

(c) During the 1820s the volume of trade moving coastwise between Philadelphia and Baltimore was apparently exceeded by that moving via a much shorter route which included two waterborne links and a land leg over the Delmarva peninsula.

(d) Arrivals in parentheses weighted according to variations in the carrying capacity of ships, brigs, schooners and sloops.

(e) The number of Philadelphia arrivals at New York was actually much greater since 'many' of the coal-laden schooners coming from the Pennsylvania city were not tallied by New York port authorities. In addition, much of the 1840 freight traffic between Philadelphia and New York went across New Jersey via the Delaware and Raritan Canal, which opened in 1834.

(f) In 1840 there was a noteworthy goods traffic between Baltimore and Philadelphia that went via the Chesapeake and Delaware Canal, which had been completed in 1830.

As intimated earlier, with few exceptions the major cities of the Southeast – New Orleans, Charleston, Mobile, Savannah, Richmond and Norfolk – carried out a comparatively small absolute volume of commodity exchange with one another throughout the pretelegraphic period. Since the principal export of four of the six largest Southeastern city-ports was cotton, and since all but New Orleans were not large by 1840 Northeastern standards, there was little reason for them to attain high absolute levels of commodity exchange. Even in relative terms, when an adjustment for population is made, the levels of commercial interaction between pairs of Southeastern ports were not really comparable with those between virtually every major Northeastern pair. The limited commercial interaction between leading Southeastern cities is entirely in keeping with the slow and comparatively low-volume movement of specialized information between most of these places suggested by the newspaper-information time-lag, postal-service and business-travel evidence.

The coastal exchange of Southeastern agricultural products for US and European manufactures coming from the major Northeastern ports was an outstanding feature of domestic trade following the War of 1812. Data for 1820 and 1840 reveal that the interregional trade involving leading Southeastern and Northeastern ports completely overshadowed the intraregional coastal activity of the Southeast. The absolute volume of traffic moving from New York and Boston to each of the six major Southeastern ports was far greater than that between any Southeastern port-pair except New Orleans and Mobile. Also, the absolute level of commerce between Philadelphia and Baltimore, at one end, and some individual Southeastern ports, at the other end, was generally somewhat higher than between Southeastern ports.

The focus usually placed on interregional trade also often obscures the importance of intraregional commodity flows between the largest cities of the Ohio and Upper Mississippi valleys. The interurban commerce of the Old Northwest was not confined to the shipment of Western products from Cincinnati, Pittsburgh, Louisville and St Louis to the Southeast and Northeast via New Orleans, plus the movement of Southeastern staples and Northeastern and European manufactures in the opposite direction. In addition, there was a sizable exchange of goods between Cincinnati, Pittsburgh, Louisville and St Louis. It consisted of agricultural products or raw materials from the hinterland of the river port of origin, products brought into the West through one of the four cities and redistributed intraregionally through the other three cities, and of manufactured goods either from the port of origin itself or from some smaller hinterland city. In this regional city-system too, the early established pattern of large-city interdependence, with two-way exchanges between every possible pair of major river ports, is in stark contrast to the interdependence pattern that is possible from a hierarchical central-place theory standpoint. With respect to the system's four largest units such a point of view would only permit a one-way flow of goods from Cincinnati to each of the next three ranked centres, and from the larger Louisville to the smaller St Louis.

The completion of the Erie Canal in 1825 opened an all-water route from Buffalo to New York. The completion of the Ohio Canal in 1833 facilitated the movement of surplus grain from a large part of Ohio and western Pennsylvania to Cleveland. Especially after these two events, the interregional trade of the portion of the West oriented toward the eastern Great Lakes helped to create intra-regional flows among that region's major centres – Buffalo, Cleveland and Detroit. Here, too, the structure of early developed large-city interdependencies did not follow a hierarchical central-place theory model. In the late 1830s two-way flows existed between Buffalo and Cleveland, Buffalo and Detroit, and Detroit and Cleveland, rather than only one-way flows from first-ranking Buffalo to the smaller-sized Cleveland and Detroit.

Large-city rank stability and city-system development in the pre-telegraphic US: a model

The largest metropolitan complexes of the US Northeast, which also have considerable national stature, solidified their regional city-system size ranks during the period from 1790 to 1840. In the decades immediately after the War of 1812 today's major metropolitan complexes of the Ohio and Upper Mississippi valleys had already established their dominance. Similarly, during the late 1820s and 1830s the now dominant metropolitan complexes of the eastern Great Lakes asserted their high regional city-system ranks.[10] Two features of the just completed sketch of pretelegraphic interurban specialized-information circulation and interurban trade are essential to the interpretation of the onset of this rank-stability phenomenon and, more generally, early city-system development in the US and other advanced economies.

First, the circulation of specialized economic information was spatially biased in such a manner that it was most readily available in the nationally largest cities. Likewise, at the regional scale specialized economic information was most easily obtainable in the urban units which were emerging as regional city-system dominants. Secondly, two-way economic interdependencies of some significance early manifested themselves between the largest cities of both the national system of cities and newly formed regional city-systems. These two-way interdependencies were in some measure synonymous with the local and hinterland specialization of economic activities. With these two generalizations in mind, a descriptive probabilistic model may be outlined of the process by which rank stability sets in among the largest units of a national or regional city-system during a relatively early period of system development. (Since the largest urban units of the pretelegraphic Southeast were not yet members of a regional city-system, the model applies to them only in so far as they were members of the national system of cities.)

Basic model structure

Imagine a comparatively large mercantile city (C_1), i.e. a city whose principal functions lie within a complex of wholesaling-trading sectors.[11] Its relative size indicates the city has begun to outdistance most competitors within its national or regional city-system. Much of the previous and ongoing growth of the city's population (and activity system) is attributable to a series of locally self-perpetuating circular and cumulative feedbacks which are here only diagrammatically represented as a submodel in Figure 2.8.[12] The feedbacks between (1) the wholesaling-trading complex and its dependent manufacturing activities and (2) local earnings and multiplier effects are collapsed into a shorthand version in the lower left-hand portion of Figure 2.9. The simplified local-growth submodel is also shown at the upper left of Figure 2.9 as simultaneously operating for other comparatively large mercantile cities $(C_2, C_3 \ldots C_n)$ belonging to the same national or regional system of cities.

While the functioning of the local-growth submodel is important, the continued population growth and high size rank of C_1, or any other large mercantile city, to a great extent spring from its trading linkages and economic interaction with other leading centres. More precisely, each sizable increment in the wholesaling-trading complex of C_1 not only enhances the activity-system employment roles and population of that city, but also either directly or indirectly causes economic interdependence, or interaction, with other large centres within the same national or regional city-system. This interdependence, by increasing the dimensions of wholesaling-trading activities in other large cities, triggers the local-growth submodel of those places and thereby brings them further economic expansion. Direct increases in interdependence occur when expansion of the

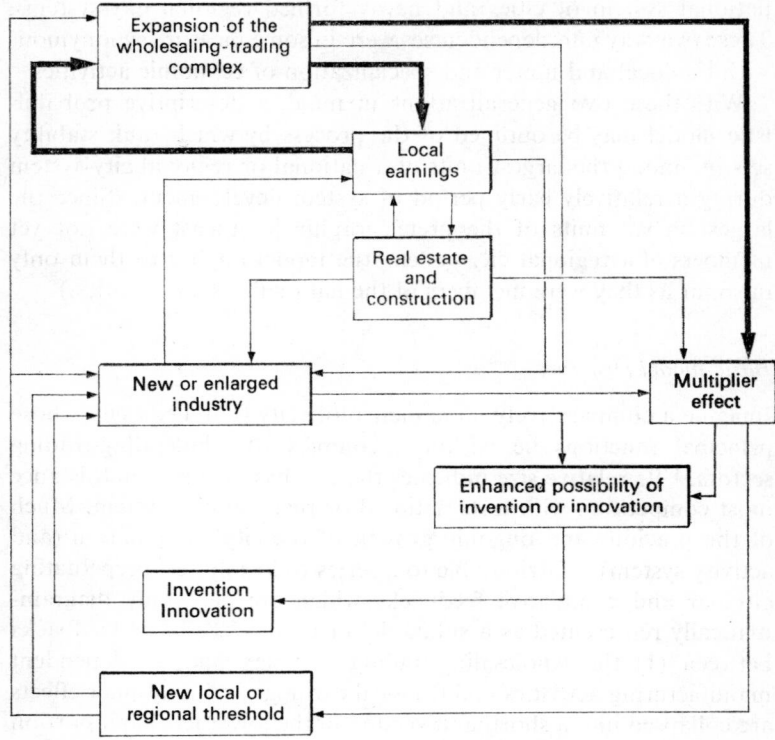

Figure 2.8: *The circular and cumulative feedback process of local urban size-growth for a single large US mercantile city, 1790–1840. Heavy lines indicate the most important relationships. For some understanding of the lower half of the diagram see the discussion below (pp. 88–92) on large-city local size growth during periods of initial modern industrialization.*

C_1 wholesaling-trading complex is a result of a larger scale of *exports* to C_2, C_3 or C_n of either local and hinterland specialities or of goods originating in another country or region. Expanded interdependence also occurs when other large cities export to C_1; i.e. when the wholesaling-trading complex of C_1 enlarges the scale of its operation by increasing agricultural or industrial *imports* originating in or passing through the hands of the expanding wholesaling-trading complex in C_2, C_3 or C_n. Indirect growth of interdependence between C_1 and C_2, C_3 or C_n results when population

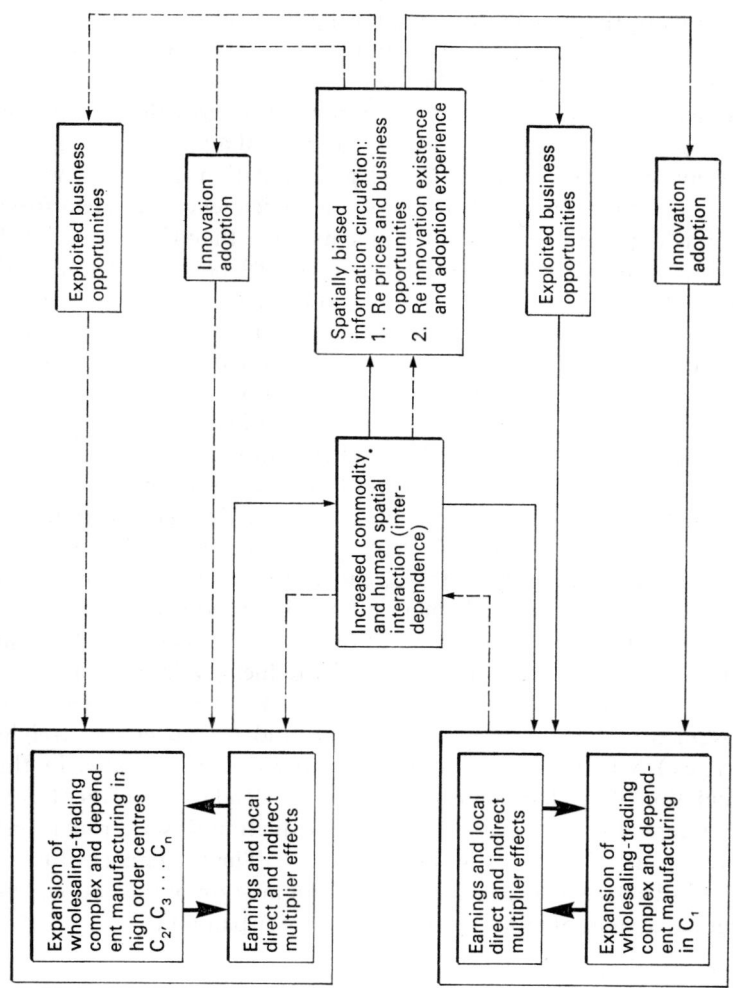

Figure 2.9: *The circular and cumulative feedback process generating large-city rank stability in national and regional city-systems during relatively early development, or pretelegraphic conditions.*

increases in the former city create a larger demand for the locally consumed agricultural and industrial goods normally received from or through the latter cities. In the same manner, indirect growth of interdependence comes about when population growth in C_2, C_3 or C_n magnifies the local demand for agricultural and industrial goods customarily secured from C_1. (The population increases which precipitate the indirect expansion of interdependence may stem from wholesaling-trading complex increments other than those associated with the direct expansion of large-city interdependence.) Enlarged commodity interaction between C_1 and C_2, C_3 or C_n is often accompanied by a widening of human spatial interaction between the same cities. This is so because of the frequent necessity for merchants or their agents to travel to the purchase-source or sales-destination city in order to bargain and consummate business transactions.

Each increment in commodity and human spatial interaction between C_1 and other large mercantile cities contributes to spatial biases in the circulation of specialized information. (Business travel is not the sole source of these spatial biases. The expansion of interdependence, or interurban trade, between C_1 and C_2, C_3 or C_n can add to spatially biased information flows by creating an incentive to improve the quality, speed and frequency of transport and postal linkages between those large centres; by inducing a larger volume of interurban business mail; and by engendering a greater interurban movement of newspapers via the mails and passenger and freight services.) Whatever their source, reinforced spatial biases in the circulation of specialized information in turn lead to yet further large-city interaction and spatially biased information flows through one of two pairs of feedback loops (Figure 2.9). The net impact of these two feedback sequences is a continued domination of the national or regional system of cities by the same large urban units.

Feedback loop details

One pair of feedback loops involves information about market changes, prices and major business opportunities in general. The information flows in question are spatially biased in such a manner that information either originating or entering the national (or regional) city-system at one large mercantile city will have a greater probability of being early acquired and exploited by the entrepreneurs of another large mercantile city than by the entrepreneurs of smaller cities. This is so because smaller cities have both fewer and less frequent contacts with C_1 and other large mercantile cities, and greater time lags from those places. Should a new business opportunity be exploited at one of the large mercantile cities such as C_1, it will eventually be synonymous with an expansion of the local wholesaling-trading complex, employment-role additions to the local activity system and population growth. For one of two reasons this in turns leads both to increased interdependence with one or more of the other large mercantile cities and to reinforced spatial biases of specialized-information circulation.

First, the previously unexploited opportunity directly involves another large mercantile city rather than a smaller city in the same national or regional city-system. Secondly, the previously unexploited opportunity or alternative involves either a smaller city, or another national or regional city-system, but the consequent population growth in C_1 fosters a greater demand for locally consumed agricultural and manufactured goods normally acquired from or through one or more other large mercantile cities.

Given the probabilistic quality of these interrelationships, any given opportunity may be exploited in one, some, or all of a city-system's largest centres. Hence, the model allows for some adjustment in the population ratios of C_1, C_2, $C_3 \ldots C_n$, and perhaps even for minor rank shifting among them. Population-ratio adjustments and minor rank shifting would follow from the occurrence of local employment multipliers in some rather than all of the city-system's leading units; and from consequent minor alterations in the distribution of probabilities among C_1 and other large mercantile cities for subsequent business opportunity exploitation.

Similarly, since the probabilistic aspect of the model sometimes permits business opportunity exploitation in low-probability smaller cities at the same time that exploitation is limited in other system units (including C_1 and other large mercantile cities), small- or medium-size cities can occasionally receive the concentrated economic stimulus necessary for relatively rapid progress through the urban size ranks.

The second pair of feedback loops involves specialized information concerning either the existence of, or demand for, commercial, financial and industrial innovations, as well as information on the experience of those who have already adopted such innovations. Here, too, the spatial biases of information circulation are such that any innovation originating or entering the national (or regional) city-system at one large mercantile city will have a significantly greater probability of being early (and multiply) adopted at other large mercantile cities than at smaller urban units. That is, the early-adoption probability is lower at those smaller and medium-size places within the national or regional city-system which have either fewer and less frequent contacts with the initially accepting city, or greater time lags from that same city. (The chances of adoption in smaller cities will be especially low when the characteristics of a particular innovation are such that its successful application depends on the fulfilment of large market or labour-supply conditions, or other scale requirements.) Adoption at one large mercantile city (e.g. C_1) leads to increased interdependence with other large mercantile cities and reinforced spatial biases in the circulation of specialized information for one of two reasons. The first is that single or multiple adoption of the innovation brings into being previously non-existent forms of interdependence between the national or regional city-system's largest units. This could take place, for example, when the adoption of a new manufacturing practice in one large city augments or creates a demand for raw materials normally procured from the hinterland of another of the city-system's dominant centres. Secondly, the adoption of an innovation brings about local employment multiplier effects and population growth in one large mercantile city, which in turn breeds a larger local demand for the agricultural and manufactured products generally imported from or via one or more other large mercantile cities.

The diffusion feedback loops of the model also allow for some adjustment in the population ratios of C_1, C_2, C_3 ... C_n, and perhaps even for minor rank shifting among them. This is so since the probabilities involved permit any particular economic innovation to be adopted in one, a few or all of a city-system's highest-ranking units, and thus permit the occurrence of innovation-derived multipliers in one, some or all of these centres. In addition, if comparable local multipliers do not occur in all of the city-system's largest cities, there also will follow some minor alterations in the distribution of probabilities among them for the subsequent adoption of economic innovations.

In a like manner the probabilistic nature of the interurban diffusion of commercial and industrial innovations occasionally can result in the relatively rapid ascension of a medium- or small-size city through the size ranks of a city-system. This would occur when an innovation was successfully adopted in a low-probability city at the same time that adoption was limited both in other comparably sized low-probability cities and, perhaps, in most or all large mercantile cities. Size-rank progress would be attributable to sizable and temporally concentrated local employment multipliers, increased economic interaction with other cities, and a higher probability of adopting commercial and industrial innovations at later dates.

The spotlight that this model places on the interdependence of large mercantile cities should not conceal the fact that such centres also grew and maintained their high ranks partially because of their interdependencies with smaller cities, most of which were located within their respective hinterlands. Local growth in a hinterland town could propagate employment multipliers in the much larger mercantile city that dominated it when that local growth sprang from the shipment of agricultural or other goods that were to be further distributed or exported by the wholesaling-trading complex of the receiving dominant centre. Local growth in a hinterland town could also generate employment multipliers in its dominant mercantile city when such local population expansion increased the demand for goods normally acquired from or via that larger place.

If the model diagrammed in Figure 2.9 is expanded explicitly to include cities of all sizes – and not merely large mercantile cities – then the entire process of pretelegraphic city-system growth and development in the US can be synthesized, in admittedly oversimplified terms, by Figure 2.10. Although the pretelegraphic national and regional city-systems of the US began to emerge in a singular historical, institutional and political environment, the feedback mechanisms summarized in Figure 2.10 are probably sufficiently general to describe the earliest city-system growth and development of economically advanced countries and regions in those instances where wholesaling-trading activities were also the main driving force behind growth and development.

Related innovation diffusion evidence

If the above model offers a reasonable depiction of the process by which large-city rank stability sets in within a national or regional city-system, then it should be demonstrable that pretelegraphic patterns of US interurban innovation diffusion were in accord with prevailing spatial biases in the circulation of specialized information. If the model is correct, it is to be expected that the largest units in the national and regional city-systems of the US were usually very

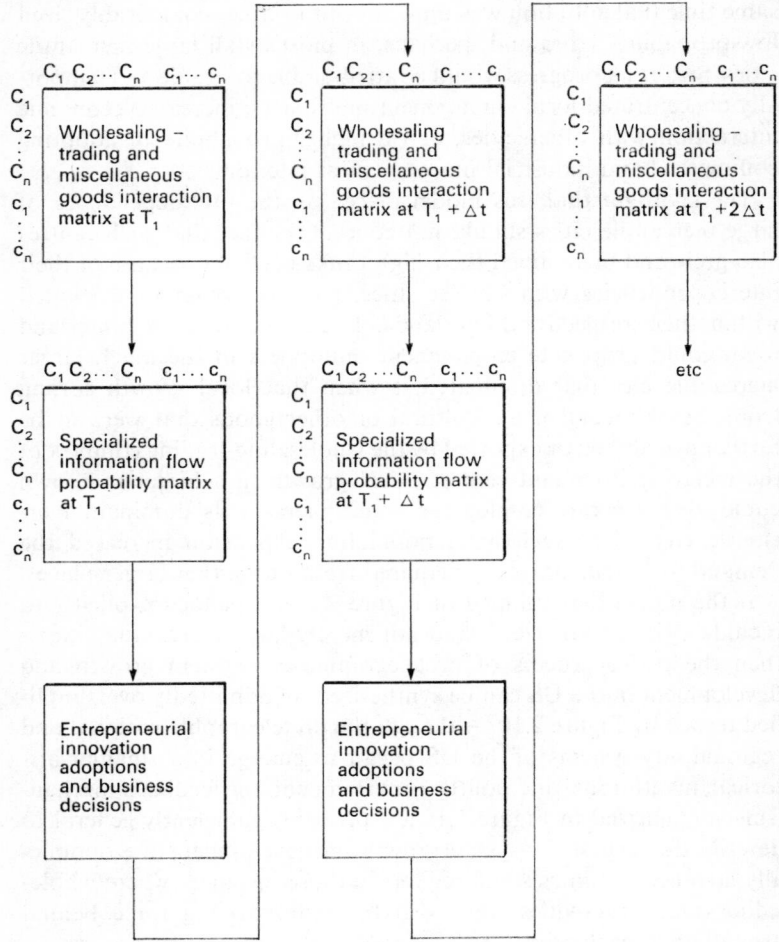

Figure 2.10: *A simplified description of the growth and development process for an entire national or regional city-system during relatively early-development, or pretelegraphic conditions.* $C_1, C_2 \ldots C_n$ *refer to large mercantile cities.* $c_1 \ldots c_n$ *refer to medium- and small-size cities in the hinterlands of* $C_1, C_2 \ldots C_n$.

early to adopt innovations – frequently being the points of innovation origin or entry – and that those same cities were often the scene of multiple adoptions when adoptions were non-existent or limited in smaller cities. Moreover, it is to be expected that diffusion between large cities frequently occurred; that innovations occasionally proceeded from smaller to larger cities; and that, owing to time lags and the strong 'distance decay' of private information, acceptance patterns were highly concentrated, or evidenced a pronounced 'neighbourhood effect'. That is, it is to be anticipated that interurban innovation adoption sequences were *not* largely confined to a hierarchical progression from the largest cities to ones of successively smaller population, as required by those interpretators of interurban diffusion who in various ways argue that innovations are channelled from place to place by the strictly hierarchical interdependencies of Christaller's central-place theory (e.g. Pyle, 1969; Pedersen, 1970; Robson, 1973; Berry, 1972, 1973; Hudson, 1969, 1972; Huang and Gould, 1974).[13]

Fragmentary evidence on the pretelegraphic diffusion of banking, horse-drawn omnibuses, intraurban street railways, daily newspapers, one-penny papers, steamboats, industrially employed steam engines, steam-engine production, and other economic phenomena repeatedly illustrates the following features: early and multiple acceptances in the leading national and regional city-system units; diffusion from one large city to another; other *non-hierarchical as well as hierarchical* adoption sequences; and neighbourhood effects (Pred, 1973b). Furthermore, US government patent records indicate that inventions – which are always in some way dependent on specialized information – were highly concentrated in the largest national and regional city-system centres. (New York, Philadelphia, Boston and Baltimore together accounted for between 24·3 per cent and 38·0 per cent of all patents in every year between 1805 and 1840.[14] After the War of 1812, Cincinnati and Pittsburgh became disproportionately important invention centres, and to a somewhat lesser extent this was so for Louisville, Buffalo, Detroit and Cleveland during the 1820s and 1830s.) If it is assumed that the great bulk of inventions which were practically converted to innovations were first put to use in the city of invention, then these data strongly suggest innovations frequently spread from smaller to larger places and between large cities of roughly the same size, as well as along larger-city to smaller-city hierarchical channels.

Somewhat more precise evidence is obtainable for the diffusion of the 'Panic of 1837', when banks stopped converting paper bank-notes into specie but otherwise remained open. Some of the key details of this process are available because newspapers reported the public resolutions in favour of suspending specie payments made by local businessmen or bankers. These resolutions, and the discussions surrounding them, usually mentioned the sources of diffusion influence. The following are some of the more significant attributes of the diffusion of the 'Panic of 1837' (Figures 2.11–2.13).

(1)   The early adoption of specie payment suspension in the national city-system's largest unit, New York, was apparently influenced by rumours from the less populous Baltimore.

(2)   New York's action was taken several days after gold and silver payments had been halted in the much smaller towns of Natchez, Mississippi (1840 pop. 3612), and Tallahassee, Florida (1840 pop. under 2500), and on the same day that a decision was reached in Montgomery, Alabama (1840 pop. 2179).

(3)   Once specie payment suspension in New York was a fact, Philadelphia, Boston and Baltimore quickly followed suit, although information sources other than New York also played some role.

(4)   A neighbourhood effect quickly spread out around New York. It eventually encompassed much of New Jersey, eastern Pennsylvania, upstate New York, and New England (Figures 2.11–2.12).

(5)   Direct hierarchical influences were exerted by New York in Providence, Albany, Rochester, Detroit, Cleveland and a host of smaller cities.

(6)   New York, Philadelphia and Baltimore jointly influenced a number of places, including Pittsburgh, which was the first city in the Ohio and Upper Mississippi valley city-system to enter the diffusion process.

(7)   Adoption influence was passed from Cincinnati to Louisville, and from Cincinnati, Louisville and Pittsburgh to St Louis.

(8)   Suspensions first appeared in the regional city-system of the eastern Great Lakes at Cleveland and Detroit.

(9)   No decision was reached in Richmond (1840 pop. 20153) until it was known that sister banks had taken action in Norfolk (1840 pop. 10920).

(10)   Events in the considerably smaller Natchez, as well as Mobile (1840 pop. 12672), had a clear impact on the stoppage of coin payments in New Orleans (1840 pop. 102193).

(11)   Although affected by news from major Northeastern centres, the bankers of Charleston (South Carolina) and Augusta (Georgia)

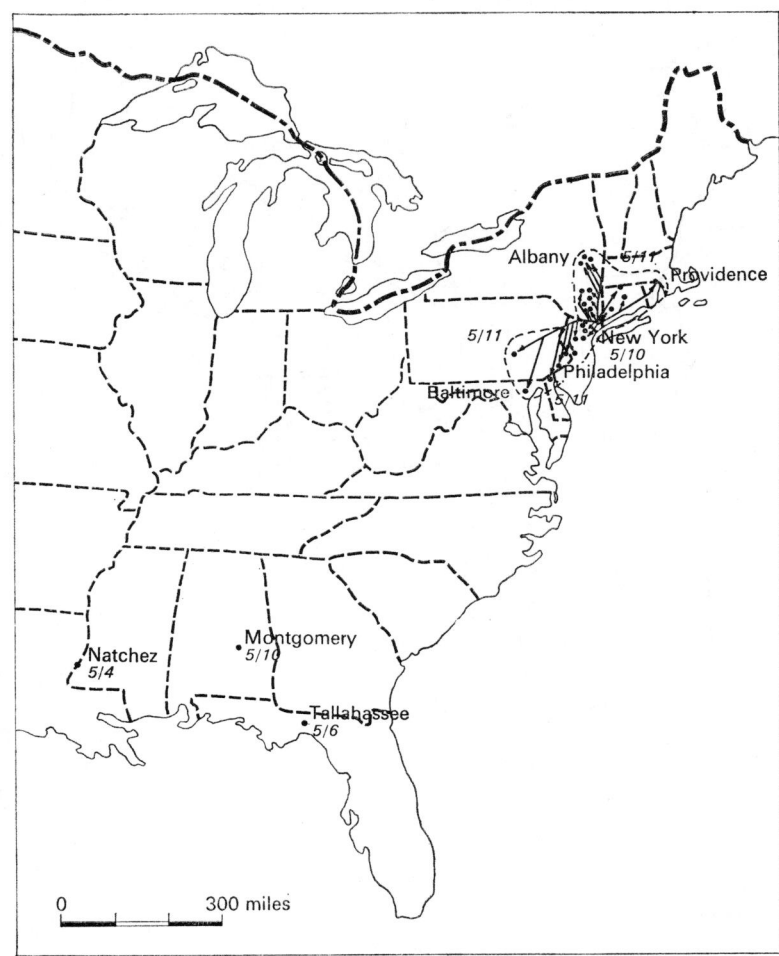

Figure 2.11: *The Panic of 1837: known specie payment suspension dates and lines of influence, May 4–11. Here, and in Figures 2.12 and 2.13, lines of influence do not necessarily represent actual routes of information circulation. Sources for Figures 2.11–2.13 are given in Pred (1973b), pp. 328–30.*

were also persuaded by information acquired from other less populous Southeastern centres.

In summary, the spread of specie payment suspensions had char-

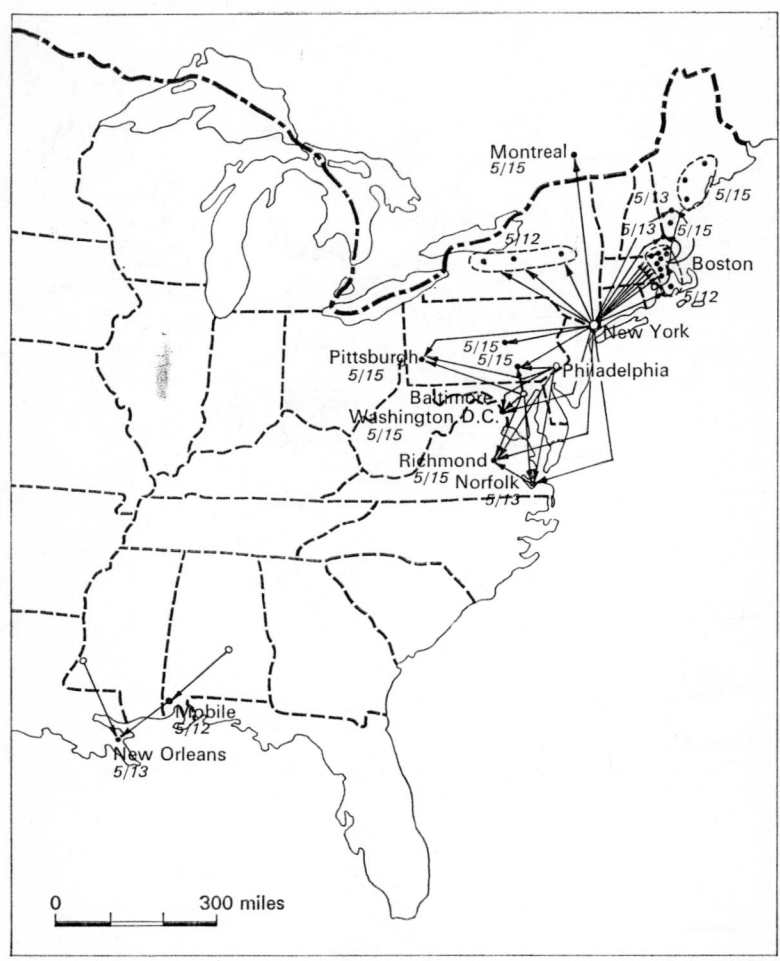

Figure 2.12: *The Panic of 1837: known specie payment suspension dates and lines of influence, May 12–15. Here, and in Figure 2.13, open dots refer to cities with earlier suspensions that influenced other urban centres during the periods in question.*

acteristics in keeping with the model depicted in Figures 2.9 and 2.10. These include non-hierarchical as well as hierarchical acceptance sequences, early acceptance by the leading cities of the national city-system, large-city first acceptances within the two Western

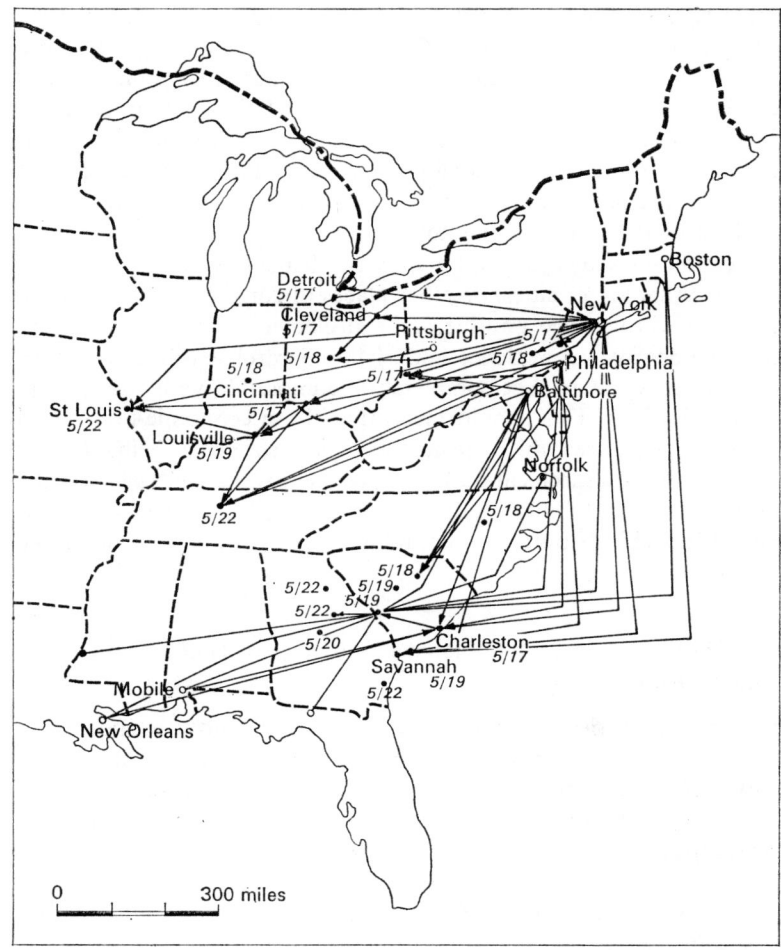

Figure 2.13: *The Panic of 1837: known specie payment suspension dates and lines of influence, May 16–22.*

regional city-systems, and a strongly expressed neighbourhood effect.

The preceding findings are apparently incompatible with hierarchical-diffusion schemes which ignore the real-world complexity of interurban economic and information-circulation linkages. This merits further comment. In no instance has an empirically based hierarchical-diffusion interpretation specified the sequence of link-ages through which adoption-influencing information passes from city to city. Instead, such studies have usually arrived at a hierarchical conclusion by the moderate to good correlations obtained when innovation acceptance dates are plotted against city size. However, even when the studied innovations are 'threshold', or market-size, sensitive, the necessary perfect correlations are never found. A com-parison of the points falling above and below any of the obtained regression lines always shows some cities being the scene of adoption before either larger cities, or other places of comparable population. In other words, since non-hierarchical elements are always present to some degree, the evidence underlying hierarchical-diffusion inter-pretations is not in fact completely incompatible with the just re-ported findings. This should mean that those economic-innovation adoption sequences which are mistakenly interpreted as being the sole product of a hierarchical-diffusion process can be generated by the large-city rank stability model whose probabilistic attributes allow *both* hierarchical and non-hierarchical information and influence chains.[15]

City-system growth and development during periods of initial modern industrialization

In those countries and regions which are currently economically advanced, the long-term rank stability of large metropolitan com-plexes in particular, and city-system growth and development in general, has usually been profoundly influenced by events that oc-curred during periods of initial modern industrialization. In a few instances true city-system formation has coincided with that period of time when manufacturing rather than wholesaling-trading activi-ties were the major contributor to urban economic growth (cf. Borchert, 1967; Lampard, 1955, 1968). More commonly, the era of initial modern industrialization was highlighted by a spatial con-centration of manufacturing in already large cities, which resulted in a strengthening of some of the major channels of interdependence within already functioning national or regional city-systems. Once again, it is instructive to examine conditions in the United States in order to gain some appreciation of the *general* feedback mechanisms that at one time or another have been operative in all advanced economies. In as much as we are dealing mostly with the historical perpetuation, rather than the initiation, of large-city expansion and city-system growth and development, conditions in the US during the period from roughly the late 1860s to 1914 can be treated in a much more summary fashion than were 1790–1840 conditions.

US urban-industrial growth, 1860–1914[16]

The late 1840s and 1850s witnessed the first burst of American industrialization outside the textile industries. However, it was not until the 1860s that modern manufacturing, with its emphasis on the specialized mass-production factory (rather than the small-volume undifferentiated workshop), became the cornerstone of urbanization and national economic growth. Despite periodic interruptions by inflation, protracted deflation and depression, the share of manufacturing in total US commodity output rose from 32 per cent in 1860 to 53 per cent in 1900. And, in the ensuing decade absolute manufacturing production burgeoned almost as much as it had in the previous thirty-year span (Table 2.6) while continued articulation of the nation's railroad network facilitated the development of mass markets. Concomitantly, the top of the US urban-size hierarchy became characterized more and more by industrial, multifunctional cities, and less and less by cities dominated by wholesaling and trading functions.

The new leading role of factory manufacturing in the growth of individual cities and entire city-systems is vividly borne out by Table 2.7, which shows the changes in employment composition and worker productivity that occurred in some of the country's most important cities between 1860 and 1890.[17]

Taken together, Tables 2.6 and 2.7 reflect the fact that, during the post-Civil War half-century of rapid intertwined industrialization and urbanization, the largest US city-system units as a group grew at a faster pace than smaller cities and that, in relative as well as absolute terms, manufacturing activities became increasingly spatially concentrated in the most populous group of centres. (In 1860 the ten cities listed in Table 2.7 collectively accounted for 24·1 per cent of all US manufacturing value added. In 1890 those same places answered for 38·1 per cent of the total.) Put otherwise, the channels of interdependence, or growth transmission, within the national and regional city-systems of the US increasingly involved manufactured goods that were produced in very highly ranked and quickly growing places.

The interrelationship between large-city growth and the absolute

Table 2.6 The urbanization and industrialization of the United States, 1860–1910[a]

Data category	1860	1870	1890	1910	Percentage increase 1860–1910
A Total US population (thousands)	31 513	39 905	63 056	92 407	193·2
B Urban population (thousands)	6 217	9 902	22 106	41 999	575·6
C Population in cities >100 000 (thousands)	2 639	4 130	9 698	20 302	669·3
B/A	19·7%	24·8%	35·1%	45·5%	—
C/A	8·4%	10·3%	15·4%	22·0%	—
Cities of 10 000–100 000/A	6·4%	8·5%	12·3%	15·0%	—
Cities of 2 500–10 000/A	5·0%	6·0%	7·4%	8·6%	—
Miles of railroad operated[b]	30 626	52 922	166 703	266 185	769·1
Index of manufacturing production (1899=100)	16	25	71	172	975·0
Pig iron production (thousands of long tons)	821	1 665	9 203	27 304	3 225·7

(a)   For sources and additional data see Pred (1966b), p. 17.
(b)   Not including yard tracks and sidings.

and relative spatial concentration of manufacturing is graphically illustrated by changes in the county-level spatial distribution of manufacturing employment in the Midwest from 1870 to 1900.[18] In spite of almost universal population increases, many Midwestern counties experienced absolute declines in manufacturing employment for one, two or all three of the decades intervening between 1870 and 1900 (Figure 2.14a). In addition, during that same thirty-year span, one of two kinds of relative industrial decline was experienced in most of those Midwestern counties that were neither diminishing in absolute importance, nor contained the most rapidly growing cities (or their young suburbs).[19] Some of the counties in

Table 2.7: Growth of manufacturing employment and productivity in ten US cities, 1860–90[a]

City	Manufacturing employment		Percentage of population in manufacturing[b]		Percentage of nation's manufacturing value added		Manufacturing value added per worker in 1879 prices	
	1860	1890	1860	1890	1860	1890	1860	1890
New York	106 216[c]	477 186[c]	9·0	19·0	10·2	13·6	$861·8	$1386·9
Philadelphia	98 983	260 264	17·5	24·9	7·8	6·6[d]	704·5	1142·9
Chicago	5 360	210 366	4·8	19·1	0·6	6·4	937·9	1347·4
St Louis	9 352	94 051	5·8	20·8	1·1	2·7	1008·8	1267·4
Boston	19 283	90 805	10·8	20·2	2·0	2·6	929·4	1299·2
Baltimore	17 054	83 745	8·0	19·3	1·0	1·7	520·8	908·8
Pittsburgh	8 837	56 438	18·0	23·7	0·7	1·4	720·6	1128·7
San Francisco	1 503	48 446	2·6	16·2	0·2	1·4	998·9	1317·0[e]
Cleveland	3 462	50 674	8·0	19·4	0·3	1·2	673·6	1051·9
Detroit	2 350	38 178	5·2	18·5	0·2	0·9	685·7	1055·9

(a) For sources as well as additional data and clarification see Pred (1966b), p. 20.

(b) Obviously, percentage of the population in manufacturing is not to be confused with percentage of the work force in manufacturing. The latter percentage was normally 2·5 to 3·0 times greater than the former. However, for a number of reasons 1860 and 1890 data on manufacturing work-force percentages are not comparable.

(c) New York as constituted under the 1898 Act of Consolidation. The 1890 manufacturing employment data for other cities *do not* include any industrial 'suburbs' that may have emerged by that date.

(d) Despite the fall-off in its percentage of total US value added by manufacturing, Philadelphia's industrial value added grew by roughly 325 per cent between 1860 and 1890 (as measured in constant 1879 prices). Philadelphia's share of total US value added by manufacturing probably would have been significantly higher if its industrial 'suburbs' were included.

(e) In order to compensate for extreme inflation in San Francisco, the city's manufacturing value added was reduced on the basis of regional wage differentials.

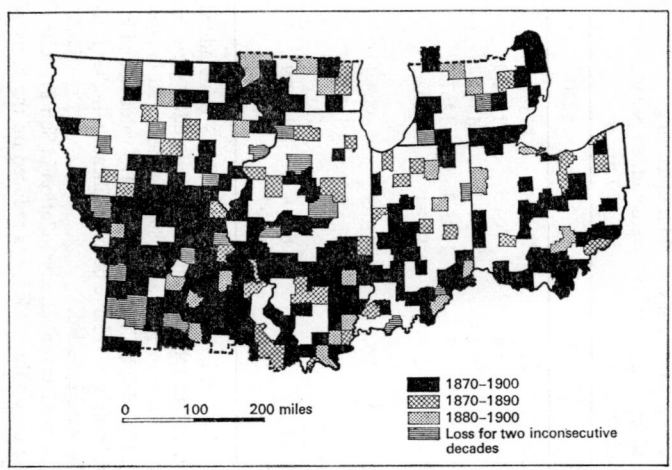

Figure 2.14a: *Counties in a selected portion of the Midwest with absolute manufacturing losses for at least two decades between 1870 and 1900. For sources see Pred (1966b), p. 62.*

question had percentage gains in population that outstripped their percentage gains in manufacturing employment (Figures 2.14b). The remainder failed to register percentage increments in their industrial work forces comparable to those of the area's largest cities – Chicago, St Louis, Cleveland and Detroit (Figures 2.14b and 2.15). Both these conditions strongly suggest that existing and potential producers in the towns and cities of the relatively declining counties had a portion of their expanded local market usurped by firms located either in nearby large metropolises, or in Northeastern centres with favoured transport rates.

Large-city growth and city-system development during periods of rapid industrialization: a model

The simultaneous perpetuation of large-city growth, or rank stability, and spatial concentration of burgeoning manufacturing activities that occurred in the US between 1860 and 1914 (and in other advanced economies at somewhat differently dated periods of initial modern industrialization) was the outcome of a number of dynamically interwoven factors. Much of what transpired can be captured through a translation of the model which portrayed both the onset of

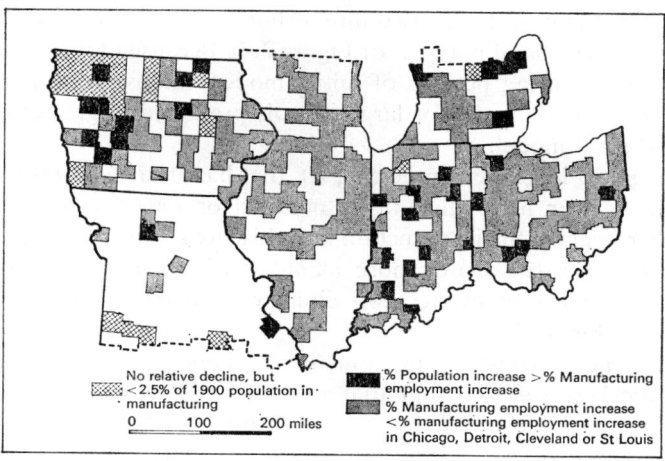

Figure 2.14b: *Counties in a selected portion of the Midwest with either relative manufacturing employment decreases between 1870 and 1900, or less than 2·5 per cent of their 1900 population employed in manufacturing.*

large-city rank stability and pretelegraphic city-system growth and development (Figures 2.9 and 2.10). The most important adjustment to be made to that model is a replacement of the submodel of locally contained growth for C_1 and other comparatively large mercantile

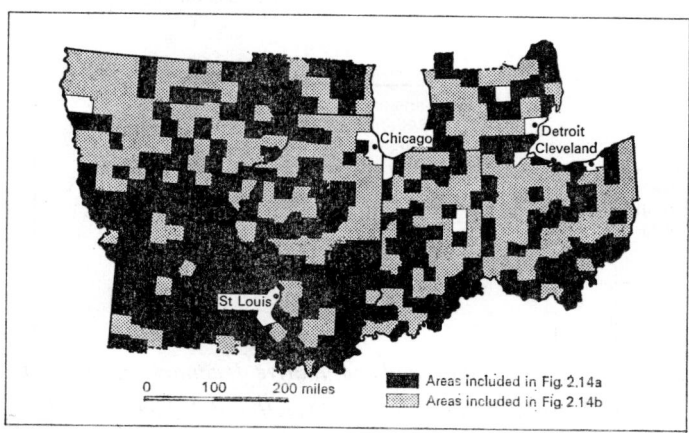

Figure 2.15: *Figures 2.14a and 2.14b combined and generalized.*

cities (i.e. the model collapsed into a shorthand version in the lower and upper left-hand portions of Figure 2.9). Because of its particular importance during periods of initial modern industrialization, the local-growth submodel for large cities is presented in greater detail than the full model.

Imagine a large mercantile city, C_1, that has attained a position of dominance, or high rank, in its national or regional city-system. Further imagine the introduction into this city of one or more large-scale factories (in one or more manufacturing categories). Sooner or later this event evokes two circular feedback chains of local reaction (Figure 2.16).[20]

First, new manufacturing functions, *whether or not they serve local markets*, will have an initial multiplier effect, creating a variety

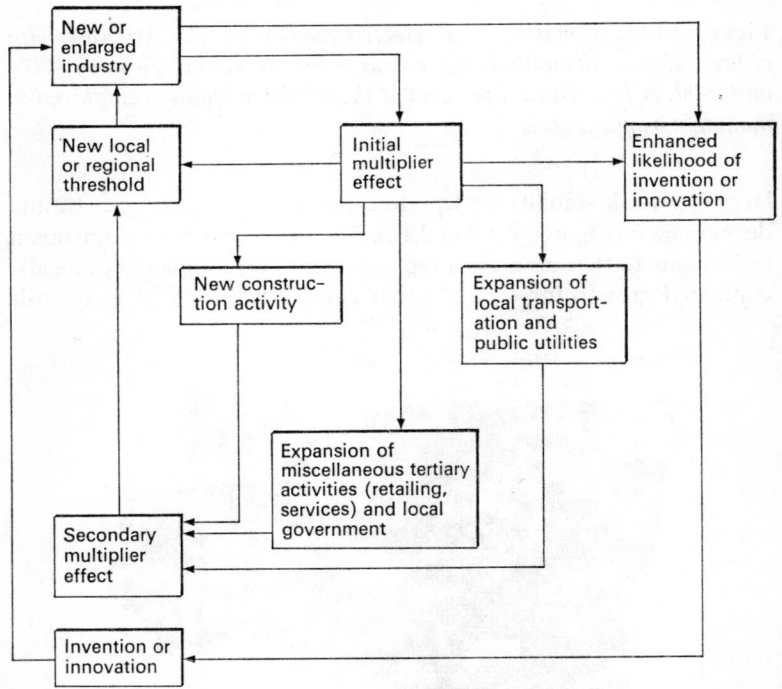

Figure 2.16: *The circular and cumulative feedback process of local urban size-growth for individual large cities during periods of initial modern industrialization. Inventions and innovations may involve* non-threshold *as well as threshold manufacturing activities.*

of additional employment roles in the local activity system. Some of these multipliers will always be of the *employee-expenditure* variety; while others will be of either the *backward-linkage* or *forward-linkage* varieties.[21] The combined effect of new industrial employment and an initial multiplier effect will be an alteration of the city's occupational structure (with the industrial sector gaining *vis-à-vis* the wholesaling-trading complex), an increase in population, and the probable attainment of one or more local or regional industrial thresholds. These higher thresholds, or larger markets, can support new manufacturing functions as well as additional plants or capacity in existing industrial categories. Once production facilities have been constructed in accordance with the new thresholds, a second round of growth is initiated, and eventually still higher thresholds are achieved. Plant construction in response to these thresholds again generates an initial multiplier effect and higher thresholds, and the process continues, at an irregular pace, in a circular and cumulative manner (unless interrupted or impeded by either local diseconomies or disadvantageous changes in the economic, technological or political environment).

This first feedback sequence is further propelled by the secondary multiplier effects deriving from the non-industrial jobs brought into existence by new or enlarged manufacturing. That is, the new construction activity, the expanded operation of local transportation and public utilities, and the increased size and variety of activities providing consumers with goods and services – all of which can be associated with an initial multiplier effect – create multiplier effects of their own that also contribute to the fulfilment of local or regional industrial thresholds.

The second cycle of local circular and cumulative feedbacks occurs at the same time and compounds and reinforces the effects of the first. This chain involves the local generation of specialized information which is most easily acquired by others in the same city. (The subsequent spread of this specialized information is influenced in a probabilistic manner by existing large-city interaction and the overall pattern of city-system interdependencies.) It stems from the continually more complex network of interpersonal communications that follows from an expanding population of economic actors. The multiplication of interactions among the growing number of individuals engaged in the manufacturing and tertiary sectors enhances the possibilities of technological improvement and invention in *non-threshold* as well as threshold industries, enlarges the likelihood of the adoption of more efficient managerial and financial practices, increases the speed with which non-locally and locally originating ideas are locally disseminated, and eases the diffusion of skills and knowledge brought in by migrants from other areas (cf. Meier, 1962). More specifically, technological improvements and inventions are stimulated since perception of demand, problem awareness, and the interindustry transfer of problem solutions – the three major sources of inventive activity – are all information-linked (cf. Feller, 1975). Once *some* inventions or ideas are implemented, or become innovations,[22] that is, once new factories have been erected, or old ones enlarged, employment and population increase, the web of interpersonal communications is again extended and densened, the chances for invention and innovation are further enhanced, and the circular process continues, perhaps even at an accelerated pace, until diverted or hindered.

In the mind's eye, the local-growth submodel just described can be collapsed and inserted into Figure 2.9 by altering the wording of the upper and lower left-hand portions of that figure from 'expansion of wholesaling-trading complex and dependent manufacturing' to 'expansion of manufacturing and dependent activities'. Once that substitution is made, the remainder of the process perpetuating large-city rank stability is easily summarized by continued reference to Figure 2.9.

Each round of manufacturing expansion in a highly ranked unit (C_1, C_2, C_3 or C_n) of a national or regional city-system calls forth increased goods interaction, or interdependence, with one or more other such dominant centres, and the triggering of the local growth submodel in those other large places. This may be due to:

(1)   the new or enlarged industry's propagation of non-local backward- and forward-linkage multipliers in other highly ranked centres;

(2)   an increased demand for specialized manufactured products or miscellaneous goods obtained from other dominant cities as a result of local population growth; or

(3)   reflexive multipliers, whereby the multiplier effects propagated by C_1 (or C_2, C_3 or C_n) at another major city magnify the demand for specialized industrial and miscellaneous goods normally obtained from C_1 (or C_2, C_3 or C_n).

Each increase in large-city goods interaction and associated business travel contributes to already existing spatial biases in the circulation of specialized information. These informational spatial biases in turn lead to yet further large-city interdependence and spatially biased specialized information flows through their probabilistic influence on the business-opportunity and innovation-diffusion feedback loops. In contrast to the pretelegraphic model, most of the exploited opportunities involve new market outlets or supply sources for local manufacturing establishments. Likewise, most of the key innovations passing through the diffusion feedback loop are in the form of manufacturing products or new production technology rather than commercial or financial novelties. (Where non-threshold manufacturing products with high-value-added, or transport-cost insensitive, characteristics are involved, the probabilistic diffusion subprocess is quite apt to be short-circuited, or concentrated on one or a very few large centres which satisfy total demand (cf. Pred, 1965b).)[23]

In passing, it should be noted that US Patent Office data support the invention and innovation-diffusion components of the thus-far outlined model and its local-growth submodel. Information circulation factors apparently contributed to a highly disproportionate concentration of inventions – and, presumably, initial innovation adoptions – in the largest city-system units. For example, in 1880 the ten nationally and regionally dominant centres listed in Table 2.7 answered for almost 34 per cent of all patents granted, but only just over 10 per cent of the nation's population. Although these data are not without their limitations (Pred, 1966b), they suggest – like pretelegraphic statistics – that innovations did not solely diffuse along larger-city to smaller-city hierarchical channels. In addition, there must have been frequent non-hierarchical spread between large cities (including Cincinnati, Buffalo and other highly ranked regional centres not listed in Table 2.7), and from smaller to larger places.

If the translated version of the model diagrammed in Figure 2.9 is extended so as explicitly to cover cities of all sizes – and not merely the highest-ranking city-system units – then the process of city-system growth and development during periods of initial modern industrialization can be summarized, again in admittedly oversimplified terms, by making a simple adjustment to Figure 2.10. There, the top row of boxes should be altered to read 'manufactured products and miscellaneous goods interaction matrix' instead of 'wholesaling-trading and miscellaneous goods interaction matrix'.

Other aspects of large-city growth and the spatial concentration of manufacturing

The concurrent spatial concentration of manufacturing and maintenance of large-city rank stability in the US between 1860 and 1914 was furthered by factors which are not directly dealt with in the translated versions of Figures 2.9 and 2.10. Improved transportation was almost certainly the most important of these factors in the US, as well as elsewhere (cf., for example, Blainey, 1966, on Australia; Whebell, 1969, on Canada; Smailes, 1957, on Great Britain; Pottier, 1963, on France).

During the period 1860–1910 the US railroad network was expanded and intensified greatly (Table 2.6) while railroad freight charges per ton-mile fell 70–75 per cent, or more. These developments favoured those new and enlarged large-scale factories which were located in major centres and had comparatively low marginal production costs because of the size of the market they served. Lowered transport costs and new rail facilities enabled the serving of yet larger market areas, the further reduction of marginal production costs, and the elimination of existing and potential small-scale, small-city producers with higher marginal production costs (cf. Pred, 1962).[24] (This event sequence was self-generating to the extent that mass production brought lower freight charges, or transport economies, to the firm and the possibility of still greater market-area expansion.) In many instances, such spatial lengthening of industrial production was synonymous with increased minimum optimal scales of operation, or the raising of thresholds beyond the reach of smaller cities. The ability to serve larger market areas also often fostered increased large-city interdependence by facilitating additional industrial specialization, or a greater division of labour, especially where non-threshold products were involved. (This is in accordance with the economic adage that the division of labour is limited by the extent of the market.)

Because ton-mile costs on railroads are usually a function of the total traffic per unit distance of track, freight-rate economies also accrued to cities as integral units, and in particular to rapidly expanding cities whose flourishing traffic included food supplies and goods in transit as well as incoming industrial inputs and outgoing manufactures. Hence, the availability of lower freight rates in a relatively few cities on the major trunk lines also helped to attract new manufacturing establishments and stimulate the expansion of existing production capacity, thereby diminishing the importance of less favoured cities. Freight-rate economies, along with an expanded railroad network, also strengthened the advantages of many large-city producers and added to their scale economies by broadening the extent of possible supply areas; by providing access to superior raw materials or semifinished goods; and by allowing the combination of new resources.

All this is in keeping with the transportation-development models of Janelle (1969) and Pottier (1963). Based on French historical materials, the latter in essence proposes the following ideal-typical chain of events.

(1) The appearance of railroad transportation routes that join leading urban-industrial centres encourages interurban, or interregional, trade between the cities served.

(2) The growth of traffic between the cities yields production scale economies and lower per unit freight costs.

(3) The resultant reduced shipping rates further stimulate interurban trade.

(4) Increased trade creates demand for new railroad facilities (e.g. double trackage, faster equipment, more frequent departures) and provides the capital for such improvements.

(5) Repeated iterations of this sequence attract economic activities and population to the railroad services and product markets paralleling the original major routes, and particularly to the most nodal *large centres*.

Once a new cost-reducing innovation was adopted in a large-city factory it could compound local growth and the overall spatial concentration of industry by as yet undepicted means. Lower per unit production costs permitted a substitution of transport spending (lengthier shipments) for labour and other per unit production costs. This, in turn, prompted a greater extension of market areas than would have occurred if only transportation improvements had been present. Such augmentation of market areas promised the division of fixed costs over an increasing volume of production (scale economies), larger optimal scales of production and higher thresholds. At the same time it hindered or arrested the growth of smaller cities that were either non-producing or had plants that failed to adopt the specific cost-reducing innovation in time. The syndrome of reduced per-unit production costs, market-area usurpation (increased spatial concentration of manufacturing), and large-city growth could also be set in motion by the cost savings resulting from external 'agglomeration' economies, or 'localization' and 'urbanization' economies. ('Localization' economies occur when many plants in a single industry acquire various cost savings – e.g. lower per unit input or service expenses – by clustering in the same urban area. 'Urbanization' economies, e.g. lower costs of information acquisition, result from the enlargement of the total economic size of all industries in a single urban area.)[25]

Among the other factors jointly influencing large-city rank stability and the spatial concentration of manufacturing the following two need brief mention.

Merger activity   Especially during the years 1897–1905, previously independent firms were combined, or merged, into the first large multilocational manufacturing corporations. Most of the firms becoming vertically or horizontally integrated were involved in industries, such as iron and steel production, that were becoming oriented toward large regional or national markets. In such industries, the emerging strategies of oligopolistic competition often prevented the appearance of new plants when minimum thresholds were fulfilled. Under these strategies, new large corporations also purchased and closed independent establishments with marginally profitable or inferior small-city locations. In other words, the piratical competitive strategies of a few industrial giants frequently hindered entry into the market, or jeopardized small-scale plant survival, thereby generally favouring the growth of large-scale production cities at the expense of inefficient and non-producing cities.

Factor availability and immobility   Many new or expanding industries had labour requirements, or activity system additions, that could only be easily met by the population system of a large city. Semiskilled and unskilled labour was readily found in most cities. However, when great numbers were needed simultaneously, or a high labour threshold had to be fulfilled, large commercial and manufacturing centres were the most probable places where a firm could satisfy its work-force requirements. The singular advantages of established industrial cities were even more pronounced with respect to skilled labour; for location elsewhere put the firm in the dilemma of finding a labour market big enough to supply a sufficient number of workers with the required aptitudes, or resigning itself to a lengthy training period for a major share of its labour force. In the US work-force availability requirements were usually satisfied with particular ease in established large urban-industrial centres. This was so because migration feedbacks steered much of the cheap labour of European immigrants into those relatively few places where relatives and friends had preceded, where foremen spoke the arrivals' native tongues, and where job-placement institutions had arisen in great numbers.

As the average scale of plant increased, and as iron, steel and other capital goods became more important *vis-à-vis* consumer goods, capital availability and costs worked to the advantage of high-ranking cities. Although post-Civil War institutional changes began to lower the barriers to interregional capital movements, investment funds remained more readily available to manufacturing interests in traditional banking capitals such as New York, Philadelphia, Boston and Baltimore, and in Chicago and St Louis, the new central reserve cities created by law in 1887. Furthermore, in each regional city-system, banks in the most rapidly growing large urban-industrial cities offered lower interest rates than most or all of their counterparts in smaller competing cities of the same region.

Finally, once manufacturing became spatially concentrated in large cities, it was not likely to shift because business management was much more prone to augment existing facilities than to relocate and repeat large initial capital expenditures.

3 Present processes of change: multilocational organizations and the interurban transmission of growth

The preceding chapter emphasized that both the long-term rank stability of large metropolitan complexes and the overall growth and development of city-systems in presently advanced economies have their roots in the feedback processes by which major channels of interdependence, or interurban growth transmission, reinforce themselves. If this interpretation is correct, an understanding of the nature of current interurban growth-transmission channels is essential in order to attain some insight into the *ongoing* processes of growth and development in economically advanced city-systems. Only when such insight is achieved is it possible to begin to grapple with problems pertaining to interregional inequalities of employment opportunity and 'quality of life'. Large multilocational business and government organizations are the most appropriate objects to focus on when attempting to understand the interurban growth-transmission structure of systems of cities in post-industrial economies. This is because large private- and public-sector multilocational organizations dominate such economies in so far as they: directly or indirectly account for most employment; are the leading implementers of explicit and implicit locational decisions; and are far and away the most important generators of flows of goods, services, capital and specialized information.

The growing role of multilocational organizations in city-system interdependence[1]

General evidence

It is widely documented that since the end of the Second World War large multilocational organizations have been gaining an ever larger share of the economy of 'post-industrial' countries. In Great Britain, for example, the proportion of assets in the sectors of manufacturing and distribution held by the 100 largest organizations burgeoned from roughly 44 per cent in 1953 to about 62 per cent in 1963 (Westaway, 1974b). In Sweden, between 1966 and 1970 alone, multilocational organizations increased their share of total office employment in the manufacturing and wholesaling sectors from 60 to 70 per cent (Engström, 1974). By 1974 150 multilocational business enterprises answered for 88 per cent of Sweden's total exports. And, partly as a result of foreign operations, the country's 200 largest domestically-headquartered business organizations had aggregate revenues that exceeded the gross national product. As another case in point, between 1960 and 1973 the number of domestic and foreign jobs controlled by the 500 largest multilocational industrial organizations in the United States grew from 9·2 to over 15·5 million, or in excess of 68 per cent. (By comparison, total US non-agricultural employment grew by only about 36 per cent during the same period.) Moreover, by early 1974, 34 million or more people worked for all those US-based multilocational business organizations – regardless of sector – that had 400 or more employees.[2] In summary, the situation in the US, as well as in other advanced economies, has reached a stage where a clear majority of private-sector employment is directly associated with domestically headquartered multilocational corporations and firms, and where virtually the entire remainder of private-sector employment is tied to one of three work-place categories: first, the single-establishment business organizations supplying goods and services to multilocational business and *government* organizations; secondly, the single-establishment businesses providing goods and services to members of the household sector, most of whom derive their income from private- and public-sector multilocational organizations; and, finally, multilocational business organizations with foreign headquarters.

The mounting economic power of multilocational business organizations has been the consequence of mergers, acquisitions, the physical expansion of existing units, and capital investment in new facilities (e.g. Blair, 1972). The often torrid pace of merger and acquisition activity, particularly during much of the 1960s, has been motivated primarily by a desire to spread risks in an era of high technological and economic instability. (It is true that the actual number of technological innovations impinging on advanced economies has grown more or less continuously from year to year. However, merger-inducing technological instability has itself been perpetuated by large business organizations who regard regular and continual invention as essential (Schon, 1971).) Mergers and acquisitions have also been spurred by the identification of management's personal goals with organizational size and growth, and by 'synergy', or the belief that the effectiveness of an enlarged organization somehow becomes greater than that of the sum of its previously separately operating parts (Ansoff, 1965; Galbraith, 1973; Lorsch and Allen, 1973). Only during the 1973–5 recession did various government decisions, tight money and lower stock prices really cut into the number of corporate acquisitions and mergers. Nevertheless, merger activity remains significant (2861 mergers were announced in the US during 1974) and capital scarcity, declining or quickly changing markets, and other recent economic hardships have further weakened the ability of small single-establishment firms to survive and compete against their large multilocational counterparts.

Through the assumption of new and expanded functions, the multilocational government organizations of advanced economies have also compiled an impressive record of increased economic significance in recent decades. In Australia the various levels of government had grown to a point in mid-1975 where they employed close to 30 per cent of the work force. In the US local, state and federal government organizations increased their job total from nearly 6·1 million people in 1950 to over 14·0 million people at the end of 1973 – a rate of expansion that was approximately double that for total employment in all non-agricultural establishments. Furthermore, the combined purchases of all levels of government currently answer for over one-quarter of the total US consumption of goods and services, while in 1929 they were responsible for only about 11 per cent of the same total.

Lacking any locational specificity, general statistics of the type just presented only provide suggestions as to the growing share of city-system interdependencies accounted for by the intraorganizational and interorganizational relationships of multilocational business corporations and government activities. Some inkling of the increased contribution of *intra*organizational linkages to the total pattern of interurban growth transmission can be obtained from charting the spatial expansion of particular multilocational organizations. For example, Jansen's (1972) study of the domestic operations of the Philips and Unilever corporations in the Netherlands for 1950 and 1970–1 revealed a rapidly densening network of intraorganizationally based city-system interdependencies.[3] While enlightening, such individual corporate portraits may be coloured by peculiarities that are misleading as to the overall picture of intra-organizationally (and interorganizationally) propagated non-local multiplier effects. Unfortunately, more aggregated statistics referring to the growth and *location* of multilocational organizational activities are not readily accessible in the literature except in those headquarters-location studies based on the uncomprehensive listings of the largest industrial and non-industrial corporations in particular countries (e.g. Ahnström, 1973; Armstrong, 1972; Goodwin, 1965; Pred, 1974b; Semple, 1973; and Westaway, 1974a). However, data specially gathered for eight metropolitan complexes of the western United States (Table 3.1) do provide a synopsis of recent trends that, if still imperfect, is more comprehensive than what is normally available.

On the basis of Table 3.1 it may be ventured that, in most US metropolitan complexes with a population of 500000 or more, the number of jobs associated with locally based multilocational business organizations has been growing at a rate of increase that far outstrips that of local population growth. (All but one of the rate differences in Table 3.1 are so great that the fact that two somewhat different time-spans are compared may be disregarded. The only anomaly, Seattle–Tacoma, is attributable to the unusual loss of almost 30000 jobs by the Boeing Company between 1959 and 1974.)[4] The assertion that Table 3.1 is representative of multilocational job-control changes in most other US metropolitan centres with over 500000 inhabitants is supported by much less extensive data pertaining to the 500 largest US manufacturing organizations. The data in question indicate that, for at least thirty-six of forty-one other US metropolitan centres with a population exceeding 500000, the 1960–72 rate of job-control growth associated with major manufacturing corporations was well in excess of the 1960–70 rate of population increase (Pred, 1974b).[5] In contrast, the 1959–74 job-control increase indicated for the Boise City SMSA in Table 3.1 is remarkably high and in no way typical of metropolitan complexes in its size class. (Only about 6·7 per cent of all the jobs affiliated with multilocational US business organizations in 1973–4 were controlled from metropolitan centres with a population of roughly 500000 or less. Smaller non-metropolitan urban places with populations under 50000 accounted for roughly another 2 per cent of the total.)

It should be recognized that some of the employment control increases shown in Table 3.1 occurred at organizational units located in foreign countries (cf. Table 3.5). Even if this is allowed there

Table 3.1: Number of jobs controlled by multilocational business organizations in selected metropolitan complexes of the western US, 1959 and 1974

Metropolitan complex	Estimated number of employees controlled by locally headquartered multilocational organizations[a]			Population		
	1959[b]	1974[c]	Percentage increase 1959–74	1960	1970	Percentage increase 1960–70
Los Angeles[d]	539 341	1 252 478[e]	132·2	6 742 696	8 452 461	25·4
San Francisco–Oakland–San Jose[f]	572 101	1 001 527	81·5	3 291 077	4 174 236	26·8
Seattle–Tacoma[g]	165 210	204 411	23·7[h]	1 428 803	1 832 896	28·3
Portland SMSA	55 732	164 073	194·4	821 897	1 009 129	22·8
Phoenix SMSA	18 625	126 685	581·7	663 510	967 522	45·8
Honolulu SMSA	18 885	92 656	390·5	500 409	629 176	25·7
San Diego SMSA	39 682	69 276	74·5	1 033 011	1 357 854	31·4
Boise City SMSA	12 702	78 302	516·5	93 460	112 230	20·1

(a) Employee estimates are based solely on units *completely owned by locally-headquartered corporations and firms, regardless of their functional specialities.* They do not include employment partially steered by locally present corporate divisional head offices. Both 1959 and 1974 totals are restricted to multilocational business organizations that employed at least 400 people as of 1974. Some no longer existing firms are included in the 1959 totals.

(b) Based on Dun and Bradstreet Company (1960–66). Some of the organizations included in the 1959 totals did not provide Dun and Bradstreet with employment figures for that year. In those cases figures were substituted from 1960 and subsequent years, as late as 1965. Thus the 1959 total for each of the eight metropolitan complexes is somewhat exaggerated and the percentage increases for 1959–74 are even greater than those indicated.

(c) Unless otherwise indicated, based on survey materials.

(d) Los Angeles–Long Beach SMSA + Anaheim–Santa Ana–Garden Grove SMSA.

(e) 1973 datum based on Dun and Bradstreet Company (1974).

(f) San Francisco–Oakland SMSA + San Jose SMSA.

(g) Seattle SMSA + Tacoma SMSA.

(h) See note 4, p. 224.

would appear to be little question that there has been *a significant upsurge in the city-system interdependencies associated with the intraorganizational linkages between the head offices of multilocational business organizations and their subordinate domestic units.* If this claim is accurate, then it follows that in many, perhaps most, metropolitan complexes and lesser cities there has been a *simultaneous absolute and relative increase in the number of local jobs controlled by multilocational business organizations headquartered elsewhere.* The validity of this second proposal is suggested by data on the expansion of non-locally controlled manufacturing employment that occurred in the Phoenix metropolitan area between 1965 and 1972 (Table 3.2). Employment control statistics for the Swedish

Table 3.2: Non-local control of manufacturing jobs in the Phoenix SMSA, 1965 and 1972[a]

	1965	1972
Total manufacturing jobs[b]	48 396	72 500
Number controlled by elsewhere headquartered multilocational business organizations	29 290[c]	53 670[d]
Percentage of total controlled by elsewhere headquartered multilocational business organizations	60·5	70·4

(a) For sources see Pred (1975c), p. 132.
(b) Including workers not involved in production.
(c) Jobs controlled by the 1000 largest US industrial corporations (corporations deriving 50 or more per cent of their revenues from manufacturing and/or mining). Since virtually all the jobs controlled from other places in 1972 were associated with the then 1000 largest industrial corporations, this 1965 figure may be regarded as reasonably complete.
(d) Not including 4289 mining jobs controlled by corporations with New York headquarters.

metropolitan areas of Norrköping and Örebro (both with 1973 populations in the vicinity of 170000) indicate the occurrence of a similar trend in the city-systems of other advanced economies (Godlund, 1972; Godlund *et al.*, 1973).

Although they lack detail, the above generalizations hint at much crisscrossing of interurban growth-transmission channels. More particularly, the two generalizations suggest that there is a high degree of interdependence between large metropolitan complexes

which arises from the intraorganizational linkages of the multilocational business organizations headquartered in those places. Put
otherwise, the generalizations point to a mounting *complexity* of
intraorganizationally based city-system interdependencies in general.
Evidence to be presented later substantiates these intimations of
the presence of a combined variety of non-hierarchical and hierarchical interdependencies.

The complexity of city-system interdependencies shaped by the
increasingly dominant multilocational business organizations of
advanced economies stems from two sources: the division of labour
within such organizations; and the more widely recognized division
of labour between all corporations and firms.

Intraorganizationally based city-system interdependence

The necessity of coping with environmental diversity and instability
has required that expanding multilocational business (and government) organizations develop increasingly intricate links of interdependence between their component units, regardless of whether
those component units are proximate to one another or spatially
dispersed (Lorsch and Allen, 1973).

To a considerable extent these links involve the flow of either administrative services, or decision-making-, control-, and coordination-
information from an organization's headquarters unit to subordinate
organizational units. In fact a number of researchers have found that
the relative share of office employment in an organization increases
as organizations become functionally and structurally more complex.
And 'the larger the size of the containing organization, the greater
will be the proportion given over to its [office and administrative]
component' (Child, 1973a; *see also* Rushing, 1967; Pondy, 1969; Blau,
1972; Child, 1973b). It is also apparent that the greater the volume of
information individual organizational units must exchange with their
extra-organizational environment as a result of expansion, the greater
will be their need to exchange information with their head office (or
some other intraorganizational unit). In short, when there is a diversification of functions, and an attendant increase of relationships and
tasks within a multilocational business organization, administrative
and bureaucratic specialization – usually at an organization-wide
or divisional headquarters unit – is often perceived as a necessary
means of environmental coping. In other words, when significant
expansion takes place within a multilocational organization at a

subordinate unit, or a new subordinate unit is opened or acquired, there is often an expansion of office employment at the headquarters unit (or other high- or intermediate-level administrative unit(s) responsible for coordinating the day-to-day routine managerial functions of several lower-level units (cf. Chandler and Redlich, 1961)).[6] When the units involved are not situated in the same city or metropolitan complex, this is synonymous with interurban growth transmission.

Much organizational expansion and functional diversification occurs via the integration (by merger or acquisition) of small-city based firms into major corporations based in large metropolitan complexes. Therefore, one would also expect the city-system interdependencies arising from the intraorganizational ties between head offices and other subordinate units to be increasingly concentrated at large metropolitan complexes. The shift of administrative functions from smaller to larger centres following merger or acquisition has been documented for the Netherlands, Sweden and elsewhere (Jansen, 1972; Nordström, 1974), and has already been suggested by Table 3.1.

Intraorganizational growth transmission linkages between cities may also occur through the flow of goods, services and specialized information among two or more units without involving an organization's head offices. Whether or not a multilocational business organization is of the extremely diversified conglomerate variety, there will be numerous functionally specialized units that must interact with one another. To take a relatively uncomplicated example, a large corporation whose sole or principal function is manufacturing is usually comprised of some combination of main and branch plants in several product lines, management and administrative offices with different levels of authority, research and development units, and marketing, warehousing and transportation facilities. In more complicated, and quite common instances, the large corporation will contain either a combination of several industrial and non-industrial functions, (e.g. organizations operating large supermarket chains frequently own bakeries, meat-packing facilities, and a variety of other food processing plants), or a number of non-industrial functions (e.g. banking, construction, and real-estate development) that allow for a wide range of intraorganizationally generated backward- and forward-linkage multiplier effects between cities.[7]

Interorganizationally based city-system interdependence

An ever greater array of interurban linkages between the units of different multilocational business organizations has been facilitated by technological advances in transportation and telecommunications. Transportation advances have lowered the relative cost of shipping goods over long distances, while jet plane and telecommunications innovations have eased the movement of specialized information and financial, insurance and other business services. At the same time, new industrial technology has fostered the appearance of plants with very specialized production and necessitated the creation of more and more elaborate physical input-output relationships. In particular: 'Manufacturing has increasingly become a matter of teamwork within vast [*inter*organizational] production systems, in which work has been divided between a great number of component units specializing in one particular aspect of [either] production [or production-facilitating service provision]' (Törnqvist, 1975). In some lines of production, e.g. the electronics and aerospace industries, the need to be able to adjust quickly to short-run demand fluctuations has also given rise to interorganizational interdependence. Furthermore, in these and other research-oriented industries, interorganizational cross-licensing and know-how agreements have become commonplace, especially among large corporations with a variety of branches and products. This is so because technological standards for the wide range of utilized components 'have reached a level where it is practically impossible to adjust research activities precisely to the needs of the [organization's] own production activities' (Krumme, 1970b).

The extent of city-system interdependence engendered by the interorganizational relationships of ever more powerful large multilocational corporations and firms is suggested somewhat by the detailed input-output analyses carried out for large metropolitan complexes such as Philadelphia (Isard and Langford, 1971), Seattle–Tacoma (Beyers 1974) and Stockholm (Artle, 1965).[8] These analyses have consistently demonstrated that many of the most important goods and service linkages of any given local sector occur with non-local units. For example, despite its highly diversified economy, the Philadelphia metropolitan complex secures nearly 50 per cent of its consumed goods and services from other locations. Likewise, the Philadelphia metropolitan complex exports roughly 50 per cent of its goods and services to other places, despite the greatly varied demands generated by its local economic activities and a population that exceeded five million in 1970. The Philadelphia data are apparently quite representative of the large metropolitan complexes of advanced economies in general. Robinson (1969) has observed that the 'normal situation today' for such complexes appears to be one where 'about 50 per cent of the expenditures are on goods and services from outside the region [*metropolitan complex*] and the immediately associated agricultural area'. From broad observations such as these it may be concluded that the non-local interdependence of the smaller and less economically diverse urban units of economically advanced city-systems is usually much greater. (In this connection it should be realized that when a merger or acquisition causes administrative functions to be shifted from a smaller city to a large metropolitan complex, the interurban linkages associated with organizational units remaining in the smaller centre may be considerably altered. In particular, if the shifted functions include the authority to make major purchasing, subcontracting and marketing decisions, then local interorganizational goods and service sources are apt to be replaced by non-local sources.)

The spatial structure of multilocational organizations

Hierarchical structures in general

Whatever their particular multifunctional attributes, private (and public) multilocational organizations are usually spatially structured along intentional or *de facto* hierarchical lines. Normally, the hierarchy consists of three or more tiers (the larger an organization the more extended its hierarchy is likely to be). Each unit at a successively higher tier serves a successively larger area. Thus, when a nationally functioning organization deliberately assigns precisely outlined areas to its component units, or sets up geographical divisions, the hierarchy takes on the following appearance.

At the peak of the hierarchy sits the controlling national headquarters. In most instances this coordinating and planning unit is situated in a metropolitan complex of national importance, but this need not invariably be so. At the next hierarchical level are the geographical division offices, which are normally located either in metropolitan areas of regional city-system significance, or in larger national-level metropolitan complexes which simultaneously function as regional city-system foci. (If the organization includes production units designed to serve the entire market area of either the country as a whole or of each geographical division, they may be found in cities of varying size, depending on their specific locational needs. However, if the plants in question either require several thousand workers, or are dependent on any of a variety of 'agglomeration' economies, they also are likely to be located in populous metropolitan areas.) Whether performing marketing, service, production, or low-level office functions, the subregionally and locally oriented units at the bottom of the organizational hierarchy may occupy a broad spectrum of locations within the national city-system, ranging from small towns and cities to metropolitan areas of regional and national significance.

Most multilocational business organizations are *not* explicitly or intentionally organized geographically. Instead, the individual units or multiunit divisions of business organizations are typically coordinated along product or other functionally specialized lines.[9] In these circumstances, in a nationwide organization, the head offices, with their great demand for specialized non-routine information, are also most likely to be found in a high-ranking metropolitan complex of national stature. Despite quite different fundamental organizing principles, the subordinate components of these organizations as a matter of practice also operate on a national, regional, subregional or local scale, and are consequently distributed among differently sized city-system members. Here too, those units having high information demands, large market thresholds, or sizable labour-force requirements are normally placed in large or very large metropolitan complexes. Other industrial and non-industrial units tend to have a greater range of city-system locations which are often influenced by labour-cost advantages, transportation facilities, raw material accessibility, or other local characteristics especially well suited to the establishments in question.

The most important multilocational business organizations in advanced economies are usually either conglomerates with many more or less completely unrelated divisions (International Telephone & Telegraph, for example, contains some 200 divisions), or multidivisional corporations comprised of semiautonomous and highly diversified divisions which are vertically integrated to some degree. For this reason it is important to distinguish between organizations with 'polycentric' and 'unicentric' hierarchical spatial structures.

In conglomerates and other large multidivisional organizations

with marked functional diversity, each division, or 'profit centre', is itself spatially structured along hierarchical lines with a quasi-independent divisional national headquarters at its peak. As a result of this, the hierarchical spatial structure of the organization as a whole is 'polycentric', with the divisional headquarters serving as the second highest level of the organization's overall internal structure. (The fact that an organization is 'polycentric' does not preclude one or more of its divisional headquarters from having the same metropolitan location as that held by the organization-wide head office.) Although the degree of divisional self-containment and decision-making autonomy varies from case to case in the type of organization under discussion (Lorsch and Allen, 1973), there are virtually always important linkages between organization-wide headquarters on the one hand, and divisional headquarters and other subunits on the other hand. Thus, while the multidivisional organization evolved largely because only a finite span of control over routine operational activities is possible (Chandler, 1962; Blair, 1972), head offices in organizations with 'polycentric' spatial structures usually remain responsible for:
(1) determining and coordinating strategic objectives;
(2) general long-term planning;
(3) resolving conflicts;
(4) granting approval of capital and major expense projects; and
(5) the allocation of funds and resources among competing operating divisions and subunits (Chandler and Redlich, 1961; Williamson, 1970; Lorsch and Allen, 1973).
From the standpoint of city-system growth and development the last two frequently overlapping functions are crucial in so far as they directly and indirectly affect where new jobs will be created. (In a nationally functioning 'polycentric' organization the spatial distribution of new employment determined by the head office over a given time is very likely to be quite widespread, partly because of the non-local multiplier effects stemming from each birth or large-scale expansion of a unit, and partly because units brought into an organization by merger or acquisition frequently add to the scatter of the organization's existing locations. The latter is so since mergers and acquisitions are usually made on the basis of growth and other criteria, rather than locational criteria (cf. Chapman, 1974).)
  In organizations with few products, services, or functions, there is generally little discretionary authority delegated to subheadquarters units – even where routine operational activities are involved. In

exceptional situations this is also true of multilocational organizations with many products, services, or functions. Whatever the case,
such centralization of authority requires that intraorganizational
control be set up within a very strict hierarchical framework that is
primarily based on chain-of-command principles rather than spatial
designations. That framework in turn means that – regardless of the
total number of subordinate organizational units – the management
of all units is responsible to a *single* national-level headquarters and
that the linkages within the organization's intentional or *de facto*
hierarchical spatial structure are very strong. Hence, such organizations may be described as having 'unicentric' hierarchical spatial
features.

Hierarchical structures at different scales

Not all multilocational business organizations function nationally.
Private-sector organizations with hierarchical spatial structures are
found at three other levels.

First, there are multiunit retailing or service-providing organizations whose operations are restricted to a single metropolitan complex and, perhaps, a portion of the surrounding 'urban field'. Here
the hierarchy is most often only two-tiered: a headquarters unit, and
district or local outlets (furniture stores, speciality clothing stores,
real estate offices, etc.). Obviously, these types of multilocational
organizations often make non-local purchases, but for the most part
they are of relatively little interest in terms of their impact on interurban growth transmission and the process of city-system growth
and development.

Secondly, there are those regional-scale business organizations
whose units are found either in a single state or province (e.g. US
banking organizations), or within the multistate (multiprovincial)
area covered by the traditionally defined hinterland of a major
metropolitan complex. In these instances the structural hierarchy
typically is made of regional, district and local units. (A similar
three-level spatial structure is often found for state- or provincial-
level government agencies.) Hierarchical spatial structures at this
scale commonly bring intermediate- and small-sized metropolitan
complexes into interdependent relationships with larger metropolitan
complexes.

Finally, in most cases very large nationally functioning business
organizations simultaneously operate at a multinational scale. This

condition adds an international tier to their hierarchical spatial structure (cf. Hymer, 1972). The international metropolitan and city-system interdependencies propagated by this extra tier are of rapidly increasing importance. Little is said here of these interdependencies, partly because the focus of this chapter is upon those interdependencies which are internal to national and regional city-systems, and partly because the topic and related issues merit extensive separate treatment.

Asymmetrical organizational spatial structures and city-system interdependence

The fact that real-world patterns of city-system interdependence are not wholly compatible with the hierarchical structure of interdependencies prescribed by central-place theory has been repeatedly emphasized in the preceding chapters of this book. Yet the hierarchical spatial structure of those multilocational organizations currently most responsible for interurban growth transmission in economically advanced city-systems has just been stressed. There is no conflict between these observations, however, since the hierarchical spatial structure of multilocational business organizations is *asymmetrical*, while both Christallerian and Löschian central-place theory would to varying degrees demand *symmetrical* organizational spatial structures.

Both the Christallerian and Löschian central-place schema require the spatial structure of all nationally functioning organizations to be symmetrical in the sense that all their organization-wide and national division headquarters should be located in the highest-ranking nationally dominant metropolitan complex. In addition, the symmetry requirements of both schema make it necessary for any plant or other non-administrative unit serving the entire nation also to be located in the single largest metropolitan complex. Christaller's central-place framework further demands symmetry in the sense that the regional- and local-level units of each and every nationally oriented business organization be present in identical city subsets. By the same token, Christallerian central-place theory requires that the spatial structure of regional-scale multilocational organizations be symmetrical to the extent that the region-wide, district (or sub-regional), and local units of each and every organization be distributed among identical city subsets. At this smaller organizational scale Löschian central-place theory only necessitates that spatial structures be symmetrical to the extent that all regionwide units should be located in the regional city-system's largest metropolitan complex.

Currently available materials for advanced economies consistently attest to the asymmetrical locational pattern of the headquarters units of the *largest* multilocational business organizations. (In any advanced economy the great majority of the largest corporations have a nation-wide – and perhaps international – market area.) Let us look at a few key pieces of evidence.

The headquarters of the 134 business organizations important enough to have their shares traded on the Stockholm stock exchange in 1972 were far from being entirely concentrated in Stockholm, the highest ranking centre of the Swedish system of cities (Table 3.3).

Table 3.3: Headquarters location of major Swedish business organizations, 1972[a]

Metropolitan area	Number of headquarters	Percentage of total	1972 population
Stockholm	50	37·3	1 447 392
Göteborg	21	15·7	722 806
Malmö	12	9·0	451 845
Helsingborg	4	3·0	211 805
Borås	4	3·0	187 654
Gävle–Sandviken	3	2·2	181 274
Uppsala	3	2·2	153 886
Linköping	4	3·0	130 126
Jönköping	5	3·7	129 827
Sundsvall	3	2·0	125 138
21 other places	25	18·7	—
TOTAL	134	100·0	—

(a) Organizations listed on the Stockholm stock exchange. Compiled from Nordström (1974).

The second- and third-ranking centres of Göteborg and Malmö also contained significant head-office clusters, and no less than twenty-eight other metropolitan areas and lesser cities contained at least one major headquarters unit.

In Great Britain the London metropolitan complex clearly contained the greatest number (532) of the head offices belonging to the 1000 private-sector manufacturing and service organizations with the largest revenues during 1971–2 (Westaway, 1973a). London's position as an administrative centre was especially accentuated among the 500 largest organizations. (Because of mergers, locational shifts and different organizational growth rates, London's share of the top 500 rose from 297 in 1969–70, to 327 in 1971–2.) All the same, in 1971–2 there was total of 222 major headquarters in seven other metropolitan complexes with a population exceeding one million (Birmingham (66), Manchester (45), Leeds (33), Sheffield (29), Glasgow (25), Liverpool (15) and Newcastle (9)). The remaining 246 headquarters were spread among about eighty-five smaller metropolitan areas and cities.

In the mid-1960s, the headquarters for the 100 largest manufacturing organizations in each of the following countries were locationally distributed as follows: *West Germany:* twelve in Hamburg, seven in Stuttgart, six each in Essen, Düsseldorf and Frankfurt, and the remaining sixty-three in thirty-nine other centres; *Italy:* forty-six in Milan, eleven each in Rome and Genoa, eight in Turin, and the remaining twenty-four in eighteen other centres; *France:* eighty-nine in Paris and the remainder in ten other centres (Ahnström, 1973). If the metropolitan areas of the advanced economies of Western Europe are viewed as a single system of cities – as is justifiable on several grounds (cf. p. 16, above) – the French case ceases to be a deviation and the total pattern of asymmetry becomes extreme.

Of the 500 largest US manufacturing corporations in 1972, only a subtotal of 147 had their headquarters in the New York metropolitan complex. In addition, fifty-five headquarters were to be found in the then third-ranked Chicago metropolitan complex, twenty in the second-ranked Los Angeles metropolitan complex, twenty-one in the ninth-ranked Cleveland–Akron metropolitan complex, and fifteen in the fourth-ranked Philadelphia metropolitan complex. Another sixty-eight major organization-wide head-office units were situated in seven other high-ranking centres with populations exceeding 2·3 million, 107 were in thirty-five widely dispersed centres with populations between 500000 and 2·1 million, and the final sixty-seven were in metropolitan areas and cities farther down the urban-size hierarchy. Likewise, of 300 leading US non-industrial organizations in 1972,[10] only seventy-two were based in New York. Of the other headquarters in this category, twenty-seven were in Chicago, twenty-two in Los Angeles, seventeen in Philadelphia, and fifty-six in eight other metropolitan complexes ranking twelfth or higher in the national city-system. Another eighty-six non-industrial organization-wide head offices were scattered among twenty-seven other metropolitan complexes with populations between 500000 and 2·1 million, and the remaining twenty were in lower-ranked urban centres (Pred, 1974b).

If those very large multilocational business organizations with a sizable manufacturing component in a given country are taken as a group, the asymmetry in their spatial structures imparted by their headquarters location pattern is generally greatly compounded by the incongruent geographic distribution of any nation-serving production units they possess. Moreover, as one descends to the regional- and local-level units of major nationally functioning multilocational business organizations, the asymmetry of their spatial structures becomes all the more apparent. When a comparison is made between the spatial structures of corporations whose organization-wide headquarters are situated in the same metropolitan complex, great dissimilarities are almost invariably found between the city subsets in which their regional, subregional and local units are located. This is illustrated in Table 3.4, which juxtaposes the US locations of units with regional-level functions belonging to Standard Oil of California (39269 employees in 1974) and Safeway Stores Inc. (117221 employees in 1974), both of which are headquartered in the metropolitan complex surrounding San Francisco Bay. Although the two corporations share regional-level locations at eleven metropolitan centres, their spatial structures are asymmetrical at thirty-two or more other urban centres. Furthermore, the number of asymmetrical metropolitan and lesser urban centres occupied by the local-level retail outlets of Standard Oil of California and Safeway Stores Inc. runs into the hundreds.

Since the spatial structures of multilocational business organizations are *asymmetrical* rather than symmetrical, one would once again expect *intra*organizationally based city-system interdependencies in advanced economies to be complex. More specifically, it is to be anticipated that the intraorganizational linkages of organizations with 'polycentric' and 'unicentric' spatial structures are synonymous with a high degree of interdependence between large metropolitan complexes. That is, it is to be expected that headquarters dominance and job-control linkages extend from large metropolitan complexes of high national or regional rank to even larger metropolitan complexes, and not merely from the single largest national or regional metropolitan unit to less populous metropolitan complexes. Likewise, it is to be anticipated that headquarters dominance and job-control linkages run between metropolitan areas of com-

Table 3.4: Metropolitan location of US units with regional-level functions belonging to Standard Oil of California and Safeway Stores Inc., 1974

Coinciding regional-level locations[a]	Asymmetrical regional-level locations[a]	
	Standard Oil of California[b]	Safeway Stores Inc.[c]
Los Angeles	New York	Washington DC
San Francisco–Oakland–	Chicago	Dallas–Fort Worth
San Jose[d]	St Louis	Kansas City
Seattle–Tacoma	Baltimore[e]	Oklahoma City
San Diego	Houston[e]	Tulsa
Denver	Miami	Richmond
Portland	Cincinnati	Omaha
Phoenix	Atlanta	Little Rock (Arkansas)
Sacramento	New Orleans	Butte (Montana)[f]
Salt Lake City	Louisville	
El Paso (Texas)	Birmingham	
Spokane (Washington)	Honolulu[e]	
	Jacksonville	
	Orlando (Florida)	
	Fresno (California)[e]	
	Mobile (Alabama)	
	Albuquerque (New Mexico)[e]	
	Des Moines (Iowa)[e]	
	Jackson (Mississippi)	
	Lafayette (Louisiana)	
	Richland–Kennewick (Washington)[e]	
	Midland (Texas)[e]	
	Achorage (Alaska)[e]	

(a) Metropolitan complexes and smaller metropolitan areas in each column arranged in order of population. For populations and definitions of centres exceeding 500000 in 1970 see Table 3.8. Metropolitan areas with 1970 populations under 500000 have their state locations indicated in parentheses.

(b) Locations may have industrial or non-industrial regional-level units. Some of the regional-level Standard Oil manufacturing units also turn out some specialized products that are marketed on a multiregional or national basis. Local-level units are also present at many of Standard Oil's regional-level locations.

(c) The listed Safeway regional-level locations perform both administrative and distribution functions. Some of these centres and additional metropolitan areas contain food-processing units which in many cases function at a regional level. Unfortunately, the information provided by Safeway did not allow any distinction to be made between locally- and regionally-oriented food-processing plants.

(d) That is, both Standard Oil of California and Safeway Stores Inc. have regional-level units in the metropolitan complex at which their national- (and

international-) level headquarters are located. In addition, both corporations have many local-level units in the San Francisco–Oakland–San Jose metropolitan complex.
(e) Local-level, but *not* regional-level, Safeway units also present at this location.
(f) Non-metropolitan urban place with population under 50000.

parable size (regardless of population class) and even from metropolitan areas of small or intermediate size to much larger complexes. Moreover, to the extent that multilocational organizations operate production and various local-level units throughout a country, one should find headquarters dominance and job-control linkages extending from metropolitan complexes of varying size to smaller towns and cities within what are normally considered the hinterlands of other distant metropolitan complexes. In addition, the asymmetrical spatial structure of multilocational corporations and firms is in some measure synonymous with the documented *inter*metropolitan specialization of economic activities (Duncan, *et al.*, 1960; Duncan and Leiberson, 1970; Bergsman, Greenston and Healy, 1972). This thereby seems to require that *inter*organizationally based flows of goods, services and specialized information should not be confined to strictly hierarchical (large- to small-centre) channels. Such growth-transmission linkages should also occur between comparably sized large (and small) urban units, and from smaller centres to both nearby and distant larger centres.

Headquarters concentration and interurban growth transmission

If multilocational organizations have been acquiring control over an ever greater share of the economy in economically advanced countries, if the headquarters of such organizations are predominantly found in large metropolitan complexes (rather than only in the highest-ranking metropolis), and if intraorganizationally and interorganizationally based city-system interdependencies are as complex as just described, then it follows that *regardless of where major new investment or activity expansion occurs, it is very likely to result in some intraorganizationally* (and interorganizationally) *based multiplier effects at a nearby or distant large metropolitan complex.* For this reason, some comments about the accumulation of organization-wide (and divisional) headquarters in large metropolitan complexes are justified. It is also important to seek some understanding of the headquarters concentration process since the activity systems of most large metropolitan complexes have recently continued to grow – in spite of absolute losses in factory employment – through the disproportionate acquisition of high-level administrative employment and related services.

Large metropolitan complexes offer headquarters units and other high-level administrative activities three specialized information advantages that are seldom available to the same degree in less populous metropolitan areas and cities. These are ease of interorganizational face-to-face contacts, business-service availability, and high intermetropolitan accessibility. With each addition or significant expansion of a high-level administrative activity these advantages tend to be strengthened (Figure 3.1). More specifically, when a high-level organizational administrative unit appears or expands at a given large metropolitan complex, there is apt to be an increase in the local occurrence of interorganizational face-to-face contacts, or an increased local circulation of specialized information. With the total number of contact-intensive administrative employees expanded, and with a consequent increase in the volume of locally circulating specialized information, the attractiveness of the large metropolitan complex is enhanced for additional administrative

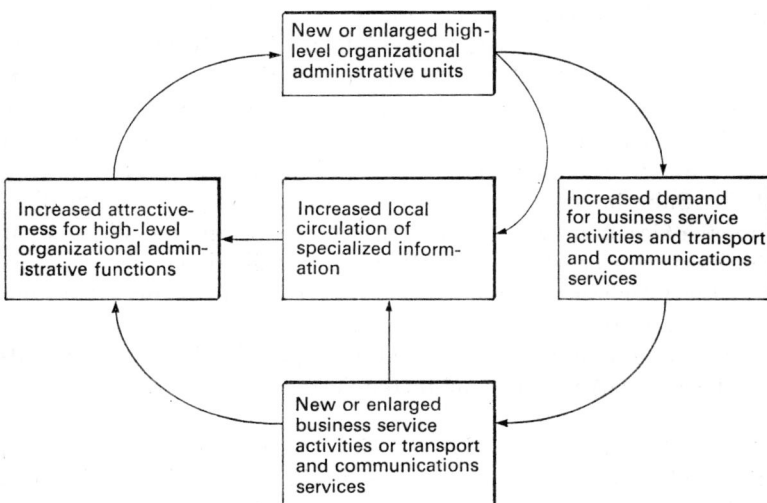

Figure 3.1: *The accumulation of high-level organizational administrative activities in a large metropolitan complex as a circular and cumulative feedback process.*

functions that are sensitive to the ease with which interorganizational personal contacts are made. At the same time, when a high-level organizational administrative unit appears or significantly expands there is very likely to be an increased demand for both specialized local business services – which the large metropolitan complex already offers in profusion – and transportation and communications services often already available to other places, especially other large metropolitan complexes. As such demand accumulates, new or enlarged business services actually materialize, and jet aeroplane and other intermetropolitan transportation and communications services are intensified. These events further the attractiveness of the given large metropolitan complex for additional administrative functions that are sensitive either to the availability of highly specialized business services, or to a high level of intermetropolitan accessibility for specialized information-exchange purposes. (Note also, that the birth or enlargement of business services also contributes to an increased local circulation of specialized information.)

This entire feedback process is reinforced by the fact that since large metropolitan complexes already possess the greatest number of multilocational business organization headquarters, they have the highest probabilities for acquiring the head-office functions that are transferred in space because of mergers and acquisitions. Finally, as the feedback between specialized-information advantages and the concentration of headquarters and other high-level organizational administrative activities continues, some organizations find they can exploit the informational spatial biases of the large metropolitan complex from a suburban location (Armstrong, 1972; Manners, 1974). Suburbanization, however, has been more typical of organizational office units which can transact much, but not all, of their business with nearby organization-wide or divisional headquarters via the telephone, computer terminals, or other modern telecommunications.[11]

A few additional words about the specialized-information advantages of large metropolitan complexes are in order.

Ease of interorganizational face-to-face contacts   In most instances, the need for frequent contacts between the high-level administrative units of different multilocational business organizations arises because they serve as one another's suppliers, purchasers, project partners or competitors. The daily time resources of contact-intensive administrative and managerial employees who have to participate in these numerous non-routine face-to-face encounters must also be allocated to other important intraorganizational work tasks. The large metropolitan complex allows such contact-intensive personnel to make many of their interorganizational face-to-face information exchanges with a minimum of time spillage and – when the quickly changing environment or other matters necessitate – on very short notice (Thorngren, 1970; Claval, 1973; Goddard, 1973b).[12] In national capital cities such as London, Paris, Tokyo, Brussels, Vienna, Copenhagen and Stockholm, and in state or provincial capitals such as Sydney, Melbourne, Toronto, Boston, Atlanta and Minneapolis–St Paul, face-to-face contacts are also facilitated with the principal administrative units of government organizations which award contracts or act as large-scale purchasers of goods and services. The promise of such contacts in capital cities is known to exert a strong attractive influence on some high-level private-sector administrative units (cf. Mera, 1975).

Availability of specialized services In recent years, rapid market and technological changes have brought about a strongly increased demand for business services. Changes in the economic and technological environment have also dictated that these business services become ever more specialized. With specialization, large markets have become necessary for survival. Most new business-service providers have tried to maximize accessibility to potential customers by locating in large metropolitan complexes. Specialization has also made business-service firms more and more dependent upon one another for supplementary and complementary services. This, along with their own more general need of specialized information accessibility, has also acted in favour of large metropolitan locations. Thus, by the mid-1960s, over 60 per cent of the US employment in specialized business services was concentrated in eighteen metropolitan complexes with populations well in excess of one million. Likewise, while containing only about 31 per cent of Sweden's 1965 population, Stockholm, Göteborg and Malmö together were responsible for roughly 65 per cent of the country's business services in general, and for an even higher percentage of the most specialized services. (In 1970 Stockholm held 59 per cent of Sweden's management consultants. The corresponding figures for Göteborg and Malmö respectively were 16 and 7 per cent. Stockholm also contained 58 per cent of all advertising agencies and 57 per cent of all computer-service firms.)

High intermetropolitan accessibility Some reference has already been made to the information economies accruing to high-level organizational administrative units located in large metropolitan complexes as a result of superior air-passenger services (pp. 24–5, above). These cost and individual time savings are especially relevant for those multilocational business organizations that are gaining control of units at an increasing number of places at the same time as they are doing interorganizational business at an ever larger number of locations. In short, the greater the variety and frequency of locally available non-stop flights or other transportation connections, the easier it is for highly paid contact-intensive employees with tightly packed schedules to fit in non-local round trips, including four or more hours of on-ground business activity, within the time limits of a single working day (Engström and Sahlberg, 1974; Törnqvist, 1973.)[13] This means a frequent saving of overnight *per diem* expenses as well as the possibility of a greater number of trips per salaried time period. It should be recognized that the frequent trips made by time-pressed contact-intensive organizational employees are not confined to situations in which intra- and extra-organizational units located elsewhere are participating in goods or service transactions with the home (headquarters) metropolitan complex. In addition, trips are often made in connection with inter-organizational goods or service transactions, or flows, between a non-local subordinate unit and a unit of another organization that is located in a third place. (Trips may be made to that third place, or to yet another centre at which the other organization is headquartered.) That is, high intermetropolitan accessibility is crucial to a head-quarters centre because non-routine information flows which originate and terminate at such a centre must involve interdependencies between other pairs of places, as well as city-system interdependencies directly involving the centre itself.

Other views of city-system interdependence and interurban growth transmission in advanced economies

This chapter has thus far placed considerable emphasis on the *supposed* complexity of city-system interdependencies in advanced economies, and especially on the importance of growth-transmission linkages between nationally and regionally highly ranked metropolitan complexes. It also has been contended that some intraorganizationally and interorganizationally based non-local multiplier

effects are quite likely to occur at a nearby or distant large metropolitan complex whenever and wherever there is some major new
investment or activity expansion. (This should be true regardless of
whether the new or expanded activity is situated in a small metropolitan area or city, a rural market centre, or a large metropolitan
complex.) These views conflict strongly with the explicit and implicit
assumptions normally made by practising regional planners,
academic consultants and interested scholars regarding city-system
interdependence and interurban growth transmission.

One of two images of city-system growth transmission underlie the
growth-centre and spatial growth-pole strategies generally adopted in
advanced economies either to stimulate regional development in
'backward', 'lagging' and 'depressed' regions, or to hinder the
expansion of major metropolitan complexes. Given the scale of
efforts made, these single-city investment concentration strategies
have met at best with limited success in terms of long-standing employment creation. The dismal performance of the growth-centre
policy implemented in Appalachia and elsewhere by the US
Economic Development Administration is well known (e.g. Hansen,
1971, 1973). That the growth-centre schemes of Canada's DREE
(Department of Regional Economic Expansion) in the Atlantic
Provinces and Alberta have also led to largely unimpressive accom-
plishments is also public knowledge (Walker, 1975). Similarly,
the achievement record of growth-centre and related policies in
France, Japan, Australia, Great Britain and other advanced economies has generally been far from highly successful (e.g. Penouil, 1969;
Kabaya, 1971; Lonsdale, 1972; Chisholm and Oeppen, 1973;
Hansen, 1974, 1975a, 1975b). In any specific advanced economy
there are doubtless numerous and often complex reasons for the
failure or relatively modest attainments of growth-centre and growth-
pole policies. However, in all likelihood, in the great majority of
instances, a substantial portion of the blame can be traced to the
grossly mistaken views of city-system growth transmission that lie
behind these policies. Before examining further evidence that appears conclusively to support the validity of this assertion, the
allegedly mistaken views must themselves be spelled out.

The hinterland-spread view

There is a considerable group of planners and regional-development experts who implicitly or explicitly assume that any significant

investment, or expansion of economic activity at a 'growth centre' or spatially defined 'growth pole' will lead to a concentration of employment multipliers and other spread effects within the target urban centre itself and its trading hinterland, or 'zone of influence' (e.g. Boudeville, 1966). This view is a descendant of Perroux's early growth-pole theory writings (1950, 1955), which were framed in terms of an abstract 'economic space', or field of forces, and which emphasized the driving *national-level* growth-generation role of large rapidly expanding and highly linked 'propulsive' manufacturing industries, or 'lead firms'. (In these early formulations there was no requirement that both the quickly growing growth-pole plants (or plants of a particular sector) and the plants providing them with either technological linkages or capital goods had to be close to one another in geographic space.) In the practically oriented, regional-level translation of growth-pole theory it is assumed that 'propulsive' manufacturing activities will always generate sizable employment-growth impacts in close proximity to the location of their operations as a consequence of the creation of strong backward and forward linkages and associated employee income expenditures (Hermansen, 1972; Earickson, 1972, 1974, 1975). That is, most of those adhering to this school of thought make the *de facto* or outward assumption that the interurban transmission of growth within economically advanced city-systems is largely or totally confined to the flow of multiplier effects *from cities of a given size to less populous nearby centres*. The possibility that sizable non-local multiplier leakages occur to more distant urban places of larger, comparable or smaller size is usually completely ignored. (Worse yet, more naive local and regional planners in effect sometimes assume that any manufacturing plant will have the same spatially confined growth-transmission impact as that supposedly generated by 'lead firms'.)

In so far as the hinterland-spread view of interurban growth transmission is inseparable from applied growth-pole theory, it is subject to the same wide range of criticisms directed toward that so-called theory (Darwent, 1969; Jansen, 1970; Kongstad, 1974; Lasuén, 1969; Mønstad, 1974; Pred, 1973a, 1974a; Todd, 1973, 1974). For example, growth-pole theory and its derivatives are often accused of overemphasizing the relative importance of manufacturing as an employment generator. The theory has also been attacked for inadequately treating innovation diffusion and specialized information circulation, and for attempting to deal with a dynamic process through the use of a static input-output approach. Here it is crucial to add that to argue that growth transmission is mostly or fully restricted to the hinterland of a growth centre is to maintain that entire regional or subregional city-systems in advanced economies have a very high degree of closure; i.e. a low degree of interaction and interdependence with urban units situated elsewhere in the national city-system. This contention is highly unrealistic in so far as regional city-systems in post-industrial economies have the characteristics of a 'complex social system', and in so far as the 'backward' region cities selected as growth centres for those regions normally stand in a 'colonial' relationship to one or more large metropolitan complexes in other parts of the country (pp. 13 ff., above). The contention is also unrealistic in so far as it ignores the extremely great likelihood that any large 'propulsive' industrial unit will belong to a multilocational organization with a variety of extra-regional linkages (cf. Krumme, 1970a, 1970b). Thus, Earickson has observed (1972): 'The foremost problem encountered in economic growth based on ['lead firm'] backward directed [linkage] impulse is the openness of most regional economies. Such openness would suggest that backward-directed pressures of demand by a lead firm may [not be met in a growth centre or its hinterland but instead] result in imports of necessary intermediate goods [or services] into the region.'

The grossly mistaken nature of the assumption that a growth centre and its 'zone of influence' can constitute a more or less closed system is somewhat suggested by the aggregate input-output relationships of the Philadelphia metropolitan complex, which has already been referred to, and by similar input-output findings for other large metropolitan complexes. That evidence, unfortunately, usually does not distinguish between hinterland and non-hinterland imports and exports. It is therefore highly significant that it has been established that the backward and forward linkages of Seattle–Tacoma's economic sectors are strongest on the whole with regions beyond the borders of the state of Washington, i.e. with regions lying *outside the hinterland* of that metropolitan complex (Beyers, 1974). Given the size of the Seattle–Tacoma complex (over 1·8 million inhabitants in 1970), it is not unreasonable to conclude that the non-hinterland growth-transmission linkages of the much less populous and economically differentiated cities normally selected as growth centres are also of primary importance.

The hierarchical-diffusion view

The second category of commonly occurring growth-transmission assumptions is phrased in hierarchical-diffusion terms derived from Christallerian central-place theory. According to Berry (1969, 1972, 1973), Lasuén (1971, 1973), and others, economic growth spreads on an interurban basis largely or entirely as a result of the 'filtering', or 'trickling down', of innovations 'downward through the urban hierarchy'. In most of these interpretations, economic innovations are supposedly always initially adopted in the largest metropolitan complex of a national or regional system of cities and their subsequent paths of diffusion are determined by the size order of cities (cf. p. 78, above). By the same token, once economic innovations are intentionally introduced in a regional growth centre they, or their 'growth impulses', will presumably sooner or later descend downward through the regional urban hierarchy, with the population rank of hinterland centres dictating the locational sequence of adoptions or felt 'growth impulses'. The possibility of interurban growth transmission occurring from a city of given size to places of comparable or larger size is therefore also denied – at least implicitly – by diffusion proponents of growth-centre planning.

Hierarchical-diffusion interpretations of interurban growth transmission rest on rather shaky empirical underpinnings. As previously indicated, there is not a single advocate of hierarchical diffusion who has actually specified a hierarchical sequence of linkages through which adoption-influencing information has been passed from city to city. Furthermore, the small number of empirical studies attempting to link diffusion with the spatial spread of economic growth have centred mostly on innovations which are artifacts of growth, such as TV-ownership, rather than on true *growth-inducing* innovations, such as new products and services, new production and communications technology, and new ways of performing or structuring the operations of business and government organizations.

Proponents of the hierarchical-diffusion view of interurban growth transmission are subject to several other criticisms that are of a more strictly conceptual nature.

First, they do not recognize that the diffusion of growth-inducing innovations is for the most part *steered* by the headquarters units of multilocational organizations, i.e. that in economic innovation diffusion processes the location of the adoption decision and the location of implementation need not be identical. In addition, when multilocational organizations steer diffusion, they are highly unlikely to be influenced by regional urban-size hierarchies unless the innovation in question is sensitive to the fulfilment of a market threshold (cf. Brown, 1975). (Even when market threshold fulfilment is important to the selection of innovation implementation locations, the threshold is often so high that only one or two adoptions are appropriate for an entire regional or subregional city-system.) More commonly, steered diffusion processes will be influenced by the already established spatial structure of the participating multilocational organizations, either because the innovation is such that it can be implemented at already operating units, or because already existing intraorganizational (and interorganizational) contact patterns are very likely to impinge upon the limited search for locational alternatives.

Secondly, by arguing that 'the role played by growth centres in regional [and city-system] development is a particular case of the general process of innovation diffusion', and that 'impulses of economic change are transmitted in order from higher to lower centres in the urban hierarchy' (Berry, 1972, 1973), these advocates underestimate or totally ignore the importance of non-local backward- and forward-linkage multiplier effects.

Thirdly, subscribers to the hierarchical-diffusion view also neglect the growth-transmission implications of post-adoption events and the accumulation of day-to-day organizational decisions. The fact that a particular growth-inducing innovation diffuses through all or part of a regional system of cities does not mean it will either survive or succeed at the same scale at all cities of adoption. Except possibly where threshold, or market, conditions are crucial, the degree of success of each innovation adoption, regardless of location, will usually depend in some measure on the accumulation of a wide range of operational decisions by the adopting organization.

Finally, to the extent that a hierarchical-diffusion view of interurban growth transmission is wedded to a growth-pole theory approach to the question (e.g. Hermansen, 1972), it is also susceptible to many of the broadsides aimed at that latter school of thought.

On the specification of interurban growth transmission channels

In order to demonstrate clearly the superiority of the multilocational organizational view of city-system growth transmission – with its emphasis on complex linkages and the interdependence of large metropolitan complexes – *vis-à-vis* the hinterland-spread and hierarchical-diffusion views, it is necessary to marshal evidence which is more graphic and detailed than that presented earlier in this chapter. There are considerable obstacles to the empirical delineation of interurban growth transmission linkages at a national or large regional scale. In economically advanced countries there is generally a paucity of data pertaining to the physical expression of interurban multiplier effects, or data relating to the movement of goods, services, and monetary payments. Even when available, such data are usually inadequate in some respect, such as their precision or locational detail (Thompson, 1974). Input-output analysis, another theoretically possible means of specifying city-system interdependencies and growth-transmission channels, is highly impractical in reality. Input-output studies of the type carried out for the Philadelphia, Seattle–Tacoma and Stockholm metropolitan complexes are expensive and extremely time-consuming. Furthermore, such studies provide little locational information, only describing the relationships of an urban complex with 'the rest of the world', or, at best, 'the rest of the state'. Thus, in order to secure details sufficient to outline growth-transmission channels at a large scale, i.e. in order to specify sectoral input-output relationships between numerous urban units of the same national or regional city-system, it would be necessary to undertake a data-gathering project of unprecedented dimensions.[14] And even if it were feasible to carry out such an enormous project, its results and utility would still be open to the variety of technical criticisms often directed toward much more modest input-output analyses.

With flow-data and input-output options closed, probably the best alternative means of specifying interurban growth-transmission channels is through a simple quantification of the spatial structure of regionally and nationally functioning multilocational business organizations. The most practical way to quantify the spatial structure of economically dominant multilocational corporations and firms is to make a determination of the location and numbers of people employed at each of their organizational units. (The well-known difficulty of obtaining financial statistics from business organizations precludes the use of unit-by-unit asset or revenue measures.) Once the exact locations of non-local job control can be specified for all the locally headquartered multilocational organizations of a particular urban centre, the relative importance of some of that centre's key intraorganizationally based interurban growth transmission linkages becomes visible. In addition, with locally based multilocational organizational job-control data in hand, some *crude* educated guesses may be hazarded as to some, but far from all, of the interorganizationaly based growth-transmission channels of a specific urban centre. This is so because of the presumed influence of existing intraorganizational (and interorganizational) contact patterns on the limited-search and uncertainty-reduction behaviour that occurs when multilocational business organizations make implicit locational decisions, i.e. when such organizations make major decisions concerning the purchase of goods and services, the award of contracts and subcontracts, and miscellaneous capital allocations.

Empirical evidence from selected metropolitan complexes of the western United States[15]

During the latter part of 1974 and early months of 1975 a survey was conducted to ascertain the spatial structure of all the multilocational business organizations employing 400 or more people that were then locally headquartered in selected metropolitan complexes of the western United States. Through mail, telephone and direct interviews the organizations were requested to indicate the location of each US and Canadian unit belonging to them or any of their wholly owned subsidiaries, the numbers of people employed at each unit, and the primary function(s) of each unit. The most important features of the virtually complete location and job-control data obtained for seven of the metropolitan complexes are condensed in Tables 3.5–3.9 (pp. 128–39) and Figures 3.2–3.12 (pp. 140–61).

When the data summarized in Tables 3.5–3.9 and Figures 3.2–3.12 are jointly considered, at least four generalizations emerge that are supportive of the argument that the views of interurban growth transmission which serve as a foundation for most regional development schemes in advanced economies are grossly mistaken.

(1) *The total volume of non-local intraorganizational linkages created within the US–Canadian system of cities by multilocational business organizations based in the selected metropolitan complexes is considerable* despite the great distances separating those complexes from the remainder of the system (Table 3.5).[16] (In view of the supposed influence of the limited-search and uncertainty-reduction decision-making syndromes, this should also be true of the non-local *inter*organizational linkages fostered by the multilocational firms and corporations in question.) Given the populations of the

Table 3.5: Aggregate job-control characteristics of multilocational business organizations with headquarters in selected metropolitan complexes of the western United States, 1974–5

	Metropolitan complex						
	San Francisco–Oakland–San Jose[a]	Seattle–Tacoma[b]	Portland SMSA	Phoenix SMSA	Honolulu SMSA	Boise City SMSA	San Diego SMSA
Number of multi-locational organizations[c]	181	53	50	24	19	12	25
Total estimated employment[d]	1 001 527	204 411	164 073	126 685	92 656	78 302	69 276
Employment accounted for by survey	974 175	203 511	164 073	124 946	92 656	77 232	68 076
Of which:							
local	244 983 25·1%	90 551 44·5%	44 699 27·2%	24 212 19·4%	19 839 21·4%	5 590 7·2%	29 019 42·6%
foreign[e]	157 930 16·2%	5 841 2·9%	14 708 9·0%	2 659 2·1%	27 065[f] 29·2%	14 265 18·5%	2 189 3·2%
non-local within the US–Canadian system of cities[g]	571 262 58·7%	107 119 52·6%	104 666 63·8%	98 075 78·5%	45 752 49·4%	57 377 74·3%	36 868 54·2%

(a) San Francisco–Oakland SMSA + San Jose SMSA

(b) Seattle SMSA + Tacoma SMSA

(c) Includes all locally based organizations with approximately 400 or more employees. Does not include organizations having divisional or subsidiary head offices in the selected metropolitan complexes, but elsewhere located organization-wide headquarters.

(d) Not including employment associated with joint ventures and partially owned subsidiaries.

(e) Exclusive of Canada. See note (g) below.

(f) Most of the comparatively large number of foreign jobs controlled from Honolulu involve plantation agriculture – the initial primary function of AMFAC, Castle & Cooke, and other major Hawaiian corporations before they became highly diversified conglomerates.

(g) The US and Canada are treated here as a single system of cities, despite the somewhat retarding effect the border between the two countries has on urban-economic interaction (Simmons, 1974a). This gesture is largely based on the fact that US-based corporations own a larger share of the assets of all Canadian manufacturing, petroleum and natural gas, and mining and smelting activities than do organizations based in Canada itself. It is to be noted also that the volume of highly business-oriented air-passenger traffic between Toronto and New York is comparable to that between Toronto and Montréal, Canada's two largest metropolitan complexes. Likewise, the air-passenger traffic between Vancouver – Canada's third-ranking metropolitan complex – and Toronto and Montréal is comparable in size to that between Vancouver and the Los Angeles and San Francisco Bay Area metropolitan complexes.

Table 3.6: Location, by general category, of US and Canadian jobs controlled by multilocational business organizations with headquarters in selected metropolitan complexes of the western United States, 1974–5

Estimated number of employees

	A All other metropolitan complexes	B Metropolitan complexes outside hinterland[a]	C Hinterland[b]	D Non-hinterland smaller towns and cities	Non-local total within US-Canadian system of cities
San Francisco–Oakland–San Jose[c]	452 904 79.3%	407 868 71.4% 364 020[e] 63.7%	63 397 11.1% 121 196[e] 21.2%	99 997 17.5% 86 046[e] 15.1%	571 262 100.0%[d] 571 262 100.0%
Seattle–Tacoma[f]	65 451 61.1%	62 225 58.1%	21 287 19.9%	23 607 22.0%	107 119 100.0%[d]
Portland SMSA	47 259 45.1%	41 248 39.4%	18 140 17.3%	45 278 43.4%	104 666 100.0%[d]
Phoenix SMSA	73 881 75.3%	71 278 72.7%	8 206 8.4%	18 591 19.0%	98 075 100.0%[d]
Honolulu SMSA	22 082 48.3%	22 082 48.3%	19 780[g] 43.2%	3 890 8.5%	45 752 100.0%[d]
Boise City SMSA	28 104 49.0%	28 104 49.0%	11 412 19.9%	17 861 31.1%	57 377 100.0%[d]
San Diego SMSA	27 330 74.1%	27 330 74.1%	1 076 2.9%	8 462 23.0%	36 868 100.0%[d]

(a) Metropolitan hinterlands defined with the assistance of Borchert (1972) and other sources in accord with central-place theory principles.

(b) Encompasses some metropolitan complexes included in column A. The Honolulu, Boise City, and San Diego hinterlands contain no metropolitan units.

(c) See note (a) in Table 3.5.

(d) Percentage total arrived at by summing the percentages listed under columns B, C, and D.

(e) Based on the inclusion of jobs controlled by San Francisco Bay Area business organizations in the hinterlands of Seattle–Tacoma and Portland. The 'nesting' of the Seattle–Tacoma and Portland hinterlands into that of San Francisco–Oakland–San Jose rests on, among other things, the smaller population class, or lower order, of the Washington and Oregon metropolitan complexes. It results in an extremely liberally delineated hinterland for San Francisco–Oakland–San Jose. One reason for this is that the Seattle–Tacoma hinterland has been defined as encompassing Alaska, as well as all the state of Washington (except Clark County which belongs to the Portland SMSA), northern Idaho, and north-eastern-most Oregon.

(f) See note (b) in Table 3.5.

(g) Predominantly composed of plantation agriculture employment. Cf. note (f) in Table 3.5.

Table 3.7: Location, by size of metropolitan complex, of US and Canadian jobs controlled by multilocational business organizations with headquarters in selected metropolitan complexes of the western United States, 1974–5

	Estimated number of employees					
	First- and second-order national centres (pop. >2·6 million)[a]	Third-order national centres (pop. 1·0–2·6 million)[a]	Intermediate-sized metropolitan centres (pop. 500 000–999 999)	(pop. 250 000–499 999)	Lesser metropolitan centres (pop. <250 000)	Metropolitan total
San Francisco-Oakland–San Jose[b]	152 585 / 33·7%	132 897 / 29·3%	54 782 / 12·1%	62 448 / 13·8%	50 192 / 11·1%	452 904 / 100·0%
Seattle–Tacoma[c]	20 615 / 31·5%	13 631 / 20·8%	4 603 / 7·0%	13 158 / 20·1%	13 444 / 20·5%	65 451 / 100·0%
Portland SMSA	11 238 / 23·8%	10 580 / 22·4%	4 953 / 10·5%	5 975 / 12·6%	14 513 / 30·7%	47 259 / 100·0%
Phoenix SMSA	22 698 / 30·7%	16 495 / 22·3%	12 704 / 17·2%	10 196 / 13·8%	11 788 / 16·0%	73 881 / 100·0%
Honolulu SMSA	9 337 / 42·3%	6 891 / 31·2%	2 353 / 10·7%	1 543 / 7·0%	1 958 / 8·9%	22 082 / 100·0%
Boise City SMSA	8 022 / 28·5%	9 505 / 33·8%	3 847 / 13·7%	1 830 / 6·5%	4 900 / 17·4%	28 104 / 100·0%
San Diego SMSA	8 247 / 30·1%	6 754 / 24·7%	2 044 / 7·5%	6 918 / 25·3%	3 367 / 12·3%	27 330 / 100·0%

(a) Cf. Borchert's (1972) definition of 'first-', 'second-', and 'third-order' US metropolitan centres. Metropolitan complexes assigned to size categories on the basis of 1970 (US) and 1971 (Canada) populations.

(b) See note (a) in Table 3.5.

(c) See note (b) in Table 3.5.

seven metropolitan complexes as of 1970 (Table 3.1), only the San Diego SMSA has a less than impressive number of jobs controlled non-locally (and locally) by multilocational business organizations headquartered within its limits.

In all seven instances the total volume of non-local intraorganizational linkages suggested by Tables 3.5–3.9 is considerably understated, in part due to the exclusion of linkages involving partly owned subsidiaries, and in part owing to the omission of linkages involving joint ventures. (For example, the 4400 San Diego employees of National Steel and Shipbuilding have not been taken into account because the company is owned 50 per cent by Kaiser Industries (based in Oakland) and 50 per cent by Morrison-Knudsen Co. Inc. (based in Boise). Were the company included, the non-local job-control totals of the San Francisco–Oakland–San Jose metropolitan complex and the Boise City SMSA would each be enhanced by 2200.) The aggregate volume of non-local intraorganizational linkages would be yet further enlarged if some account was taken of the job control of locally occurring divisional or subsidiary head offices belonging to corporations with organization-wide headquarters situated elsewhere. (Job-control figures for the San Francisco–Oakland–San Jose metropolitan complex, for example, do not include the almost 100000 employees of Pacific Telephone, despite the presence of its head administrative unit in San Francisco. Pacific Telephone is a subsidiary of the New York-based American Telephone & Telegraph Co.)

The San Diego exception with respect to non-local intraorganizational job control arises mainly because of the leading part played in its economy by the federal government, especially the military establishment. That is, a very substantial portion of the linkages originating and terminating in the San Diego metropolitan complex are associated with multilocational government organizations rather than multilocational business organizations. Moreover, as with the other selected metropolitan complexes, a large share of the local San Diego job-market and economy is directly tied into multilocational business organizations based in other metropolitan complexes, such as St Louis (e.g. General Dynamics Corp.), Detroit (e.g. Burroughs Corp.), and San Francisco–Oakland–San Jose (e.g. Safeway Stores Inc. and Bank of America) (also note Table 3.8).

The San Diego case is counterpointed by the situation prevailing in the Boise City SMSA. On a *per capita* basis Boise's non-local job control approaches that for the New York City metropolitan

Table 3.8: Jobs controlled at seventy major metropolitan complexes by multilocational business organizations based in seven western US metropolitan complexes, 1974–5

	1970 population	Estimated number of employees controlled from[a]							
		San Francisco–Oakland–San Jose[b]	Seattle–Tacoma[c]	Portland SMSA	Phoenix SMSA	Boise City SMSA	Honolulu SMSA	San Diego SMSA	Total for selected centres
New York[d]	16 894 371	23 537	2 180	1 430	3 837	227	66	98	31 375
Los Angeles[e]	8 452 461	92 346	3 603	3 392	3 301	2 124	3 161	5 383	113 265
Chicago[f]	7 612 314	11 863	564	2 470	4 837	929	542	843	22 048
Philadelphia[g]	5 317 407	4 918	7 115	1 076	2 978	155	121	42	16 405
Detroit SMSA	4 431 390	1 517	179	746	1 395	39	4	207	4 087
San Francisco–Oakland–San Jose[b]	4 174 235	—	6 428	1 314	2 237	2 141	5 079	1 454	18 653
Boston[h]	3 388 795	4 760	110	536	1 223	28	7	64	6 728
Washington DC SMSA	2 908 801	8 326	111	103	785	823	254	35	10 437
Cleveland–Akron[i]	2 743 433	2 923	96	479	1 407	1 342	70	85	6 402
Montréal[j]	2 743 208	342	2	25	318	100	3		790
Toronto[j]	2 628 043	2 005	227	146	380		5	36	2 799
St Louis SMSA	2 410 163	3 397	768	493	904	801	44	211	6 618
Pittsburgh SMSA	2 401 245	820	48	96	1 099	177	3	98	2 341
Dallas–Fort Worth SMSA	2 377 979	13 213	654	156	1 417	308	462	462	16 672
Baltimore SMSA	2 070 670	3 176	114	370	171	2	5	3	3 841
Houston SMSA	1 999 316	8 561	180	419	1 116	165	211	555	11 207

Minneapolis–St Paul SMSA	1 965 159	876	410	640	3 374	150	4	169	5 623
Miami[k]	1 887 892	1 645	641	108	1 006	26	3	99	3 438
Seattle–Tacoma[c]	1 832 896	11 445	—	2 895	387	2 469	1 435	397	19 028
Cincinnati[l]	1 611 058	1 539	376	132	577	39	97	87	2 847
Atlanta SMSA	1 597 816	3 187	919	987	803	267	7	219	6 389
Milwaukee[m]	1 574 526	1 652	79	306	503	32	3	57	2 632
San Diego SMSA	1 357 854	11 516	247	316	349	448	274	—	13 150
Buffalo SMSA	1 349 211	2 206	50	338	182		38		2 814
Kansas City SMSA	1 271 515	4 588	1 679	91	1 442	158	41	260	8 259
Denver SMSA	1 228 801	8 105	608	315	795	1 469	1 468	343	13 103
Riverside–San Bernardino SMSA	1 143 146	18 282	124	369	83	257	226	2 154	21 505
Indianapolis SMSA	1 109 882	1 121	78	84	381	28		36	1 728
Tampa–St Petersburg SMSA	1 088 549	855	113	55	332	28		257	1 640
Vancouver[j]	1 082 352	4 583	1 669	1 112	245	210	505	17	8 341
New Orleans SMSA	1 045 809	4 137	261	143	507	10	32	39	5 129
Columbus SMSA	1 017 847	1 035	121	676	232	76	247		2 387
Portland SMSA	1 009 129	21 939	4 046	—	590	2 129	1 220	266	30 190
Phoenix SMSA	967 522	5 019	250	192	—	392	540	830	7 223
Rochester SMSA	961 516	484	75	140	92	192		49	1 032
Providence SMSA	905 558	983	58	103	41			26	1 211
San Antonio SMSA	888 179	1 385	21	58	282	6	261	192	2 205
Louisville[n]	867 330	1 766	62	33	583	137			2 581
Hartford[n]	866 120	433	81	75	62		26	25	702
Dayton SMSA	850 266	154	12	66	127	6			365
Memphis SMSA	834 006	2 016	67	538	1 161	288	21		4 091
Sacramento SMSA	800 592	16 020	429	422	317	214	2 144	132	19 678

Table 3.8 continued

Albany–Schenectady–Troy SMSA	777 793	475	48	126	114	505	2		1 270
Birmingham SMSA	767 230	1 270	39	54	300	2		4	1 669
Toledo SMSA	762 741	437	232	28	73	2			772
Greensboro–Winston–Salem SMSA	723 304	2 016	193	252	282	68			2 811
Salt Lake City SMSA	705 458	5 761	648	224	241	1 724	43	144	8 798
Nashville SMSA	699 144	497	1 151	310	577	24		22	2 581
Oklahoma City SMSA	698 180	2 908	42	81	210	2	22		3 265
Norfolk SMSA	687 576	618	13	244	297	6		49	1 252
Syracuse SMSA	636 507	315	74	147	187	2			725
Honolulu SMSA	629 176	4 134	416	67	750	290	—	38	5 695
Northeast Pennsylvania SMSA	621 830	589	68	46	50	19			753
Jacksonville SMSA	621 519	1 239	227	52	649			628	2 814
Allentown–Bethlehem SMSA	594 124	521	16	45	1 295	263		36	2 176
Charlotte SMSA	557 785	419	120	71	858	57		49	1 574
Tulsa SMSA	550 835	2 495	27	52	166		7	2	2 749
Winnipeg[j]	548 573	1 740	55		910	2			2 707
Richmond SMSA	542 242	1 977	33	243	297	2			2 552
Springfield–Holyoke SMSA	541 752	479	143	58	27	12	19	90	564
Omaha SMSA	540 142	1 621		722	2 531	2	70	24	5 138
Grand Rapids SMSA	539 225	332	58	492	93	2	60		1 071
Orlando SMSA	453 270	636	113	85	350	372		981	2 597

Lansing SMSA	424 271	221			26	45		499	761
Raleigh–Durham SMSA	418 841	220	811	258	191	41	1		1 526
Fresno SMSA	413 053	5183	176	82	423		354	342	6 601
Knoxville SMSA	409 409	3360	29	43	149				3 582
Wichita SMSA	389 352	698	8 768	45	60	2		36	9 609
Mobile SMSA	376 690	373	8	50	110	2			543
Baton Rouge SMSA	375 628	1488	8	1 180	59				2 735

(a) See caption to Figure 3.2.
(b) See note (a) in Table 3.5.
(c) See note (b) in Table 3.5.
(d) New York–New Jersey SCA + Bridgeport SMSA + Norwalk SMSA + Stamford SMSA. The combination of metropolitan areas into larger metropolitan complexes in this and preceding tables is based upon heavily overlapping commuting patterns and the sharing of major airport facilities. Cf. Chapter 2, note 1 (p. 220).
(e) Los Angeles–Long Beach SMSA + Anaheim–Santa Ana–Garden Grove SMSA.
(f) Chicago–Northeastern Indiana SCA.
(g) Philadelphia SMSA + Wilmington, Del., SMSA.
(h) Boston SMSA + Brockton SMSA + Lawrence–Haverhill SMSA + Lowell SMSA.
(i) Cleveland SMSA + Akron SMSA.
(j) 1971 population datum.
(k) Miami SMSA + Fort Lauderdale–Hollywood SMSA.
(l) Cincinnati SMSA + Hamilton–Middletown SMSA.
(m) Milwaukee SMSA + Racine SMSA.
(n) Hartford SMSA + New Britain SMSA.

Table 3.9: Deviation of job-control linkages from central-place theory and hinterland assumptions of interurban growth transmission (based on multilocational business organizations headquartered in selected western US metropolitan complexes, 1974–5)

	Percentage of *all non-local* job-control linkages within the US–Canadian system of cities unaccounted for by Christallerian central-place theory		Percentage of *metropolitan* job-control linkages within the US–Canadian system of cities unaccounted for by Christallerian central-place theory		Ratio of non-hinterland *metropolitan* linkages to all hinterland linkages	Ratio of *all* non-hinterland linkages to all hinterland linkages
	I[a]	II[b]	III[c]	IV[d]	V	VI
San Francisco–Oakland–	44.2	88.9	33.7	90.0	6.4:1	8.1:1
San Jose[e]	41.8[f]	78.8[f]	33.7[f]	80.4[f]	3.0:1[f]	3.7:1[f]
Seattle–Tacoma[g]	53.9	80.1	52.3	95.1	2.9:1	4.0:1
Portland SMSA	64.1	82.7	46.2	87.3	2.3:1	4.8:1
Phoenix SMSA[h]	58.9[h]	91.7	53.0[h]	96.5	8.7:1	10.9:1
Honolulu SMSA	49.1	56.8	84.2	100.0	1.1:1	1.3:1
Boise City SMSA	80.1	80.1	100.0	100.0	2.5:1	4.0:1
San Diego SMSA	63.7	97.1	54.8	100.0	25.4:1	33.5:1

(a) Based on all jobs controlled in non-hinterland smaller towns and cities (column D, Table 3.6), plus jobs controlled in all non-hinterland metropolitan complexes belonging to the same or larger population size classes (appropriate columns Table 3.7).

(b) Based on all jobs controlled in non-hinterland smaller towns and cities plus all jobs controlled in *every* size class of non-hinterland metropolitan complex (columns B and D, Table 3.6).

(c) Based on all jobs controlled in metropolitan complexes belonging to the same or larger population size classes (appropriate columns Table 3.7).

(d) Based on all jobs controlled in *every* size class of non-hinterland metropolitan complex (column B, Table 3.6).

(e) See note (a) in Table 3.5.

(f) See note (e) in Table 3.6.

(g) See note (b) in Table 3.5.

(h) During the early 1970s the Phoenix SMSA probably had the most rapid relative rate of growth of all major US metropolitan complexes. By 1974 it had an estimated population of 1·2 million. For this reason Arizona's largest metropolitan centre was assigned to the 'third-order national centre' size category (Table 3.7) when computing columns I and III. Had the Phoenix SMSA been instead assigned to the 500000–999999 size class on the basis of its official 1970 population (967 522), then the percentage of deviating linkages would have risen to 71·9 in column I and 70·2 in column III.

Figure 3.2: *US and Canadian metropolitan complexes with jobs controlled by multilocational business organizations headquartered in the San Francisco–Oakland–San Jose metropolitan complex, 1974–5. (Here, as in Figures 3.3–3.12, circles are proportional to the number of jobs controlled. Unavoidably, there were some dissimilarities in the*

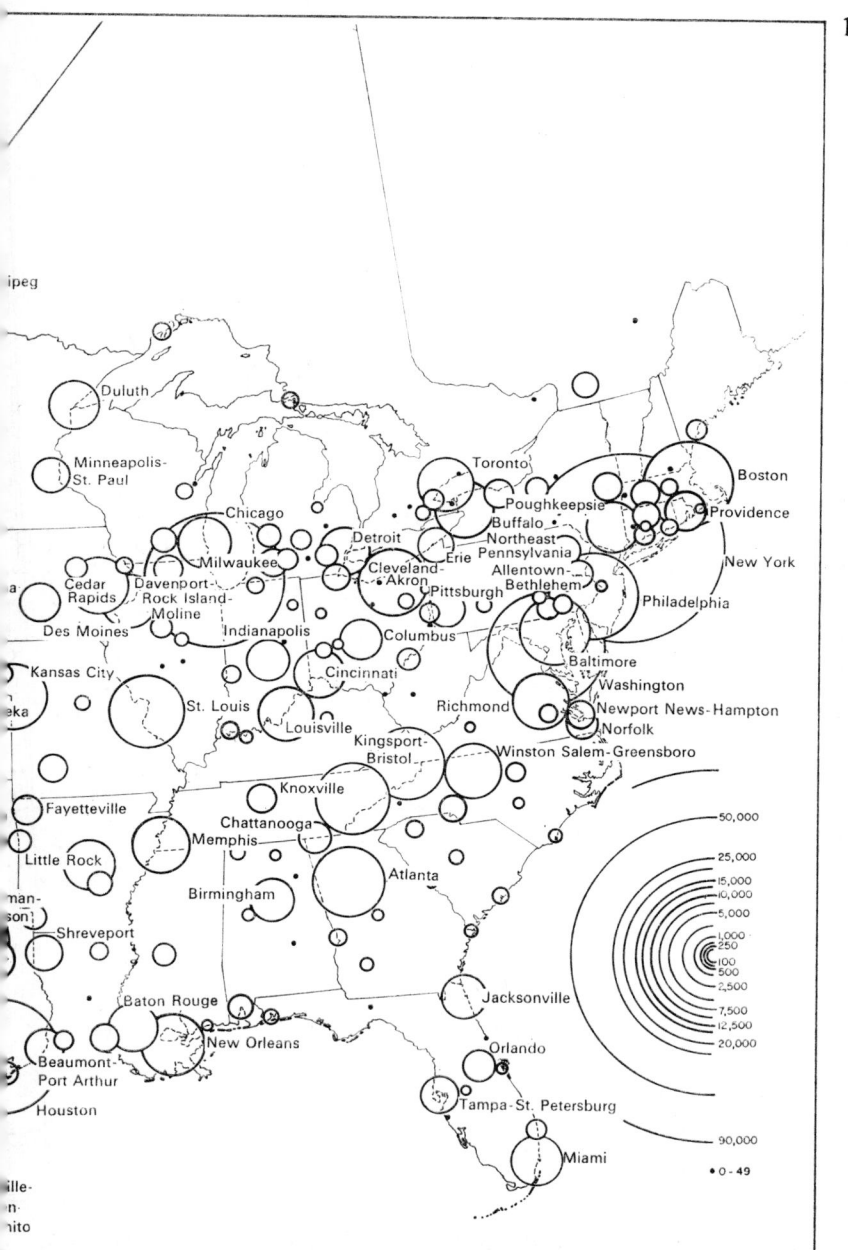

quality of data provided by the surveyed organizations. In some instances it was necessary to make estimates based on such criteria as output, sales and production capacity. Consequently, there is a margin of error of 100 or more for some of the larger employment totals shown in Figures 3.2–3.12 and Table 3.8.)

142

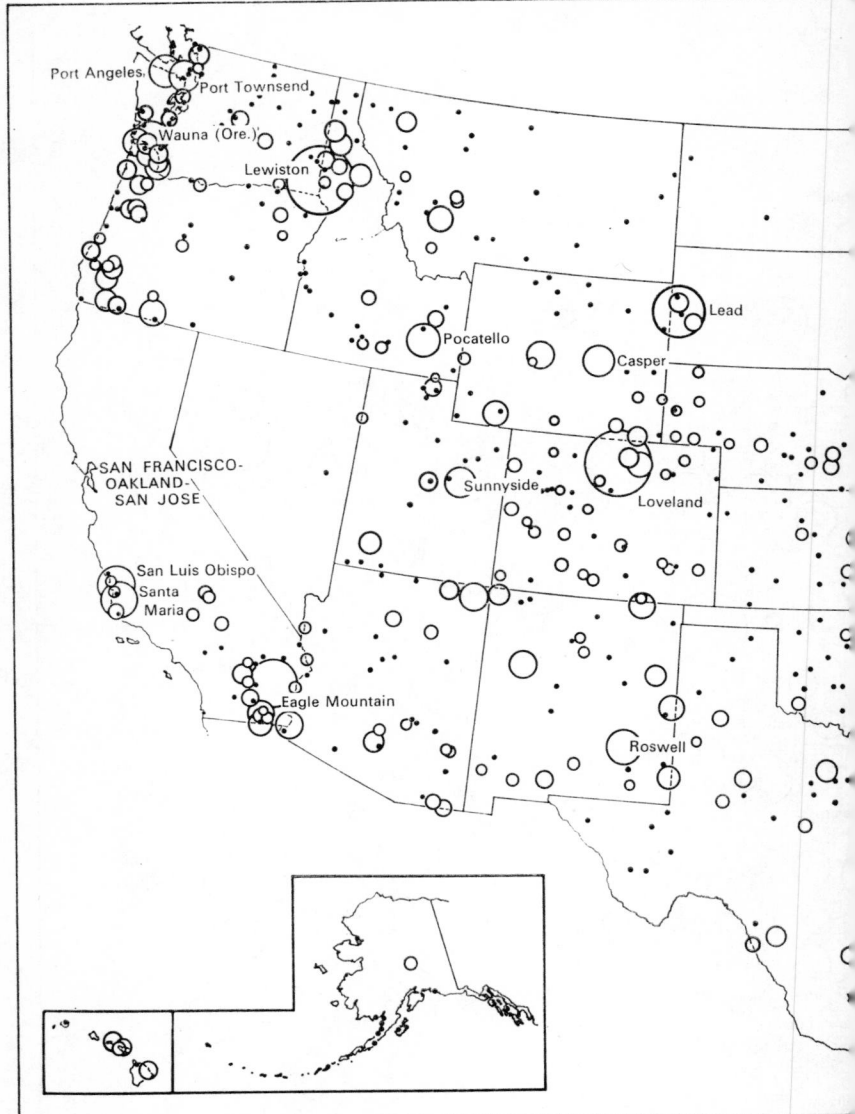

Figure 3.3: *Jobs controlled in non-hinterland smaller cities and towns by multilocational business organizations headquartered in the San Francisco–Oakland–San Jose metropolitan complex, 1974–5. (In order to maximize the detail of this map, the hinterlands of the Seattle–*

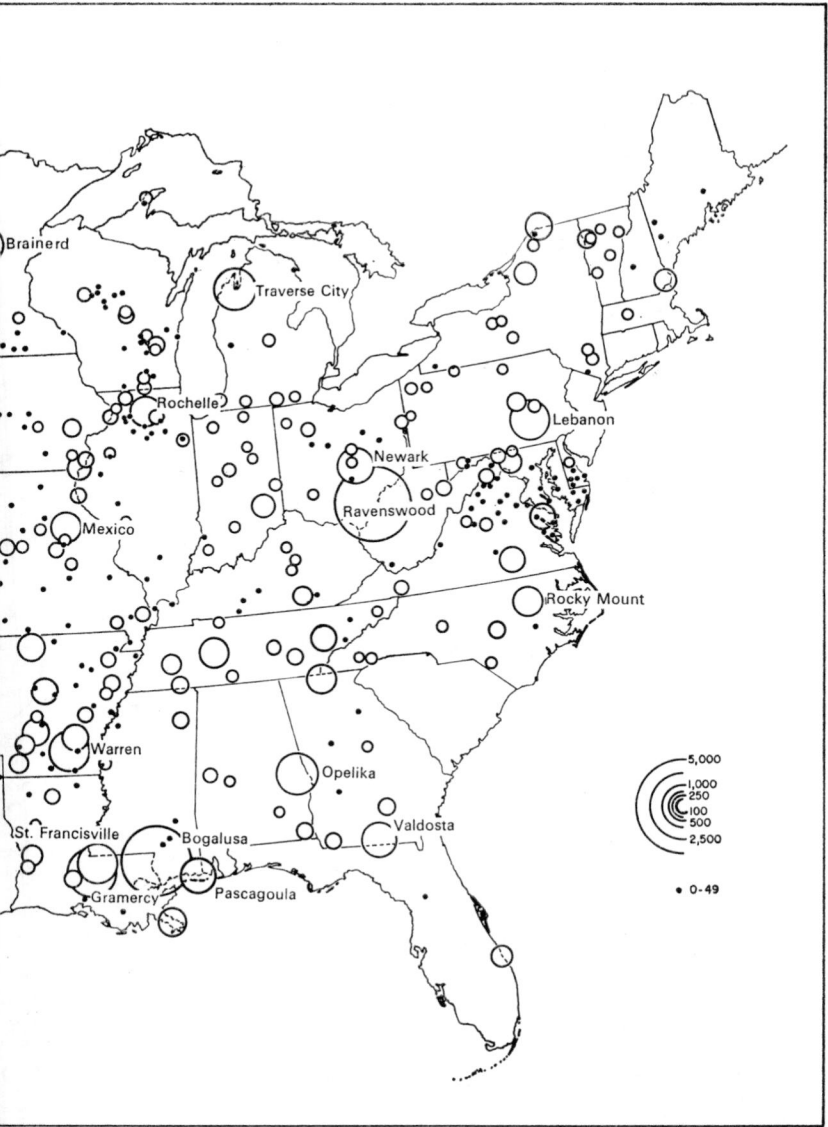

Tacoma and Portland metropolitan complexes have not been 'nested' into that of the San Francisco–Oakland–San Jose metropolitan complex (cf. note (e), Table 3.6). 10 581 jobs occurring in non-metropolitan places scattered throughout Canada are not shown.)

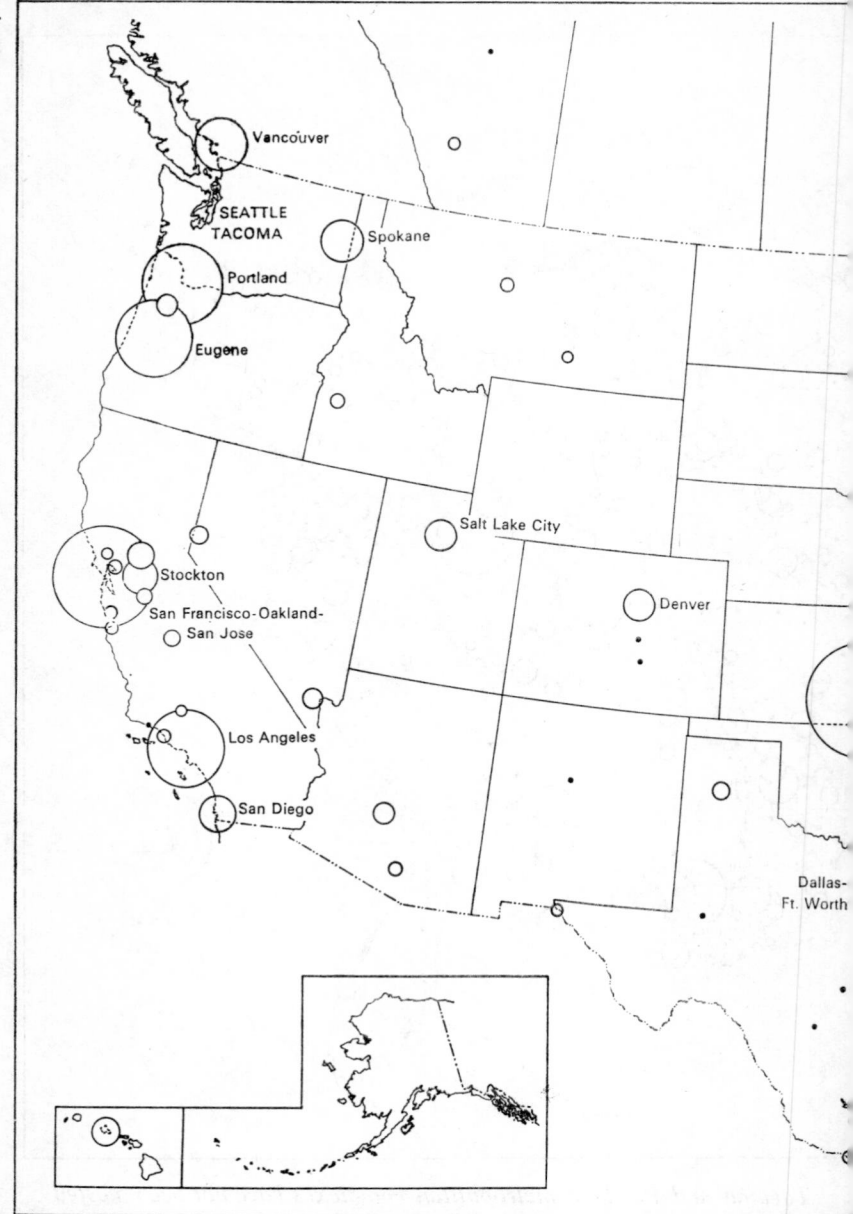

Figure 3.4: *US and Canadian metropolitan complexes with jobs controlled by multilocational business organizations headquartered in the Seattle–Tacoma metropolitan complex, 1974.*

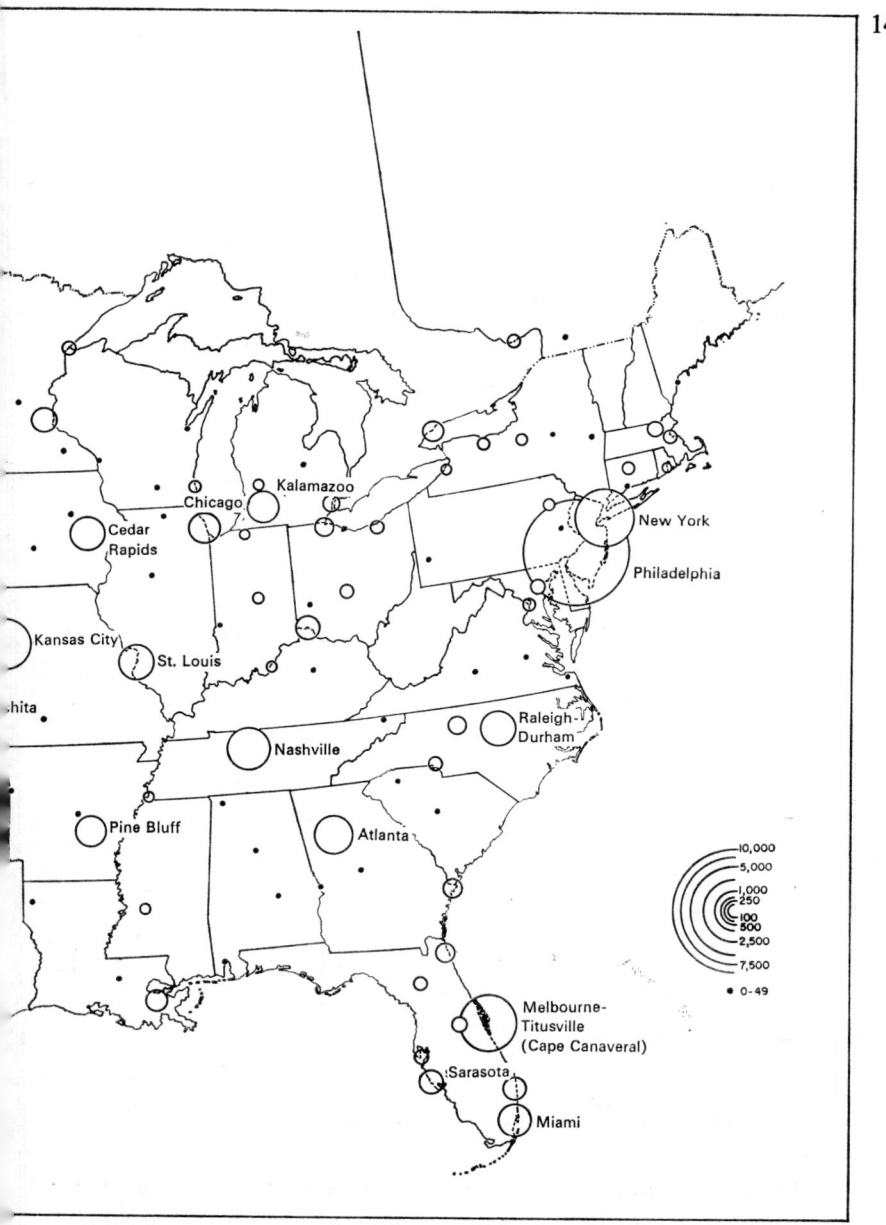

Cedar
Rapids

Chicago

Kalamazoo

New York

Philadelphia

Kansas City

St. Louis

hita

Raleigh-
Durham

Nashville

Pine Bluff

Atlanta

10,000
5,000
1,000
250
100
500
2,500
7,500

• 0-49

Melbourne-
Titusville
(Cape Canaveral)

Sarasota

Miami

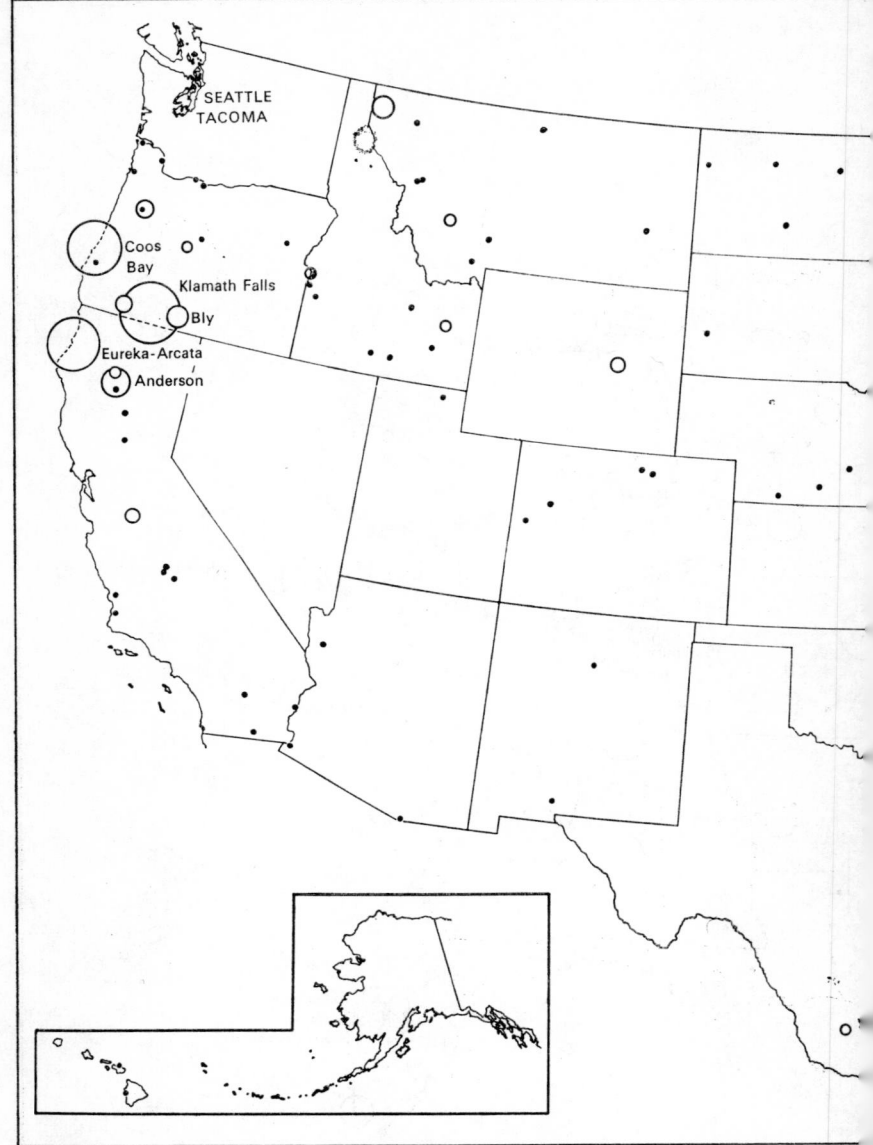

Figure 3.5: *Jobs controlled in non-hinterland smaller cities and towns by multilocational business organizations headquartered in the Seattle–Tacoma metropolitan complex, 1974. (2661 jobs occurring in geographically widespread Canadian cities and towns are not shown.)*

Marshfield

Lewiston
Plymouth
New Bern
Jacksonville

Wright City-
Valiant-
Craig

Hot Springs
Decherd

Dierks
De Queen

Philadelphia

2,500
500
100
250
1,000

• 0-49

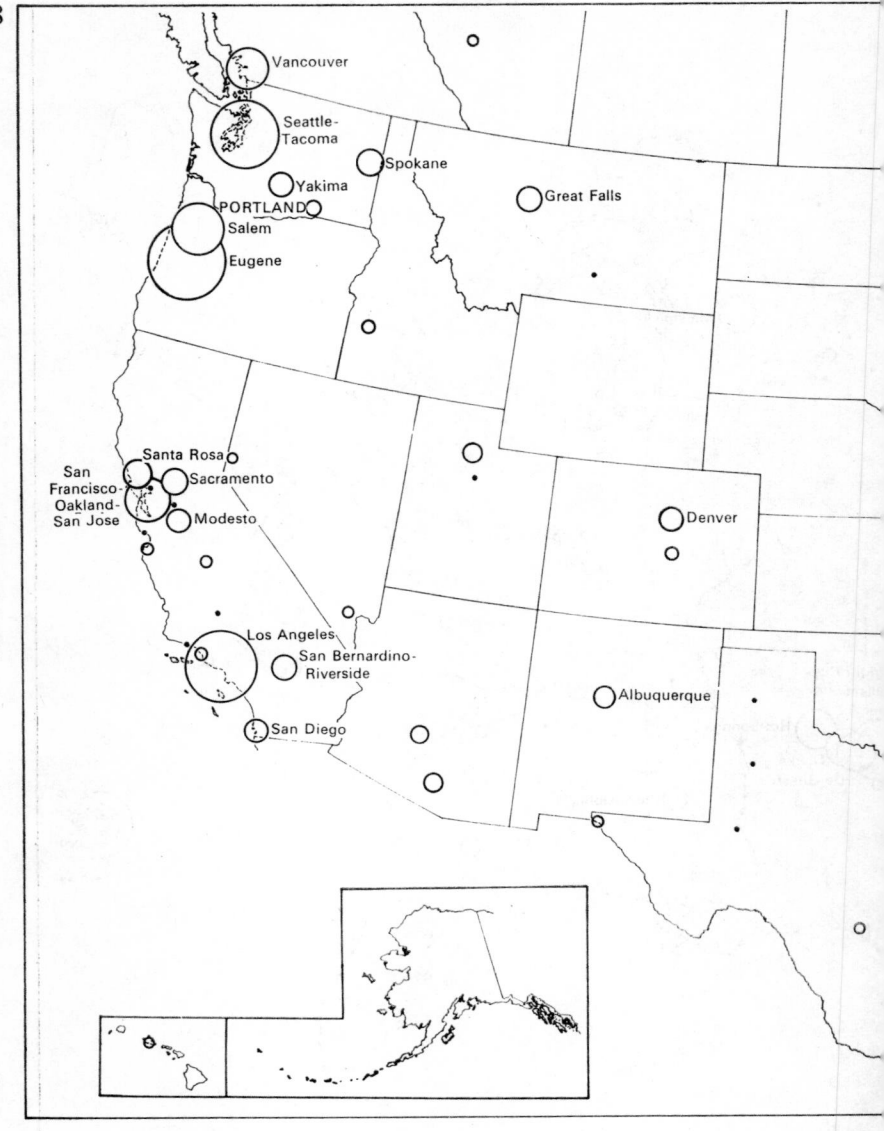

Figure 3.6: *US and Canadian metropolitan complexes with jobs controlled by multilocational business organizations headquartered in the Portland SMSA, 1974–5.*

Minneapolis-St. Paul

Milwaukee

Kitchener-Guelph

Buffalo

Boston

Grand Rapids

Detroit

Davenport-Rock Island-Moline

Chicago

Kalamazoo

Cleveland-Akron

New York

Omaha

Peoria

Champaign-Urbana-Danville

Springfield

Columbus

Philadelphia

Baltimore

St. Louis

Roanoke

Winston Salem-Greensboro

Raleigh-Durham

Nashville

Memphis

Atlanta

Savannah

2,500
500
100
250
1,000
5,000

• 0-49

Baton Rouge

Houston

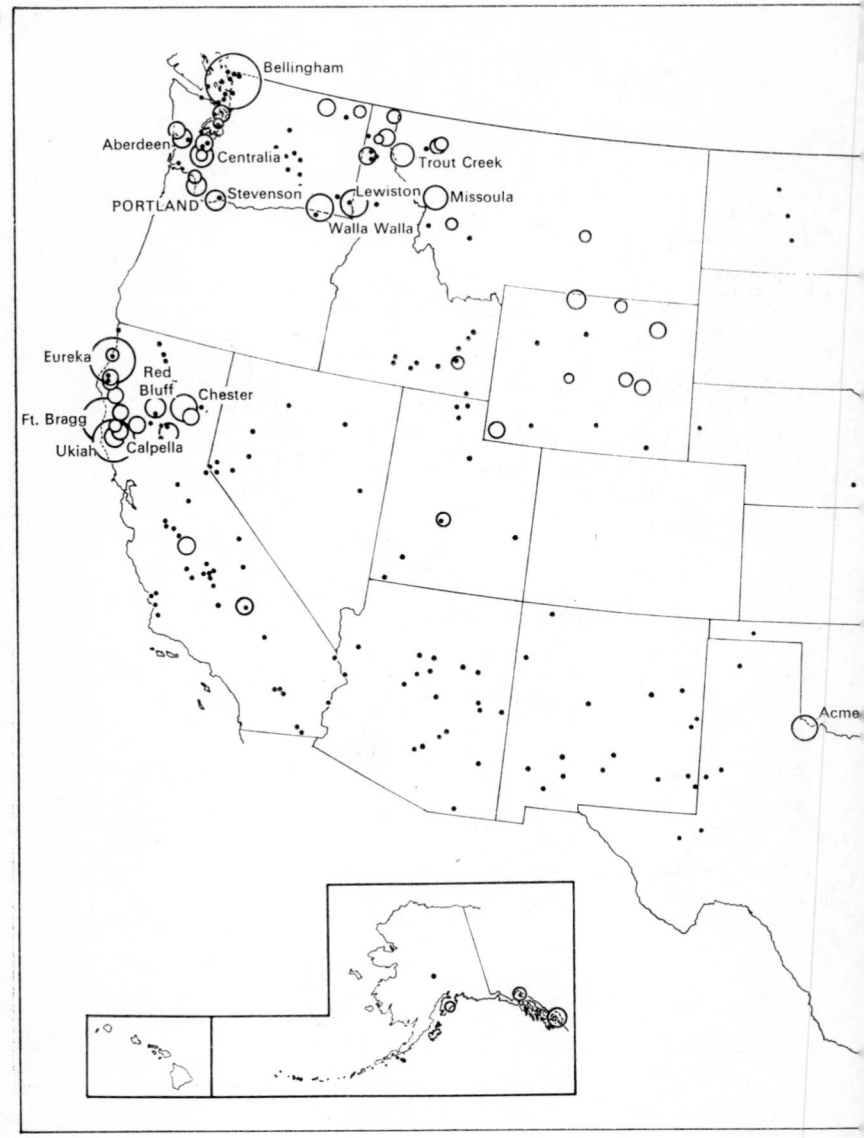

Figure 3.7: *Jobs controlled in non-hinterland smaller cities and towns by multilocational business organizations headquartered in the Portland SMSA, 1974–5. (1617 jobs situated in smaller cities and towns scattered throughout Canada are not shown.)*

Woodland
Bingham
Plattsburgh
Lyons Falls
Mohawk
Mellen
Escanaba
Goodman
Gagetown
Ft. Dodge
Coldwater
Washington
Emporia
Conway
Statesville
Whiteville
Seneca
Sumter
Russellville
Fordyce
Crossett
Sulligent
Louisville
El Dorado
Ruston
Monticello
Dodson
Vienna
Urania
Brunswick
Taylorsville
Dothan
Gloster
Chiefland

2,500
500
100
250
1,000
5,000

• 0 - 49

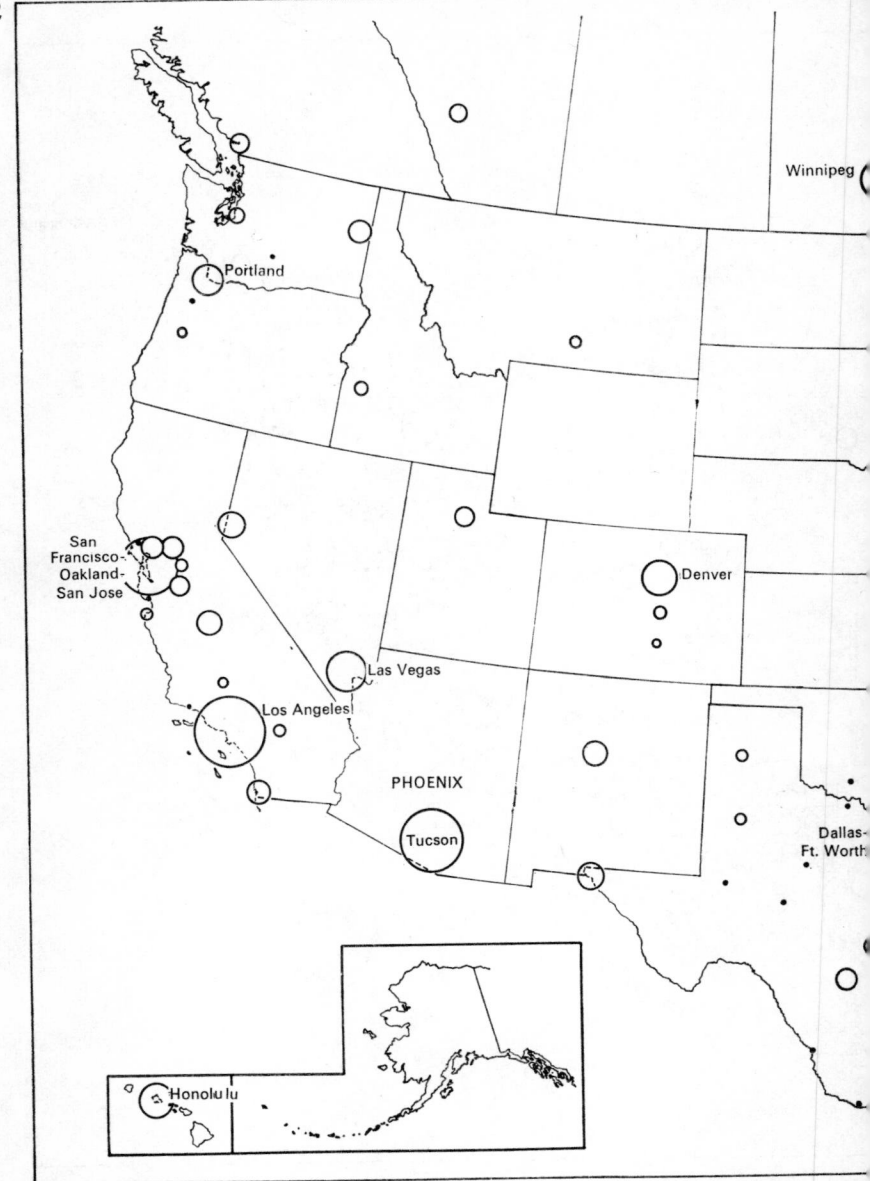

Figure 3.8: *US and Canadian metropolitan complexes with jobs controlled by multilocational business organizations headquartered in the Phoenix SMSA, 1974–5.*

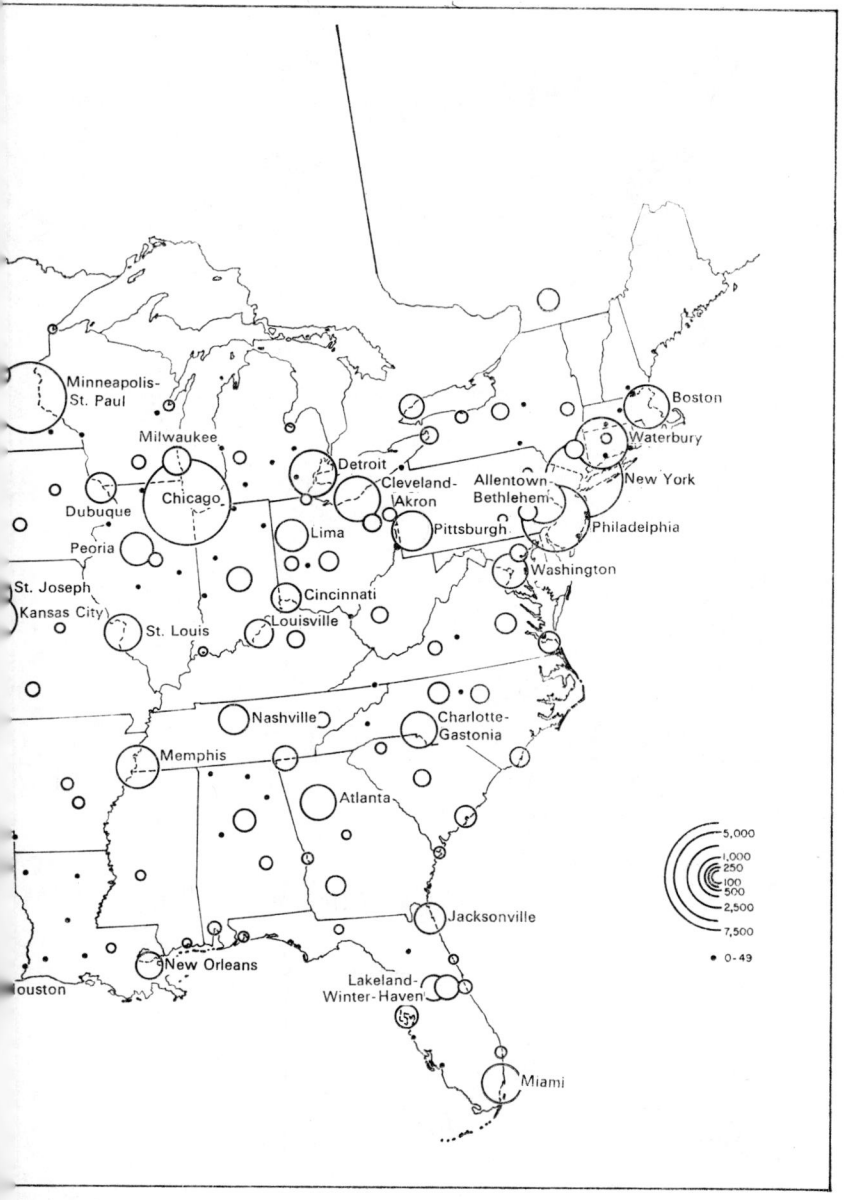

Minneapolis-
St. Paul

Milwaukee

Detroit

Dubuque

Chicago

Cleveland-
Akron

Allentown-
Bethlehem

Boston

Waterbury

New York

Peoria

Lima

Pittsburgh

Philadelphia

St. Joseph

Kansas City

Cincinnati

Washington

St. Louis

Louisville

Nashville

Charlotte-
Gastonia

Memphis

Atlanta

Jacksonville

New Orleans

Houston

Lakeland-
Winter-Haven

Miami

5,000
1,000
250
100
500
2,500
7,500

• 0-49

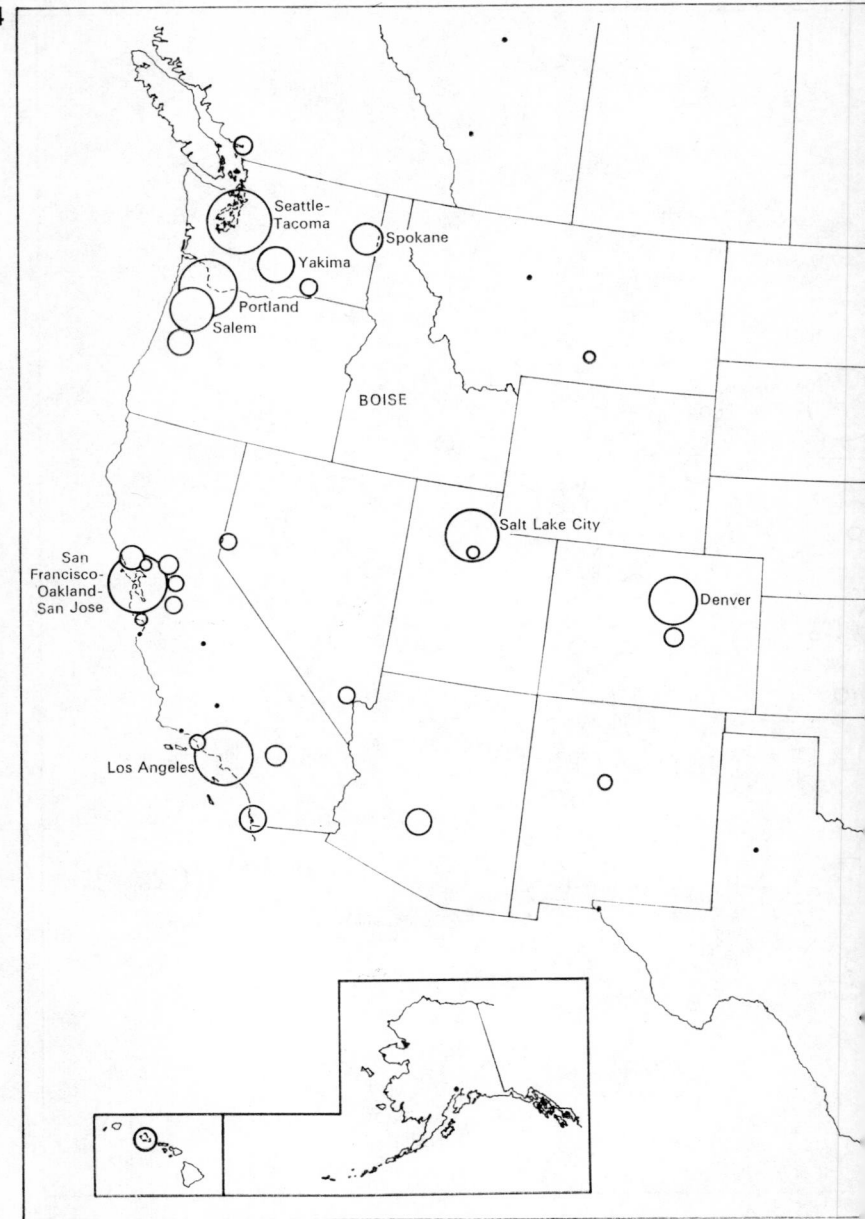

Figure 3.9: *US and Canadian metropolitan complexes with jobs controlled by multilocational business organizations headquartered in the Boise City SMSA, 1974–5.*

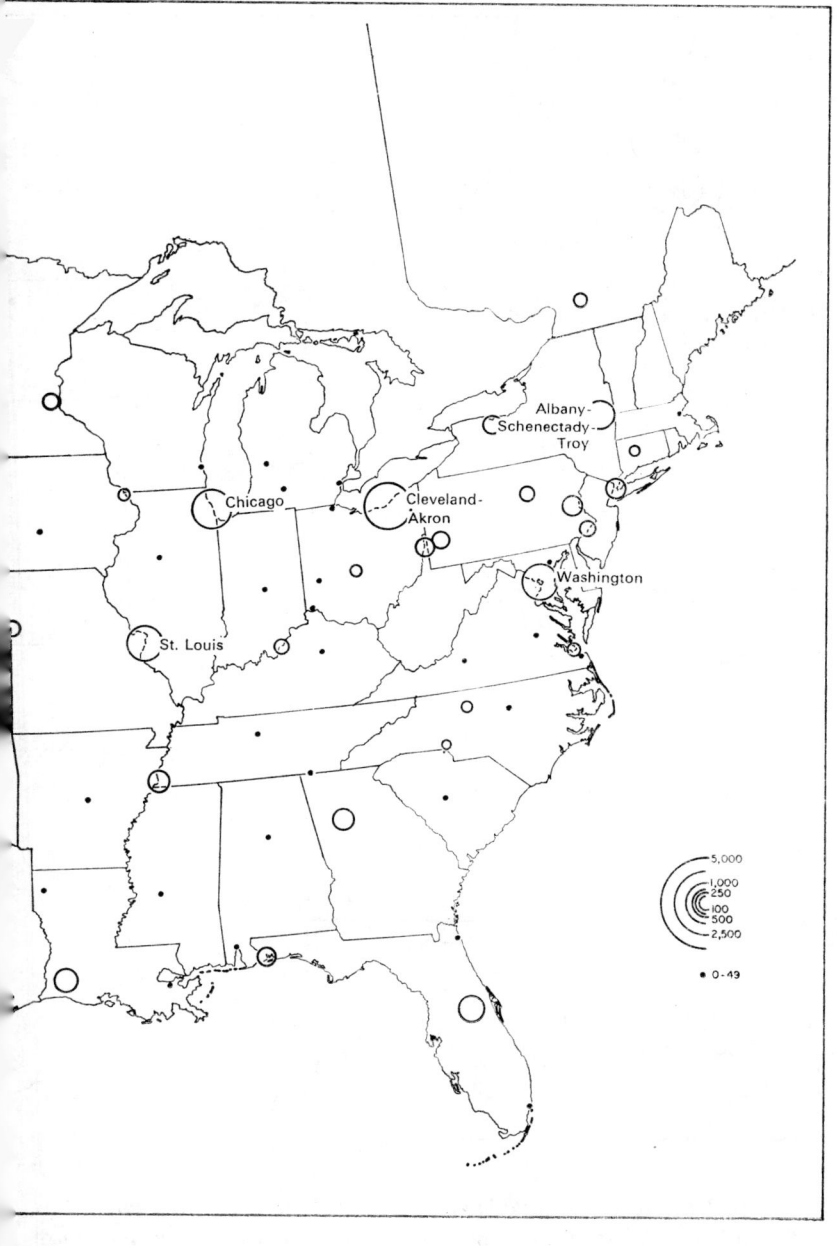

Figure 3.10: *Jobs controlled in non-hinterland smaller cities and towns by multilocational business organizations headquartered in the Boise City SMSA, 1974–5.*

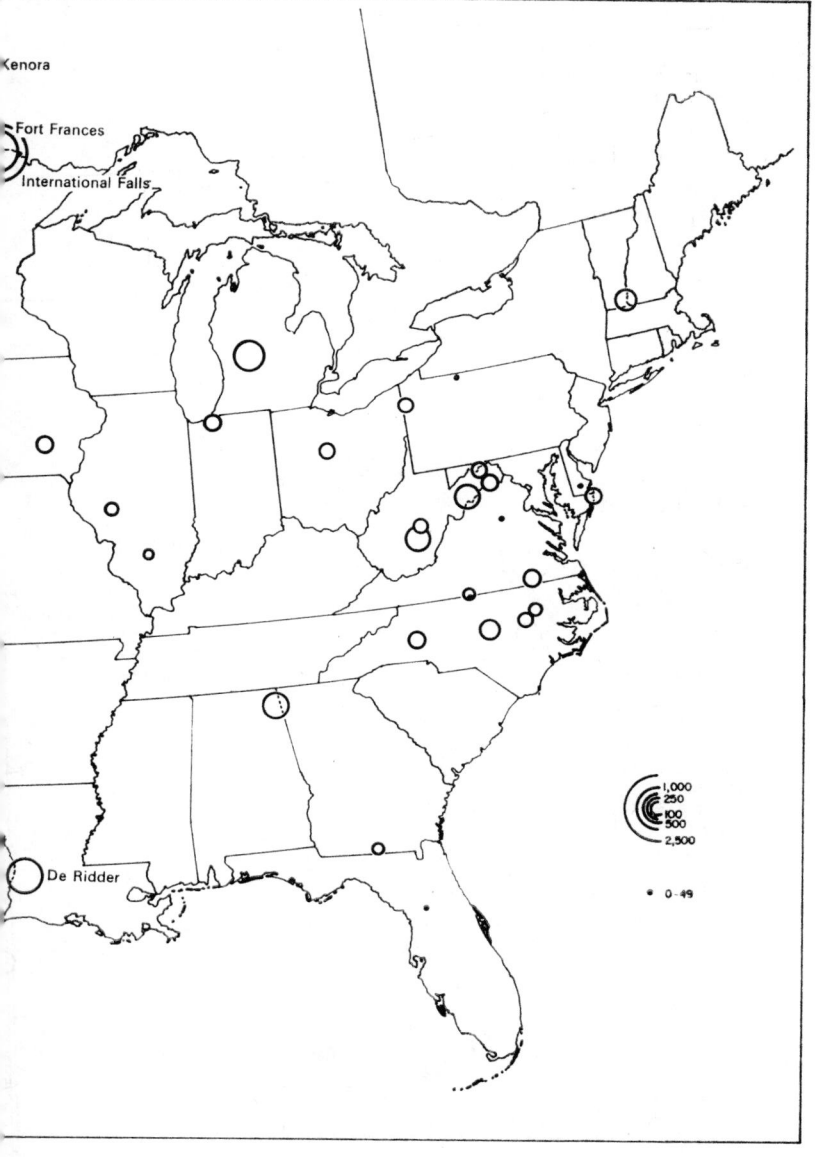

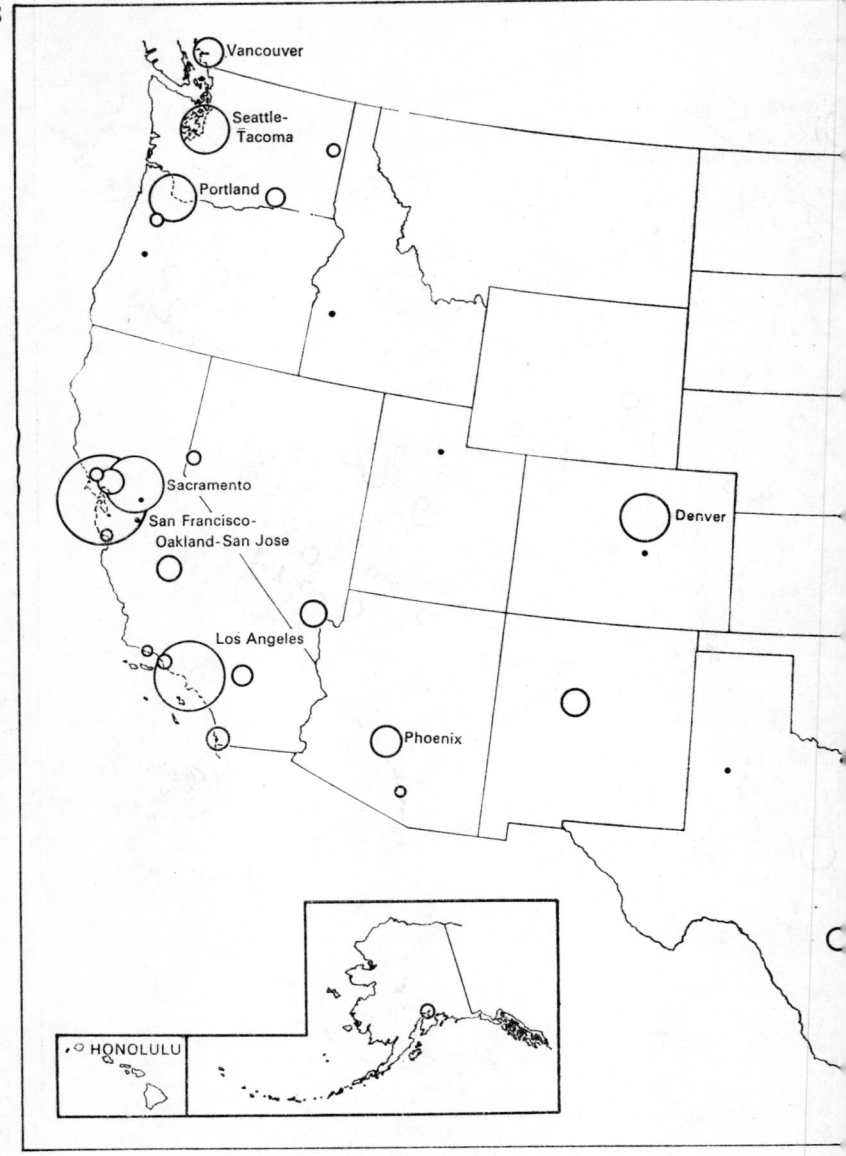

Figure 3.11. *US and Canadian metropolitan complexes with jobs controlled by multilocational business organizations headquartered in the Honolulu SMSA, 1974–5.*

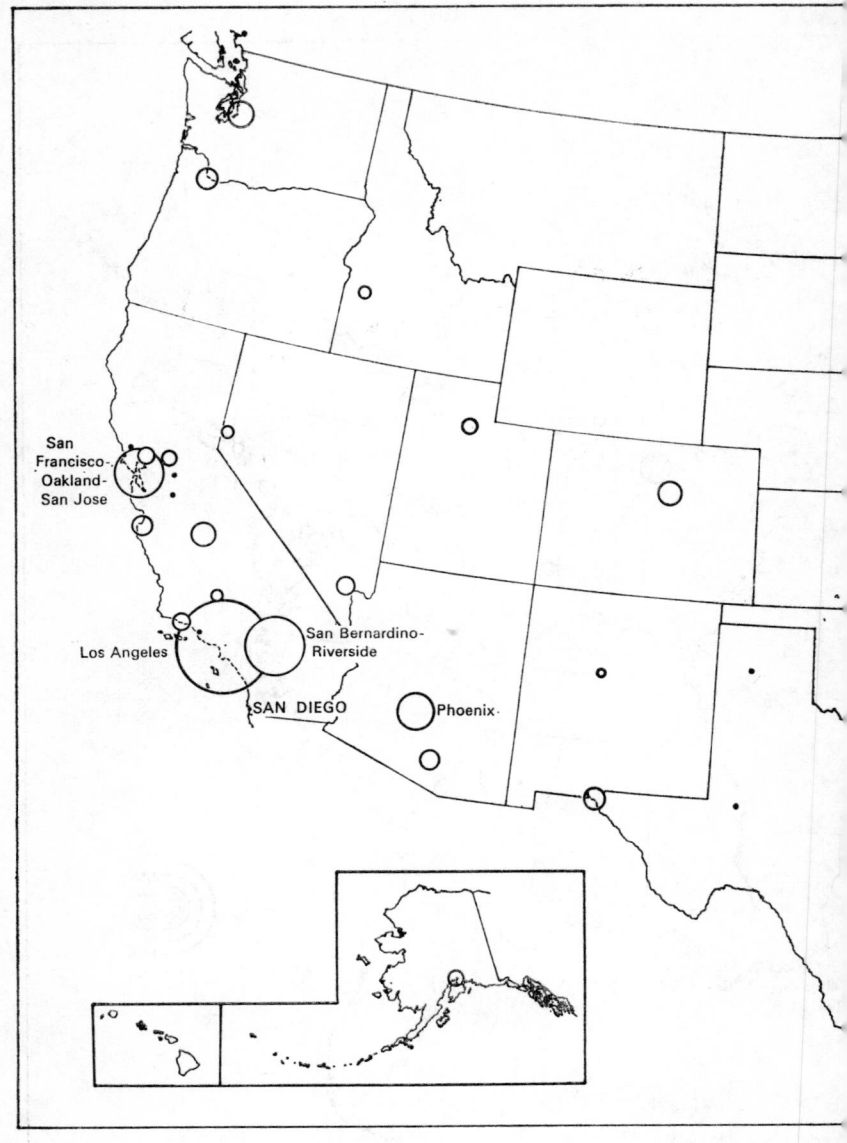

Figure 3.12: *US and Canadian metropolitan complexes with jobs controlled by multilocational business organizations headquartered in the San Diego SMSA, 1974–5.*

complex. (The New York complex controls roughly 33 per cent of the jobs associated with all US multilocational business organizations.) Boise's extremely high relative level of non-local intraorganizational linkages is mostly the product of four organizations: the Boise Cascade Corp. (forest-products conglomerate with 29000 domestic and foreign employees), Morrison-Knudsen Co. Inc. (diversified heavy construction and engineering firm with 21000 employees, mostly overseas), Albertsons Inc. (retailing concern with over $1.0 billion in sales during 1974 and almost 14000 employees), and J. R. Simplot Company (principal functions: food processing and fertilizer mining and production; 6000 employees).

(2) Despite the exclusion of relationships involving partly owned subsidiaries, joint ventures, and divisional or subsidiary head offices, *the overall pattern of interurban growth transmission stemming from the spatial structure of multilocational organizations is complex in several senses.* The spatial distribution of intraorganizational job-control linkages for most metropolitan complexes exhibits either rather limited distance decay – as in the San Francisco–Oakland–San Jose, Seattle–Tacoma, Boise City, and San Diego cases (Figures 3.2–3.7, 3.9–3.10, 3.12) – or virtually no distance decay – as in the Phoenix SMSA example (Figure 3.8). The distance decay of Honolulu's intraorganizational job-control linkages (Figure 3.1) is not an unanticipated exception, given both the extreme physical and time-zone distance separating that island metropolis from the eastern US and Canada, and the relatively recent and cautious entry of its major conglomerates (AMFAC, Castle & Cooke, Dillingham Corp.) into the operation of mainland retailing, production, and engineering units.

The complexity of the intermetropolitan pattern of intraorganizationally-induced growth transmission is also reflected by the number of centres at which linkages from individual metropolitan complexes terminate. Multilocational business organizations based in the San Francisco–Oakland–San Jose complex, for example, control units in 234 other US and Canadian metropolitan centres. Multilocational business organizations headquartered in Seattle–Tacoma operate offices, plants and establishments in 144 other US–Canadian metropolitan complexes; while the multilocational corporations based in the much less populous Boise City SMSA function in no fewer than 108 other metropolitan complexes scattered across the entire US–Canadian economic landscape. Moreover, as multilocational business organizations grow, there is both a frequent elaboration in the number of centres at which job-control linkages terminate, and an emergence of new intraorganizational ties with already related centres. For example, as a result of the merger and acquisition activity of a single organization (Combine Communications Corp.), in a brief period Phoenix's job-control linkages with Chicago, Detroit, Cleveland–Akron, Cincinnati and Atlanta were pushed to levels beyond those indicated in Table 3.8.

Many linkage-pattern details are additionally complex in the sense that they are unexpected from a gravity-model perspective.[17] Three arbitrarily selected examples illustrate this point. The most important job-control linkages of the Phoenix SMSA are with the Chicago metropolitan complex, rather than with the comparably sized but physically much more proximate Los Angeles metropolitan complex (Figure 3.8). The intraorganizationally generated interdependencies between San Francisco–Oakland–San Jose and the eastern Tennessee centres of Knoxville and Kingsport–Bristol are of greater importance than those with such metropolitan complexes as Detroit, Cincinnati, and Indianapolis, which lie at similar distances from northern California but have much larger populations (Figure 3.2.). The leading job-control linkages of Seattle–Tacoma are with the Wichita SMSA and the Philadelphia metropolitan complex rather than with larger and more locationally accessible metropolitan centres (Figure 3.4).

The job-control distribution eccentricities of specific metropolitan complexes often lose much of their mystery once one is familiar with the nature of the corporations that dominate the local headquarters scene. The Seattle–Tacoma pattern of intraorganizational growth-transmission ties with other metropolitan complexes is much influenced by the Boeing Company (mainly aircraft production and aerospace activities with about 68 000 employees). Likewise, the Portland pattern of job-control linkages with non-hinterland smaller cities and towns (Figure 3.7) is highly affected by the forest-resource requirements of three corporations with a total of over 67 000 employees (Georgia Pacific, Louisiana Pacific, and Evans Products) and several smaller organizations that are also primarily associated with wood, pulp and paper products. Also, Phoenix's pattern of intraorganizational linkages with other metropolitan complexes (Figure 3.8) becomes somewhat clearer in light of the fact that the Arizona centre houses the headquarters of the Greyhound Corp. (nationwide bus transportation and manufacturing conglomerate with over 35000 employees). Furthermore, in the context of earlier limited-search and uncertainty-reduction observations, it is noteworthy that whenever a large metropolitan complex has a major corporation – such as Boeing – operating on a very sizable scale in an 'unexpected' less important metropolitan centre – such as Wichita – it usually also has several other multilocational organizations controlling units in the same centre.

(3) *The total array of non-local intraorganizational growth-transmission linkages of business organizations based in any particular metropolitan complex is highlighted by ties with other metropolitan complexes.* That is, the most important non-local intraorganizational (and, by extension, interorganizational) growth-transmission channels of any single metropolitan complex *do not* extend between that urban unit and smaller places situated within its traditionally defined retail-trade, or central-place, hinterland. For the seven centres covered here, the percentage of non-local intraorganizational linkages involving other metropolitan complexes ranges from 45·1 to 79·3. In contrast, the percentage of intraorganizational interdependencies involving hinterland locations is clustered between 2·9 and 21·2, with the exception of Honolulu (Table 3·6). More significantly, again with the exception of Honolulu, the ratio of non-hinterland metropolitan linkages to all hinterland linkages varies from a low of 2·3:1 to a high of 25·4:1 (Table 3·9, column V).[18] Incomplete data unmistakably indicate that this third generalization is also true for the intraorganizational growth-transmission linkages generated by multilocational corporations and firms headquartered in the Los Angeles metropolitan complex.

(4) In every instance *non-hinterland smaller towns and cities constitute an important element in the overall pattern of interurban growth-transmission channels of intraorganizational origin* (Table 3.6 and Figures 3.3, 3.5, 3.7, 3.10). For five of the seven metropolitan complexes under discussion, the absolute number of jobs controlled by locally-based multilocational organizations is greater for non-hinterland smaller towns and cities than it is for the hinterland as a whole. This statement also holds for the San Francisco–Oakland–San Jose metropolitan complex if its hinterland is circumscribed in a less than liberal manner (Table 3.6).[19] As a consequence of the magnitude of job-control interdependencies involving non-hinterland smaller towns and cities, the ratio of all non-hinterland linkages to all 'hinterland' linkages is typically 3.7:1 or greater (Table 3.9, column

VI). Modern communications and computer technology has contributed significantly to this repeatedly high level of non-hinterland intraorganizational linkages, since it has allowed large volumes of routine information to be moved cheaply over long distances, thereby easing the physical separation of administrative units from production and other subordinate units.

It is admittedly not possible to pinpoint the extent to which the *intra*organizational transmission of growth between cities is related to the *inter*organizational transmission of growth between cities. Nevertheless, the above generalizations, and especially generalizations (3) and (4), would seem to indicate that the hinterland-spread and hierarchical-diffusion assumptions normally made by regional planners concerning the spatial transmission of growth are both over-simple and flagrantly incorrect. If the data presented here are at all representative of the interdependencies to be found in economically advanced systems of cities, if the ratio of all non-hinterland linkages to all hinterland linkages elsewhere is also typically 3·7:1 or more, then *any assumption that the non-local growth impact of large-scale investments in a growth centre will be mostly or totally concentrated in the centre's hinterland is quite likely to be very wrong.* On the contrary, Figures 3.2–3.12 not only underline the significance of non-hinterland linkages in general, but further undermine the hinterland-spread assumption by indicating that non-local multiplier-effect leakages can frequently flow to head-office metropolitan complexes situated at considerable distances involving hundreds or thousands of miles.

The incompatibility of hierarchical-diffusion, or Christallerian central-place theory, growth-transmission assumptions with the empirical materials presented above can be summarized in a number of ways. Firstly, we can give the hierarchical-diffusion assumption an extremely free interpretation, allowing it to mean that growth can be *directly* transmitted from a centre of given size either to any other urban place occurring within its hinterland, or to any less populous metropolitan complex outside its hinterland – regardless of the distances involved and regardless of the existence of intervening larger metropolitan complexes.[20] Even in these relaxed circumstances 41·8 to 80·1 per cent of the non-local job-control linkages for the metropolitan complexes observed here go unaccounted for (Table 3.9, column I). Secondly, we give the hierarchical-diffusion assumption a strictly literal interpretation, disallowing the possibility that growth can be transmitted to any metropolitan complex located beyond the borders of a specific centre's physically contiguous retail-trade market area, or hinterland. Now the spectrum of non-local linkages unaccounted for is shifted upward considerably, spreading from 56·8 to 97·1 per cent (Table 3.9, column II). Thirdly, because of their importance, we focus solely on intermetropolitan linkages, allowing the hierarchical assumption to mean that growth can be transmitted from a metropolitan centre of given size to any other metropolitan complex which is not of comparable or larger population – regardless of whether or not it occurs within the centre's hinterland. Under these comparatively loose constraints, between 33·7 and 100 per cent of the intermetropolitan job-control linkages associated with the seven metropolitan complexes studied cannot be accounted for (Table 3·9, column III). Finally, a strictly literal interpretation of hierarchical diffusion is again applied, requiring intermetropolitan growth transmission to be confined to hinterland metropolitan complexes. The percentage of unanswered-for inter-metropolitan linkages now reaches impressively high levels that fall between 80·4 and 100 per cent (Table 3.9, column IV).

Under any of these four alternatives, observed deviations are so great that it seems safe to suggest that *only under quite unusual conditions can there be a firm basis for the assumption that growth is transmitted solely via hierarchical diffusion from cities of a given size to less populous nearby centres.*

Swedish empirical evidence

Several Swedish studies of the economic flows generated by business organizational units also vividly illustrate the inappropriateness of the hinterland-spread and hierarchical-diffusion views of interurban growth transmission (e.g. Bylund and Ek, 1974; Erson, 1974; Fredriksson and Lindmark, 1974; Herlitz, 1974).

Malmö, located across the Öresund from Copenhagen, is a metropolitan complex with a population of about 450 000. It is generally observed that, along with Stockholm and Göteborg, this centre dominates the smaller metropolitan centres and urban places within the Swedish system of cities. Table 3.10 partially summarizes findings concerning the interdependence patterns created in 1970 by the flow of goods, services and specialized information to and from national-, regional- and local-level organizational units located in

Malmö metropolitan complex, 1970[a]

Type of flow	Origin or destination					Percentage total
	Local (within Malmö)	Stockholm	Göteborg	Smaller hinterland places	Other smaller metropolitan centres, cities and towns	
Outputs *sold* by Malmö manufacturing units	34	27	9	11	19	100[b]
Services *sold* by Malmö business-service units	60	10	4	11	15	100[b]
Physical inputs *purchased* by Malmö manufacturing units	32	12	5	15	35	100[b]
Business services *purchased* by Malmö manufacturing units	66	14	1	3	16	100[b]
All goods and service flows to and from the locally present units of ten selected Malmö organizations	47	20	7	9	18	100[b]
Information exchange of the locally present units of ten selected Malmö organizations	45	17	4	8	26	100

(a) Derived from Bylund and Ek (1974).
(b) Percentages based on monetary values.

Malmö. Aside from the category-to-category variations in the importance of local flows, at least four features stand out from this table.

First, business organizational units in Malmö sell substantial quantities of goods and services to the even larger metropolitan complexes of Stockholm and Göteborg. In fact, the magnitude of goods and business-service sales to Sweden's first- and second-ranking metropolitan complexes clearly outstrip those to places within Malmö's own hinterland. (In terms of the nature of large-city interdependence in general, it is notable that the business services sold to Stockholm are for the most part highly specialized.)

Secondly, more goods and business services are sold by Malmö's units to smaller metropolitan centres, cities and towns outside its hinterland than to such places within its own hinterland. These geographically widespread interorganizational linkages mean, of course, that hinterland forward-linkage multiplier effects are of secondary importance.

Thirdly, the backward-linkage multiplier effects extending from Malmö to its hinterland are also comparatively unimportant. That is, the purchases of physical inputs and business services made by organizational units belonging to Malmö's private sector from smaller hinterland places rank lower than the purchases made from both Stockholm and Göteborg combined, and from non-hinterland metropolitan centres, cities and towns. (The physical goods obtained from smaller places include slightly processed raw materials and intermediate goods, while those purchased from Stockholm and Göteborg are virtually all of the latter type.)

Finally, a rather limited sample of the total number of studied Malmö organizations appears to indicate a reasonably close parallel between the pattern of goods and service flows and the pattern of personal contacts, or specialized information flows.

Comparable evidence based on 1970 input and output flows exists for the 'metropolitan areas', or labour-market regions, of Borås, Falun-Borlänge, and Skellefteå.

In the case of Borås (a loosely defined metropolitan complex in southwest central Sweden with a population of over 185000), locally present industrial units – principally in the textile and apparel branches – provide very little in the way of backward and forward growth-transmission linkages to the surrounding hinterland. A total of 39 per cent of the domestic physical-input purchases of these units comes from the larger complexes of Stockholm (12 per cent), Göteborg (23 per cent), and Malmö (4 per cent). Another 25 per cent is secured from comparably and smaller-sized non-hinterland urban centres, but no more than 6 per cent is acquired from hinterland locations. Likewise, a total of 58 per cent of the domestic sales of these units go to Stockholm (36 per cent), Göteborg (18 per cent) and Malmö (4 per cent), while the corresponding non-hinterland and hinterland figures are 16 per cent and a mere 5 per cent respectively. In addition, although manufacturing activities in Borås obtain a total of 64 per cent of their business services from Göteborg and Stockholm (in contrast to only 4 per cent from hinterland places), the city's own business-service units manage to make 14 per cent of their admittedly limited sales in the country's two largest metropolitan complexes.

In the case of Falun–Borlänge (a metropolitan area in central Sweden with about 140000 inhabitants), locally operating manufacturing plants – mostly in the steel and paper sectors – also provide rather limited backward and forward growth transmission to the adjacent hinterland. In spite of their considerable dependence on essentially unprocessed raw materials, 25 per cent of the total value of domestic purchases made by these plants originate in Stockholm (18 per cent), Göteborg (5 per cent), and Malmö (2 per cent). An additional 42 per cent is obtained from comparably and smaller-sized non-hinterland urban centres, but only 11 per cent is procured from hinterland places. (Over half of Falun–Borlänge's factories create no hinterland backward linkages whatsoever.) On the sales side, a total of 41 per cent of the value of all domestic linkages is associated with Stockholm (23 per cent), Göteborg (11 per cent), and Malmö (7 per cent). A further 36 per cent is sold to non-hinterland locations; a figure that heavily outweighs the 4 per cent registered by all hinterland places in combination.

Two quite important generalizations emerge when the findings for Malmö, Borås and Falun–Borlänge are jointly considered with similar evidence for Skellefteå, a smaller urban-centred area in the north with a population of about 82000. First, manufacturing plants belonging to large multilocational organizations consistently make a greater fraction of their sales and purchases at non-hinterland locations than do industrial units belonging either to single-location firms or to smaller multilocational corporations. To the extent that this is true in other economically advanced countries, and to the extent that there is a very great likelihood that the industrial facilities attracted to a planned growth centre will belong to a large multilocational organization, this seems to suggest that most growth-centre regional development schemes are foredoomed to have a very limited impact on hinterland employment opportunities (The only hinterland segment likely to benefit is that small 'local' area within commuting radius of the growth-centre, or targeted 'metropolitan area', itself.) Secondly, there is a tendency for the percentage of non-local (and non-hinterland) purchases and sales – and related multiplier effects – to increase as urban size decreases. That is, the smaller the selected growth centre in a 'backward' or 'depressed' region, the smaller is the likelihood that agglomeration advantages (or linkages) will spontaneously arise in the centre and its environs, and the greater the probability that interorganizational (and intraorganizational) multiplier leakages will occur to non-hinterland locations in general, and larger metropolitan complexes in particular.

Other empirical findings on interurban growth transmission

Several researchers posing questions somewhat different from those raised in this book have produced a variety of evidence that also points to the inaccuracy of the hinterland-spread and hierarchical-diffusion views of interurban growth transmission widely held by regional planners and academics in advanced economies. Only some of the most cogent of these findings are summarized in this section.

Based on data acquired 'from a sample of manufacturing establishments located within 40 miles of downtown Montréal', Gilmour (1974) found that the most important input-output linkages, or growth-transmission channels, occurred outside the local metropolitan complex (1971 pop., 2·74 million). Most notably, large establishments with 100 or more employees aggregately made 'over half of their transactions' outside the Province of Québec, or *well outside* the hinterland of the Montréal metropolitan complex. It is also significant that Gilmour was able to attribute some of the 'spatial expansiveness' of Montréal's manufacturing linkages to the economies obtained from interacting with distant units belonging to the same corporation or firm.

Britton's service-linkage study (1974) of eighty-seven Ontario manufacturing plants reveals that key auditing, legal and financial services are usually procured either from Toronto (1971 pop., 2·63 million) or more distant non-Ontario metropolitan complexes *if* – as in most instances – the observed factory is part of a multilocational organization. The services obtained from Toronto or more distant large metropolitan complexes apparently involve economies of scale. These economies are provided either intraorganizationally (i.e. by divisional or organization-wide headquarters which also supply the same services to other subordinate units), or interorganizationally (i.e. by service firms which cater to both head offices and many or all of their dependent units). Whichever the case, such non-local service acquisition is synonymous with multiplier-effect leakages, or growth transmission, *upward rather than downward* through the urban hierarchy. Growth is transmitted to *non-hinterland* locations whenever service multipliers leak to Toronto and other large North American complexes from, for example, the London and St Catherines – Niagara Falls metropolitan areas (1971 pops., around 300000), or from lesser Ontario urban places.

A detailed analysis of the income and *inter*organizational input linkages generated by the Boeing Company of Seattle–Tacoma has led Earickson (1975) to conclude that the 'hinterland spread [or growth-transmission] effects' of 'propulsive' manufacturing activities 'may be more illusory than real'. While some understandable local impact of the wage and salary expenditures of Boeing employees was discovered, the total impact of Boeing's interorganizational purchases on hinterland economic activities was comparatively small. In 1967 nearly 90 per cent of Boeing's purchases originated from beyond the Seattle–Tacoma hinterland, and 'the firm's inter-industry linkages generated income in the hinterland equal to only 0·003 of total hinterland value added'. Furthermore, the most important metropolitan suppliers to Boeing's Seattle–Tacoma activities fell into three categories, none of which are in keeping with hierarchical-diffusion interpretations of interurban growth transmission. The major input providers were located in the smaller but quite distant *non-hinterland* metropolitan complexes of Hartford, Conn., and Rockford, Ill., in the *larger* metropolitan complexes of Los Angeles, New York, Detroit, and Cleveland–Akron, and in the San Diego, Phoenix, and Dallas–Fort Worth metropolitan complexes – all of which belong to the *same general population-size category* as Seattle–Tacoma.[21]

Moseley's investigations (1973a, 1973b) into the growth-transmission impacts of growth centres in East Anglia and Brittany have caused him to observe that 'severe doubts must be cast on the notion that "growth impulses" . . . trickle down' to smaller places. With respect to Haverhill and Thetford, two East Anglian growth centres, it was observed that expansion 'has improved the choice of employment and presumably the prosperity of many residents of the small towns and villages [immediately] surrounding them, but in terms of the generation of supplementary economic activity, such impulses appear to have "trickled up".' For example, in 1971 roughly 93 per cent of the material inputs of the bigger Haverhill and Thetford factories came from beyond East Anglia and Essex. Furthermore, most of the intraregional growth transmission resulting from industrial purchases terminated at *larger* urban units, particularly Cambridge and Norwich. With respect to Rennes, the leading metropolitan centre of Brittany (1970 pop., 200000), trend surface analyses showed that the transmission of growth to hinterland locations was probably largely confined to places within a commuting radius of a mere 20–25 kilometres.[22]

Research involving the Central Clydeside Conurbation, or Glasgow metropolitan complex, and other parts of Scotland further confirms the leakage of multiplier effects to non-hinterland metropolitan complexes (Firn, 1974; Lever, 1974). Approximately 80 per cent of the 1970–1 purchases made by twenty-four glass, electrical machinery, paper, tool, paint and clothing factories involved centres outside Scotland, i.e. non-hinterland locations (Lever, 1974). Here too, the non-hinterland transmission of growth is intimately related to the spatial structure of organizations. Most of Scotland's manufacturing capacity belongs to multilocational organizations whose primary administrative and headquarters functions are carried out in London, elsewhere in Great Britain, or overseas. Non-Scottish headquarters units frequently make decisions concerning the procurement of raw materials, semi-finished goods, and services. 'Economies of scale in transport and information collection' give these head-office units 'an advantage in identifying and using more distant [non-Scottish] suppliers' (Lever, 1974).

A number of other British studies (e.g. Moseley and Townroe, 1973; Salt, 1967) similarly indicate that the input linkages of branch plants controlled by multilocational corporations based elsewhere typically 'extend over wide geographical areas'. These studies also indicate that the local and hinterland component of branch-plant suppliers is in most cases relatively unimportant. It also has been observed that 'regional', or hinterland, multiplier effects in general are 'comparatively small' in Britain (Steele, 1969; Chisholm, 1974).

An examination of wholesaling, correspondent banking,[23] and other statistics has allowed Borchert (1972) to conclude that 'the major [US] metropolitan centres [with over 1·0 million population] are less important as regional capitals [i.e. as *hinterland-oriented complexes*] than they are as major components in the national system of labour, entrepreneurship, and capital'. In conjunction with this evidence of complex city-system interdependencies, Borchert also found that the economic linkages of lower-order metropolitan areas with populations under 500000 are far from monopolized by the nearest major metropolitan complex within whose hinterland they are situated. More specifically, in addition to its correspondent banking links with the major metropolitan centre to whose hinterland it belongs, 'each lower-order [metropolitan] centre also has financial ties with other places of the same or higher order in other parts of the country. These links with other centres, in the aggregate, greatly exceed those with the [nearest major metropolitan complex and parallel] . . . the links between parent and branch plants, raw material producers and processors, . . . [and] specialized distributors and major industrial plants.'

Multilocational organizations and city-system growth and development in advanced economies: a model

It has been demonstrated rather clearly that the hinterland-spread and hierarchical-diffusion views of interurban growth transmission are grossly inaccurate. Substantial support has also been provided for the view that complex interurban linkages, especially between large metropolitan complexes, are the most prominent feature of city-system growth transmission in advanced economies dominated by multilocational business and government organizations. It now remains to present a probabilistic model which describes the process by which employment levels are perpetuated in nationally and regionally highly ranked metropolitan complexes (and their surrounding 'urban fields'), and by which interregional economic inequalities are prolonged. More precisely, the model attempts to depict the means by which the interurban circulation of specialized information and the actions and spatial structure of organizations feed back upon one another to influence the process of city-system growth and development in advanced economies.

At least three points made previously are to be kept in mind when digesting this heuristic model. First, in so far as multilocational business and government organizations dominate advanced economies, their explicit and implicit locational decisions are directly or indirectly responsible for the creation and perpetuation of most employment opportunities. Secondly, explicit and implicit locational decisions are typically reached after a limited search for satisfactory alternatives and often influenced by a desire to reduce uncertainty. Thirdly, as yet incomplete evidence appears to indicate that both the limited-search and uncertainty-reduction syndromes of locational decision-making lead to choices which at one and the same time are greatly influenced by existing spatial biases in the circulation of specialized information (i.e. existing organizational contact patterns) and contribute to subsequent spatial biases in the circulation of specialized information. The model should also be recognized as little more than a paraphrasing of the model which summarized the process relationships prevailing when wholesaling-trading activities were the main driving force behind city-system growth and development (pp. 70–78). That is, although technology, economic institutions, and the forms of business operation have undergone enormous changes over the last 100–150 years, it can be asserted that the process of city-system growth and development in currently advanced economies remains dominated by the constantly repeated interplay between existing local and interurban economic linkages, spatial biases in the interurban circulation of specialized information, and new and expanded local and interurban economic linkages.

Local-growth submodel

Imagine a large metropolitan complex (C_1) situated within an advanced economy. Its size indicates that the complex has previously outdistanced most of its competitors within its pertinent regional city-system or the entire national city-system. Since the complex is in an advanced economy, its economic functions and those of its nearby surrounding area are dominated by the job-providing activities of multilocational private or public organizations. All but a small portion of its ongoing and recent population growth is in one way or another associated with the expansion of already existing organizational activities and the local birth of new organizational units. Much of the growth process of the metropolitan complex is locally self-sustaining in a circular and cumulative manner which is collapsed into a shorthand ideal-typical version in the lower left-hand portion of Figure 3.13. The simplified local-growth submodel is also shown at the upper left of Figure 3.13 as simultaneously operating for other regionally or nationally highly ranked metropolitan complexes $(C_2, C_3 \ldots C_n)$. In particular, each major increment

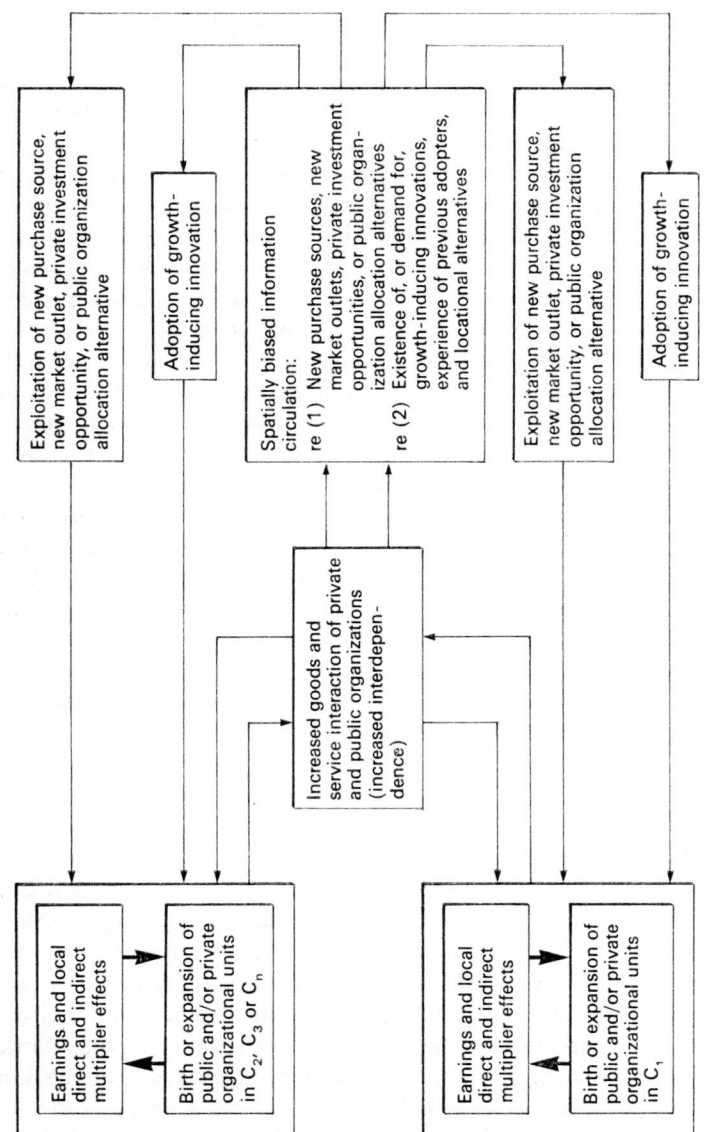

Figure 3.13: *The circular and cumulative feedback process of urban-size growth for large metropolitan complexes in advanced economies.*

or birth of organizational activity propagates *local* employment multiplier effects. These occur either directly, as backward- or forward-linkage multiplier effects, or indirectly, as employee-expenditure multiplier effects.[24] Initial direct and indirect multiplier effects may call forth secondary multiplier effects; e.g. an activity expanding via the backward-linkage mechanism may itself call forth backward- or forward-linkage multiplier effects, as well as employee-expenditure multiplier effects. The combined impact of all these direct and indirect local multipliers, or *addition of employment roles to the metropolitan activity system*, is apt to be an increase in population and the attainment or duplication of one or more local or regional thresholds. The surpassing of new thresholds sooner or later leads to the establishment of new major organizational units and another round of local-growth feedback. Additional rounds of local direct and indirect multiplier effects also come about as a result of the investment of earnings from previous rounds in non-threshold activities, or new and expanded organizational units which are not particularly sensitive to the scale of the local or regional market. Such a local ploughing back of earnings is likely to be stimulated by, first, the increasingly complex *intra*urban network of organizational information exchange that accompanies urban size growth (and, among other things, influences the perception of local opportunities); and, secondly, the availability of 'agglomeration' economies of either the 'localization' or 'urbanization' variety.

Increased interdependence and its feedback consequences

While the functioning of the local-growth submodel is crucial, the continued high size-rank and employment growth of C_1, or any other large metropolitan complex, depends greatly on its organizational linkages and economic interaction with other leading centres. Each major increment or birth of organizational activity in C_1 not only increases the size of that complex, but also directly or indirectly engenders organizational and economic interdependence, or interaction, with other large metropolitan complexes within the same regional or national city-system. This interdependence, by enhancing the scale of organizational activity in C_2, C_3 or C_n, contributes to the local-growth submodel of those metropolitan complexes and thereby brings them further economic expansion. Direct increases in interdependence occur when the initial major increase in organizational activity at C_1, through backward or forward goods and service linkages, causes interorganizational or intraorganizational *non-local* multipliers at C_2, C_3, or C_n.[25] Indirect growth of interdependence between C_1 and other large metropolitan complexes results when local multipliers at C_1 itself generate additional demands for goods and services from those complexes. Interdependence can also arise indirectly when the direct and indirect non-local multipliers propagated by C_1 at another major centre are reflexive, i.e. increase the demand for goods or services normally obtained at C_1. In the same manner, each major increment or birth of organizational activity in another large metropolitan complex, e.g. C_2, not only enhances the size of that complex, but is also capable of directly or indirectly producing organizational and economic interdependence with other major centres.

By definition, each expansion of interdependence between any pair of large metropolitan complexes has a physical manifestation in the movement of goods and services – and monetary payments when interaction occurs on an *inter*organizational basis (Figure 3.13). Each new or enlarged interurban goods and service linkage also has a parallel, or dual, flow of routine or non-routine specialized information (cf. Dunn, 1970). In addition, when subordinate organizational units are involved, increased goods and service interaction between two metropolitan complexes may, at least initially, be further accompanied both by specialized information flows between those complexes and the head-office metropolitan complexes of the involved organizations, and by specialized information flows between the two headquarters centres. Whatever the case, each increment in goods and service interaction between C_1 and other large metropolitan complexes *contributes to spatial biases in the availability of specialized information*. These spatial biases, in turn, through one of two pairs of feedback loops, lead to yet further interaction between major metropolitan complexes and yet further spatial biases in the availability of specialized information (Figure 3.13). The net impact of these two feedback sequences is a perpetuation of employment and population growth at metropolitan complexes of high national or regional rank, i.e. a continued dominance of national and regional city-systems by the same large metropolitan complexes *and their immediately peripheral areas*.

One pair of feedback loops involves specialized information capable of affecting the implicit locational decision-making of organizations, e.g. information regarding purchase sources, new market outlets, new contracting or subcontracting possibilities, and investment opportunities in already functioning, or previously diffused activities. The spatially biased flows in question operate so that any specialized information of this variety either originating or entering the city-system at one large metropolitan complex will have a greater probability of being early acquired, and non-locally exploited, in or near one or more other major metropolitan complexes than in less populous urban centres within the city-system.[26] This is so largely because the aggregate non-routine organizational contacts of smaller cities with C_1 and other large metropolitan complexes are fewer and less frequent than those among C_1 and its size-group peers. That is, more non-routine contact-generating organizational activities occur in large metropolitan complexes. Should an organizational unit in one large complex, e.g. C_1, implement a major implicit locational decision that involves another city, it sooner or later will entail local (C_1) expansion of the organization and some local employment growth. This is quite likely to be accompanied by both increased interdependence with one or more other large metropolitan complexes and reinforced spatial biases in the circulation of specialized information for one of two reasons. The first is that the major implict locational decision directly involves another large metropolitan complex, rather than a smaller city in the same national or regional city-system. The other reason is that the major implicit locational decision involves either a smaller city, or another national or regional city-system, but the resulting local multipliers at C_1 create a greater organizational demand for goods and services normally acquired from one or more other large metropolitan complexes.

Since this pair of feedback loops operates in a probabilistic fashion, any given implicit locational opportunity or alternative may be exploited in one, some, or all of a city-system's largest centres. Thus, this model, like its earlier counterpart (Figure 2.9), permits some adjustment in the population ratios of large metropolitan complexes, and perhaps even some minor rank shifting among them. Such changes could follow from the occurrence of local multipliers of varying scale in or near some rather than all of the city-system's leading centres; and from consequent minor alterations in the distribution of probabilities among C_1 and other large metropolitan complexes for the subsequent exploitation of implicit locational opportunities and alternatives.

In addition, since the model functions in a probabilistic manner, it sometimes allows implicit locational opportunities and alternatives to be implemented in low-probability smaller cities at the same time as implementation is limited in other system centres (including C_1 and other large metropolitan complexes). The model thereby occasionally enables small- or medium-size cities to acquire the economic impetus necessary for relatively rapid progress through the size ranks of the city-system.

The second pair of feedback loops involves specialized information concerning the existence of, or demand for, new product or service innovations, and other growth-inducing innovations whose adoption often requires an explicit locational decision. This pair of feedback loops also involves specialized information regarding both the experience of previous organizational adopters of particular innovations, and alternative locations for implementation. The spatial biases of innovation-relevant information circulation are normally such that any growth-inducing innovation perfected or introduced within the city-system at one major metropolitan complex is more likely to be adopted early and on a larger or multiple basis at other major complexes than at smaller places within the system. That is, early-adoption probabilities are lower at those medium- and small-size cities within the national or regional system which have fewer and less frequent contacts with the large metropolitan complex where an initial or very early acceptance has occurred. (However, if the innovation in question is a new manufactured item, competition may eventually force the adopting organization to 'trickle down', or diffuse, production units from a large metropolitan complex to a smaller hinterland or *non-hinterland* city where labour, tax or other cost savings are available.)

For one of two reasons, the consequences of organizational adoption at one large metropolitan complex (e.g. C_1) are apt to be increased interdependence with other large metropolitan complexes and reinforced spatial biases in the circulation of specialized information. First, single or multiple organizational adoption of the innovation itself requires the establishment of new forms of interdependence between the national or regional city-system's largest metropolitan complexes.[27] Secondly, the organizational adoption of an innovation brings local multiplier effects and population growth in or around one large metropolitan complex which, in turn, breed a larger demand within other local organizations for goods and services normally secured from other major centres.

Here, too, the feedback process allows for some adjustment in the population ratios of a city-system's largest complexes and for occasional minor rank-shifting among them. This is because the probabilities involved allow any specific growth-inducing innovation to be adopted in one, a few, or all of the system's leading metropolitan complexes and thereby permit the occurrence of innovation-derived multipliers of varying magnitude in one, some, or all of those complexes. Furthermore, if comparable local multipliers do not occur, the distribution of probabilities among large metropolitan complexes for the adoption of subsequent growth-inducing innovations may be slightly adjusted.

Similarly, the probabilistic aspect of the interurban diffusion of growth-inducing innovations sometimes can cause a medium- or small-size city to advance comparatively rapidly through the size ranks of a national or regional city-system. This would happen when a growth-inducing innovation was successfully adopted by an organizational unit in a low-probability city at the same time as adoption was limited both in other comparably sized low-probability cities and, perhaps, most or all large metropolitan complexes. Size-rank advance would follow from large and temporally concentrated local multipliers, greater economic linkages with other cities, and a higher probability of adopting additional growth-inducing innovations.

In keeping with the empirical evidence presented earlier in this chapter, it must be granted that large metropolitan complexes – or their immediately contiguous peripheries – also continue to grow and maintain their high ranks due to their interdependencies with smaller cities both inside and *outside* their respective central-place hinterlands. In particular, when an organizational unit is born or significantly expanded in a small- or medium-size city, interorganizational or intraorganizational multipliers are likely to occur either in a nearby or more distant large metropolitan complex. This is partly because of the variety of goods, services, and market outlets available in large metropolitan complexes, and partly because of the concentration of organizational headquarters in such complexes. Conversely, a major increment or birth of organizational activity at a large metropolitan complex can precipitate intraorganizational or interorganizational multipliers at a place of smaller population. This is possible because of the highly scattered distribution of production and various local-level units operated by multilocational organizations. If, on these grounds, the model diagrammed in Figure 3.13 is expanded to encompass cities of all sizes – and not merely large metropolitan complexes – then the entire process of city-system growth and development in advanced economies can be synopsized, in again admittedly over-simplified terms, by Figure 3.14.

A final qualification concerning the operation of this model is in order. The very recent decline of some large metropolitan complexes

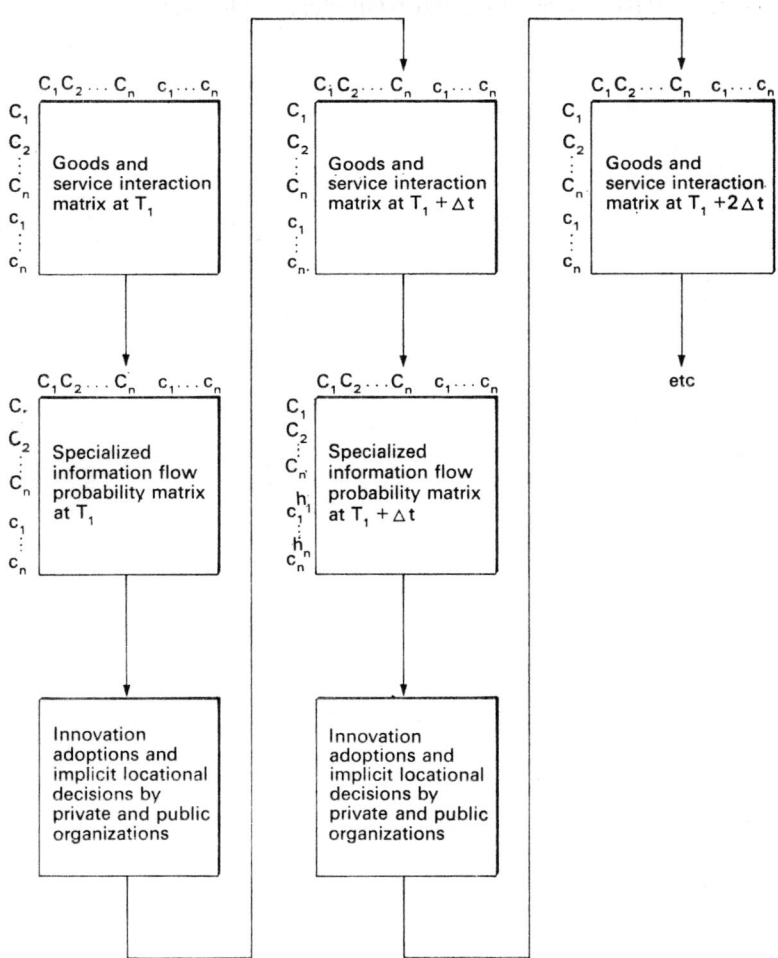

Figure 3.14: *A simplified description of the growth and development process for an entire national or regional system of cities in an advanced economy. Cf. Figure 2.10 (p. 78).*

in advanced economies is at least partly explained by the increasing frequency with which multilocational organizations are exploiting the cost or amenity advantages of non-metropolitan urban places when locating factories and other units with routine functions. This, in turn, is partly attributable to the ease with which routine units can be physically separated from administrative offices when modern communications and computer technology is employed.[28]

4 Future development options: office activities, services and the quality of life

What are the implications of the ongoing processes of city-system growth and development for efforts to reduce or largely eliminate interregional inequalities of employment opportunity? What are the implications of the ongoing processes of city-system growth and development for efforts to stimulate long-term 'quality-of-life' improvements in 'backward', 'lagging' or 'depressed' regions? One way in which to provide at least provisional answers to these difficult interrelated questions regarding advanced economies is to consider some basic regional development and national settlement policy alternatives and some of the issues surrounding them. Before taking such a step, it is perhaps best to set the stage by restating some of the most pertinent observations and findings of previous chapters.

First, to an increasing extent the growth and development of individual urban units, regions and entire city-systems in advanced economies are dominated by multilocational business and government organizations. Such organizations, especially in the private sector, dominate growth and development processes because they are the most significant implementers of explicit and implicit locational decisions, because they directly answer for the majority of job opportunities and indirectly account for almost all other employment, and because they are clearly the most important propagators of interurban flows of goods, services, specialized information and capital. (Thus, for example, it has been argued that Australian growth has been disproportionately concentrated in the Sydney, Melbourne, Adelaide, Brisbane and Perth metropolitan areas, 'not because of the inherent unsuitability of other areas, but because of the general inability' of private multilocational organizations to change their decision-making behaviour (Stilwell, 1974).) Therefore, unless the unemployed of disadvantaged regions are induced to migrate, any policies that are to influence the composition of specific local activity systems, or the location of employment and economic growth at the regional or national level, must be directly aimed at such organizations.

Secondly, the structure of city-system interdependencies in advanced economies resulting from intraorganizational and interorganizational relationships is extremely complex. Typically, the greatest volume of non-local growth transmission linkages crisscrosses between nationally and regionally highly ranked metropolitan complexes. In addition, the intraorganizational and interorganizational linkages extending between a large metropolitan complex and smaller towns and cities outside its hinterland are usually much more important than the sum of those extending to all hinterland places – regardless of population. Consequently, whenever and wherever major new investment or activity expansion occurs some non-local multiplier effects are quite likely to appear at a nearby or distant large metropolitan complex. In particular, the implementation of a major implicit or explicit locational decision anywhere in a 'backward', 'lagging' or 'depressed' region will very probably foster an employment multiplier in one or more nearby or distant metropolitan complexes where organizational administrative functions, business services and nonroutine purchase-source decision-making are concentrated.

Thirdly, the spatial distribution of job-providing activities in any economically advanced country or large region is but one of many possible outcomes resulting from the reiteration of probabilistic feedbacks deeply embedded in the past. That is, the process of city-system growth and development in presently advanced economies apparently basically consists of constantly repeated feedbacks between existing local and interurban economic linkages, spatial biases in the interurban circulation of specialized information, and new and expanded local and interurban economic linkages.

Finally, the occupational composition of the work force in advanced economies has been undergoing profound changes. In general, a stable or decreasing number of jobs is associated with the processing and movement of natural resources and intermediate- and final-demand goods. At the same time a growing fraction of jobs is associated with the processing and exchange of specialized information. This is in no small measure due to the corporate and government planning activities necessitated by a swiftly changing technological and economic environment. Another contributing factor is the need for coordination and administrative specialization created within multilocational organizations by their increasing size, functional diversification and structural complexity. Perhaps most importantly, a substantially disproportionate share of highly salaried office employment – which is expanding more rapidly than clerical employment – has been accumulating in major metropolitan complexes.

The manufacturing option

Specific government policies

For a long time, since their beginnings in the UK during the 1930s, the vast bulk of policy strategies utilized by national or provincial (state) governments in trying to combat regional unemployment were single-mindedly centred on efforts to influence the location of manufacturing production units. (Virtually all the few remaining policy strategies involved the much criticized offering of relocation grants or other migration stimuli to the unemployed individuals of problem regions.)[1] In recent years the regional employment-creation and settlement policies put into action in some advanced economies have been somewhat more diversified. Nevertheless, in just about every highly industrialized capitalist country, attempts to influence the location of manufacturing production units remain the cornerstone of regional development, or employment-creation, policies.

In striving to attract privately controlled factories either to particular 'growth centres', or a problem region as a whole, governments have used a variety of measures that fall into one of three broad categories. First, there are the 'carrot' incentives provided directly to firms or corporations in conjunction with the creation or expansion of production facilities at the desired centre(s) or region(s). Secondly, there are infrastructure improvements to enhance the attractiveness of the target location(s) or region(s); and, thirdly, 'stick' controls and permission obstacles have been used to discourage manufacturing investments in the largest metropolitan complexes (cf. Sundqvist, 1975).[2] (The assessment of special taxes or other monetary penalties to divert new factory construction from large metropolitan complexes and expansive regions to high-unemployment regions has been much debated but little practised.) A few arbitrary examples give some idea of the range of strategies presently or previously used.

In the Netherlands grants have been made available to cover 25 per cent of new factory construction costs, 25 per cent of new machinery purchases, and 50 per cent of the cost of land acquisition. In Great Britain, outside the 'development areas', or highest unemployment regions,[3] no construction or expansion of manufacturing facilities of more than 10000 square feet in the Southeast, and 15000 square feet elsewhere, can occur unless an 'industrial development certificate' has been issued by the Board (Department) of Trade. The British Board of Trade also offers the following inducements for plants to be established or relocated in development areas.

(1) 'A regional development grant of 20 per cent of the cost of new plant and machinery and of new industrial building with free depreciation on the plant and machinery, and an initial depreciation allowance of 40 per cent on buildings.'

(2) 'Selective assistance, normally [distributed] in the form of low interest loans but also [paid] by interest relief and removal grants.'

(3) Also, when justified, 'training grants [can be awarded] to offset the cost of training or retraining labour' (Cameron, 1974).

The Japanese offer help toward the payment of local taxes and higher than normal rates of machinery and equipment depreciation to corporations placing factories in designated places or areas. The French have attempted to discourage plant construction in Paris through the assessment of a construction tax and a construction-permit hurdle. Additionally they have offered investment subsidies, low-interest loans and tax benefits (including selective property tax exemption and reduced purchase taxes on buildings and equipment) to business organizations establishing production units in selected cities and 'zones', mostly in the western part of the country (Prud'Homme, 1974).

In Sweden a grant is given to firms and corporations for each manufacturing job created in the 'inner aid area', or the sparsely populated interior of Norrland (approximately $1,600 for each of the first two years of employment, and about $800 for the third). The Swedish government also provides factory construction or conversion grants varying from 35 to 65 per cent of total costs (depending on whether located in the 'inner aid area' or other unemployment problem areas), and transportation subsidies ranging from 15 to 35 per cent of normal freight rates on goods produced or processed in the 'aid areas'. (In order to counteract locational disadvantages, preferential rail rates also are given on manufacturing inputs consumed in the 'aid areas'; but no industrial products which might compete with 'aid-area' goods may be brought in under reduced freight charges.)

Policy limitations

Despite long-term governmental efforts, the regional rank order of unemployment in Great Britain has remained unchanged for at least a half-century (Brown, 1972). Based on this and similar general evidence for other countries, plus the very limited success of manufacturing dominated growth-centre schemes, it would appear that the primary emphasis still given to production-unit employment in the regional development policies of advanced economies is highly questionable. Although little doubt exists that some fraction of regional inequalities of employment opportunity may yet be removable or reducible through governmental influences on the location of production units, there are a number of arguments that may be marshalled against policy strategies which give first place to manufacturing jobs.

Most obviously, since the total number of factory jobs in any 'post-industrial' country is either stable or declining, all efforts to rescue troubled cities or regions with such employment must in the long run prove futile. That is, manufacturing oriented policies unwittingly seek to 'solve' unemployment problems by shuffling a dwindling or more or less fixed supply of jobs from one place to another. Moreover, to the extent that new or expanded factories are capital-intensive units belonging to multilocational organizations, the size of intraorganizational and interorganizational multipliers transmitted to the offices and work-places of 'undesirable' large metropolitan complexes in other regions is apt to be large.

The current nature of product life cycles is a somewhat less obvious but perhaps equally important reason for faulting regional development plans that focus on industrial employment opportunities (cf. Krumme and Hayter, 1975). Manufactured articles have always undergone a life cycle once they have survived the often lengthy 'development' phase that occurs between invention and commercial production.[4] During this cycle three event sequences are staggered after one another.

(1)   The number of establishments involved in production grows slowly and then increases rapidly as diffusion occurs on the supply side, only to diminish later owing to competition and falling demand.

(2)   The number of employees mounts as demand expands and then decreases because of productivity improvements and demand reductions.

(3)   After a slow start the volume of business burgeons as diffusion

occurs on the consumption side; but it too eventually declines as demand turns to either substitute or completely different products.

Over the last few decades product life cycles have tended to become increasingly telescoped, covering ever shorter durations of time, largely because of the accelerated pace of technological change and fluctuations in demand. Faced with an environment which is characterized by a quick tempo of technological change and unstable demand, multilocational industrial organizations normally attempt to cope by constantly broadening their range of products and by modifying, or differentiating, existing products. This coping strategy, by bringing a greater number of products into competition with one another, and by altering the demand for intermediate goods (or already manufactured inputs), only serves to reinforce the trend toward abbreviated product life cycles. As a consequence of this trend, the manufacturing engendered at specific places in problem regions by government measures very often has proved to be no more than a temporary medicine for the illness of unemployment. It is highly probable that this will continue to be the case in the near future. The grounds for such a dismal forecast become clear from an examination of two of the most significant classes of manufacturing activity attracted to regions plagued by persistent unemployment.

Plants 'trickled down' by multilocational business organizations
When a large corporation initiates the manufacture of a new product, it is most likely to do so in that metropolitan complex where its principal management functions are located and where a variety of external economies exist alongside the technicians and skilled labour that are readily available either intraorganizationally or from other local sources. However, if standardized output becomes feasible and there are prospects for expanded sales, the original production unit may appear inadequate or costly when confronted by competition. If replacement by one or more new facilities is decided upon, problem-region smaller-city locations may frequently – but not always – appear attractive because of tax benefits, subsidies, lower wages, or other cost savings. At a late intermediate stage in the product life cycle, or during a general economic boom, when peaking demand requires relatively quick accommodation, problem-region smaller-city locations may also seem appealing to multilocational organizations, especially if the necessary building and machinery are not highly capital-intensive. Once a plant has been 'trickled down' (cf. Thompson, 1965), the controlling multilocational or-

ganization is unlikely to sense any allegiance to the labour-market or local economic concerns of the receiving city. When delivery contracts expire, or when domestic demand begins to dwindle, or when import substitution occurs in foreign markets, the plant's entire work force may be laid off at short notice. (Whereas a single-plant firm may react to a certain percentage fall-off in demand by a corresponding cutback in output, the mutilocational organization may find it more 'efficient' to shut down completely one of its marginal units.) 'At times, neither employees nor regional planning authorities are notified of impending closures in advance, nor are serious attempts made to sell such plants to competitive corporations with a more suitable spatial or organizational structure or a more appropriate "temporal composition" of their product mix' (Krumme and Hayter, 1975). Moreover, the total cessation of factory operations by multilocational organizations is sometimes facilitated by tax regulations; e.g., in the US the entire cost of production buildings and equipment can be depreciated over a period as short as five years. Even if the abandonment or modification of a product does not lead to the closure of a 'trickled-down' plant, its total number of jobs will be temporarily or permanently reduced by layoffs until the controlling multilocational organization again steers resources in its direction. 'Trickled-down' plants are also particularly vulnerable to layoffs during periods of general recession (cf. Phillips, 1972).[5] At the same time, whether closure or layoffs are involved, administrative and office personnel at other organizational units may be unaffected, as the corporation continues about the business of starting up or acquiring new types of production that sooner or later will foster job opportunities at other locations.

Independent plants providing inputs to multilocational business organizations The technology of the automobile industry, aircraft manufacture, and a growing number of other types of production require the assembly of hundreds or even thousands of component units. We also know that a mounting share of the total value of manufactured goods in advanced economies is accounted for by multilocational business organizations. Because of these two facts it is increasingly likely that any independent plant, or single-location firm, that is established in a problem region will be either a supplier or a subcontractor for one or more multi-plant manufacturing corporations. Consequently, in more and more cases the employment total and very existence of independent plants – whether or not in problem-region cities – is vulnerable to any adjustment in the implicit locational decision-making of its market-providing larger organization(s). Many an independent plant has great difficulty in surviving the full time-period during which the more complex product it provides an input for is manufactured by a multilocational organization. (Survival is frequently particularly difficult for smaller single-location firms with limited capital resources.) In the process of modifying or differentiating a complex product, a multilocational organization will steadily and deliberately substitute one input for another; for example, automobile manufacturers annually alter door handles, dashboard dials and instruments, hubcaps, and a multitude of other details. In the process of improving the technology of production so as to increase cost efficiency and to remain competitive, multilocational organizations will also be frequently compelled to substitute one slightly different input for another. In the process of responding to demand decreases – either during a recession or toward the end of a complex product's life cycle – multilocational organizations are often forced to terminate purchases from one or more duplicate suppliers of a particular input. (This often happens in conjunction with a marginal-plant closure on the part of the purchasing multilocational organization.) In short, therefore, the expected lifetime of input-providing independent plants established in the cities of high-unemployment regions in many – perhaps most – instances must be regarded as comparatively short.

Many of the other hazards associated with regional development policies emphasizing manufacturing jobs stem from the specific planning strategies employed. For example, attempts to improve the viability of existing or potential production units in target cities (regions) by making highway network or other transportation improvements are subject to backfire. After all, roads lead into a region as well as out of it. Hence, the massive investment of highway construction funds, as in Appalachia, may fail to attract new plants and instead cause local producers to have their markets encroached upon as distant extraregional manufacturing units acquire better accessibility. When the strategy is that of focusing on a single very large-scale capital-intensive manufacturing project, such as a new high-capacity steel mill or petroleum refinery, there is a grave danger that the local economy will become extremely 'overheated' by the housing and other demands created by hundreds or thousands of *temporary* construction workers.

The inappropriateness of manufacturing-oriented regional development policies is additionally self-evident if one also equates the goal of interregional equality of employment conditions with geographically comparable spectrums of occupational opportunity – and thereby geographically comparable levels of *per capita* income – rather than merely with geographically comparable levels of employment or unemployment. If the urban activity systems of problem regions primarily receive manufacturing employment-role increments (or very few employment-role increases of any kind) then many of the recently educated and intellectually skilled members of their corresponding population systems will be driven to migrate to other cities, where they hope the activity system contains an appropriate assortment of available office (and professional) employment roles (cf. pp. 29–32, above). Such out-migration contributes to a downward spiral of economic and social events, diminishing the attractiveness of the region's larger cities for administrative functions, related business services and office activities in general, and magnifying the chances that further out-migration will occur in the future owing to inadequately matched activity and population systems.[6] By the same token, the steering of a stable or declining volume of factory jobs to problem-region cities leads to a falling-off of such jobs in large metropolitan complexes, i.e. to a highly unbalanced array of employment roles in the activity systems of large metropolitan complexes. Such activity system distortions, heightened by the concentration of high-level administrative and business-service employment opportunities in large metropolitan complexes (cf. pp. 116–20, above), means that the poorly educated or otherwise handicapped elements of large metropolitan population systems have difficulty securing steady work. The widespread local activity system/population system matching difficulties that arise in connection with manufacturing-oriented regional development, or employment creation, policies leads naturally to the consideration of the next alternative.

The office and business-service activity option

Specific government policies and experiences

To suggest that industrial production activities be given less emphasis, and that administrative functions, related business services and office activities in general be given greater emphasis in the formulation of regional development policies, is not to suggest that office employment has been completely ignored by the policy makers and planners of advanced economies. In the United Kingdom, the Netherlands and Sweden some plainly visible measures have been implemented and in other countries (e.g. Denmark and Norway) initial steps have been taken.

Since the early 1960s British efforts to influence the locations of office activities have for the most part fallen into three categories: first, the dispersal of existing private-sector offices from Central London; secondly, the control of new private-sector office construction in London and elsewhere; and, thirdly, the decentralization of government civil service offices from London.

Since 1963 the quasi-independent Location of Offices Bureau has been responsible for promoting private-sector office dispersal from the highly congested Central London area. The Bureau, which has aided in the decentralization of roughly 10000 jobs per year, supplies information and advice to firms and corporations contemplating a move, but lacks the executive power either to make consultation obligatory, or to encourage movement to any particular city or region. Consequently, the Bureau's efforts have met with limited success and considerable criticism (e.g. Rhodes and Kan, 1971; Burrows, 1973; Goddard, 1973a). In the early 1970s most of the jobs decentralized via the Bureau involved the routine office functions of multilocational organizations which chose locations well within the urban field of London (Goddard and Morrison, 1975; Daniels, 1975) where they could still 'borrow' some of the communications advantages of that metropolitan complex. In fact, approximately 71 per cent of the moved office jobs were to be found within a sixty-mile radius of Central London, another 16 per cent were situated 60–100 miles away, and only 1 per cent had made their way to the country's highest unemployment regions, or 'development areas'. Moreover, Westaway (1974a) has shown that during the 1960s Glasgow and the other metropolitan area labour markets of the development areas actually experienced a negative shift in their share of total British high-level office employment. Given this situation, plus the limited achievements recorded by the programme of construction controls, the government in late 1973 finally began to offer relatively substantial inducements to corporations and firms willing to shift office employment to the development areas. These new incentives, which took the form of rent subsidies and a grant for each employee moved, have not been in effect long enough to have their full impact judged. (Small construction grants previously had been tried as an inducement, but demonstrated little success, especially since most employers preferred to rent office facilities.)

The control of business office construction has been under the jurisdiction of the Department of the Environment since 1964. Permits to build office structures containing 3000 or more square feet of space were initially only required for London, but later were also made mandatory both for the entire surrounding Southeast and for Birmingham and the remainder of the Midlands. Under the control system, developers in theory may obtain a permit for London office construction if they can argue that the proposed occupants have linkages in London that cannot be matched elsewhere. In practice 'The fact that most office development in London and the Southeast is speculative (i.e. built in advance of demand and not for a particular client) makes it difficult . . . to discriminate between one type of activity and another in the granting of . . . permits' (Goddard, 1973a). Furthermore, the geographically selective administration of construction controls has not been able to prevent the occurrence of sizable office developments in prosperous uncontrolled centres (e.g. Bristol, little more than 100 miles from Central London) rather than cities in the 'development areas'.

Since the government of the United Kingdom has a direct say in the matter, the decentralization of civil service jobs has been somewhat more successful in creating jobs in the highest unemployment regions. Of the 50000 government office jobs removed from London between 1963 and 1972, roughly 38 per cent were obtained by the development areas. However, numerous places received only a handful of new posts and many of the moves involved 'low-level clerical jobs which brought only limited benefits to the receiving' cities (Goddard, 1975). In late 1973 the government's Hardman Report proposed the further decentralization of 31000 headquarters jobs from London, 17 per cent of which were to go to the development areas.[7] The report was criticized on a number of grounds, including its failure to consider the potential mobility of government research and development offices from the surrounding Southeast (e.g. Goddard, 1975; Stephens, 1975). Most importantly, as Cameron (1974) has pointed out, even if the government were to decentralize its own offices at a more rapid pace, it is unlikely that the highest unemployment regions plus the so-called 'intermediate areas'[8] in combination will gain more than 3000–4000 jobs *per annum*, which is far from enough to make a large contribution to interregional labour-market equilibrium.

In March 1974 the government of the Netherlands approved a long-discussed plan to disperse 16 000 jobs tied to central government agencies from The Hague, which along with Amsterdam, Rotterdam and Utrecht form the Randstad metropolitan complex (Toby, 1973; Sundqvist, 1975). (The Randstad contains about 36 per cent of the Netherlands' less than 14 million inhabitants.) Close to 75 per cent of the first employment shifts were destined for the comparatively thinly populated, highly agricultural and unemployment-beset provinces of the north. In particular, the largest portion of the shifts – which were to include the headquarters of the national postal, telegraph and telephone service – were to go to the cities of Groningen (1972 pop., 172 000) and Leeuwarden (1972 pop., 88 000). All the remaining jobs were to be relocated to the South Limburg region, where unemployment is a problem because of the instability of coal mining. There has also been much debate about various government proposals to use taxes or licensing controls to limit office and other commercial construction in the Randstad, where congestion and preservation of open spaces are considered major problems. In so far as other advanced economies are concerned, whatever lessons are eventually learned from any Dutch measures should be of limited general applicability. This is because almost the whole physical area of the Netherlands lies within a 100-mile radius, or the 'urban field', of the Randstad metropolitan complex, and can therefore benefit from its external economies to some extent.

In 1974 the Swedish government also began to implement a coordinated policy of decentralizing jobs connected to central government agencies operating in Stockholm.[9] By 1980 the relocation scheme is to cover 11 330 jobs, or roughly 25 per cent of all national-level government employment found in the capital city in 1974. This gesture is primarily, but not entirely, seen as a *supplement* to the manufacturing incentives designed to aid unemployment problem areas. It will eventually affect all or part of fifty-six agencies, many of which contain a large share of high-rank, high-salary positions. (Agencies with a high percentage of lower-salaried workers performing tasks that mainly involve routine information were not considered desirable because of their lower propensity to generate local employee expenditure multiplier effects.) Quite significantly, before the final formulation of policy and the first move took place, a study of the face-to-face contacts and other communications behaviour of 20000 civil servants in selected government agencies was undertaken so as to determine, among other things, which agencies were unsuitable for dispersal from Stockholm; which agencies had a high percentage of contacts with one another or with regional and local institutions; and which cities were most suitable for the reception of office employment positions (Thorngren, 1973; Persson, 1974). Consequently, it was decided that agency clusters would be assigned to fifteen urban centres, most of which had populations in excess of 100000 and which were presumably capable of providing the most basic related services. The clusters designated for Umeå, in Norrland (1270 jobs) and Gävle, 115 miles north of Stockholm (920 jobs), are illustrative of the importance attached to the cost savings and other benefits of locally contained specialized information contacts. In the former case, the National Bacteriological Laboratory, the National Defence Research Institute, the College of Forestry, and the National Institute of Occupational Health offer obvious linkages to the local university and its medical school. In the latter instance, the Geographical Survey office, the National Land Survey Board, the Central Board for Real Estate Data and the National Institute for Building Research already possess overlapping and mutual contacts of vital importance. While the Swedish government has not taken any direct action concerning the location of private-sector office employment, there are those who hope – perhaps unrealistically – that the decentralization of government agency clusters will exert some significant attractive influence on business offices.

Advantages of the alternative

It has just been shown that existing British, Dutch and Swedish policies have been mostly confined either to the relocation of government employment in numbers that are quite modest in terms of problem-region labour markets, or to essentially unsuccessful strategies for influencing the location of private-sector office activities. It is possible to make some suggestions as to what steps might be taken in order to create greater interregional equality of employment opportunities through influencing the location of both *new* and existing office jobs *on a large scale*. However, it would be premature to do so without first comparing the supposed advantages of stressing office employment in regional development with the supposed limitations and negative side effects of such a policy.

Among the advantages that might possibly materialize in conjunction with a regional employment-creation policy that gave
primary emphasis to administrative functions, related business
services and office activities in general, the following are most
worthy of enumeration.

(1)   The office activities either shifted to, or established in, a high
unemployment region could lead to a reduction of interregional
multiplier leakages to large metropolitan complexes. Extensive
office-employment multiplier leakages – which are a typical characteristic of high unemployment regions in advanced economies – would
have particularly good prospects for reduction if some high-level
administrative units of multilocational business organizations could
be established in one of the more important cities of the region in
question. (While the population of the largest urban units varies
considerably from one problem region to another, it is seldom that
such units lack either the status of a small metropolitan area of
100000 or more, or the ability or potential to provide some essential
business services.)

(2)   As earlier suggested, the out-migration of educated and skilled
population elements from problem regions would not be as great if
the activity systems of the larger cities of those regions contained a
more representative mix of employment roles. New office jobs may
not only be filled by the recently trained or currently unemployed,
but also by those who are overqualified for the job they already
have and desire a more stimulating or better-paid position. When the
latter occurs, local unemployment can be relieved via 'chains of
opportunity' (cf. pp. 29–30, above). Of course, to the extent that new
high-level office jobs are filled by organizational personnel brought
in from other regions, the employment-role benefits accruing to the
problem region are restricted to those associated with multiplier
effects.

(3)   In many, and perhaps most, circumstances, regional employment-creation policies emphasizing office activities could be less
demanding of scarce government resources than other policy alternatives. The subsidies or costs to be incurred for creating one office
job are apparently considerably less than those to be incurred for
establishing one factory job. According to calculations made by
Rhodes and Kan (1971), the subsidy cost of moving manufacturing
production jobs to British 'development areas' in the early 1970s
was at least four times greater than that for shifting office jobs.[10]

(4)   In certain instances office location in a problem-region city

will yield intraorganizational or interorganizational efficiencies that are not necessarily available in the larger metropolitan complexes of other regions. The multilocational business organization may find it profitable to bring a new or existing office unit into direct or closer proximity with other of its own office or non-office units if there is some promise of considerable internal informational exchange, and if that office unit will not have to maintain a large quantity of geographically widespread interorganizational contacts. New branch offices, even in 'backward' regions, may make for more efficient communications with existing customers and at the same time facilitate market expansion. Organizations providing business services are especially likely to benefit from starting new branch operations at a given location if other types of office activity are simultaneously being attracted to the same location. By spinning off routine or other functions away from a high-level administrative unit in a major metropolitan complex, an organization may obtain sizable rental savings and also relieve congestion or other accommodation problems that are otherwise often 'solved' by shifting from a central city to a nearby suburb. Obviously, such a move enables a greater devotion of time and space to co-ordination and non-routine decision-making activities at the major metropolitan unit. In addition, staff turnover in a problem-region city may turn out to be lower by one-third or more than in the more fluid labour market of a large metropolitan complex (Rhodes and Kan, 1971). Note, however, that the propensity to exploit possible intraorganizational and interorganizational efficiencies varies from business sector to business sector, and from corporation to corporation, depending largely on variations in organizational spatial structure and overall contact pattern.

(5) Yannopoulos (1973) has contended that office activities generally are capable of generating greater *local* multiplier effects than manufacturing production activities. Whether or not this is true in specific instances depends, of course, on which type of office activity is being compared with which type of plant, as well as on the linkage potentialities offered by the location under consideration. However, average office salaries tend to be higher than average factory earnings, especially when an office contains some high-level administrative functions. Locally contained employee-expenditure multipliers will thus tend to be higher. Moreover, a larger share of the more basic inputs required by offices – including printing services and paper supplies – should be obtainable from local sources than is

usually the case for production units. On the other hand, the total value of such office inputs may be relatively small.

Limitations and negative side effects of the alternative

Perhaps the most telling criticism that can be levelled against a regional development strategy that emphasizes office-employment creation is that non-routine communications costs will be either increased for office units that *relocate* to high-unemployment regions, or higher for *new* office units that are placed in the cities of such regions rather than in traditionally selected large metropolitan complexes. Evidence from Sweden indicates that decentralized government offices have encountered, or will encounter, non-routine communications costs that are substantially higher than those incurred at Stockholm (Thorngren, 1973; Persson, 1974; Törnqvist *et al.*, 1975). Prior to relocation from Stockholm, positions involving numerous face-to-face contacts have an average of 4·5 per cent of their working time allocated to *local and non-local* travel. It has been estimated that twice as much travel time will be necessary from decentralized locations. Higher non-routine communications costs have apparently also been the rule for private offices leaving London (Goddard and Morris, 1975). The time and travel costs of *maintaining* fixed, irreplaceable or habitual[11] face-to-face contacts from problem-region cities will be especially great either when a high percentage of such contacts are situated in the abandoned office centre, or when the air (and rail) transport network is so connected that many contact locations can only be reached over a roundabout route through the abandoned office centre or some other large metropolitan complex. (Infrequent and time-consuming travel connections may also necessitate that face-to-face encounters be arranged with considerable advance notice.)

All the same, it should be realized that much of the face-to-face contact work occurring in the office districts of large metropolitan complexes could readily be replaced by telecommunications. A communications survey covering Central London revealed that 'around 20 per cent of all meetings have characteristics similar to telephone calls, i.e. short and specific discussion between two familiar people'. It was also found that 5 per cent of impromptu non-routine contacts could easily be replaced through the use of document transmission facilities and the holding of regularly scheduled meetings at widespread intervals (Goddard and Morris, 1975). It is additionally possible that new or relocated offices in problem-region cities will be able to establish or maintain non-routine contacts – and sizably reduce the need for trips – by utilizing conference telephone calls, telephonic document transmission, video telephone connections, and communications satellites. (Although the experts are far from being in total agreement, there is some consensus that, in the near foreseeable future, such advanced and often costly communications technology will facilitate a reduction in the need for *intra*organizational meetings, but will only have a limited impact on the psychological need for high-level *inter*organizational face-to-face contacts, particularly those involving complicated and unstructured specialized information and unfamiliar individuals.) It is also conceivable that, when confronted by the time and travel costs of a high-unemployment region location, office units will be forced to hold better planned and more structured meetings. Such meetings may prove more productive than quickly arranged informal talks, and may reduce the total number of contact trips necessary by lasting longer and covering more items. Cost savings may be similarly attained by accumulating several meeting commitments with different contact partners for each trip. Furthermore, relocated offices may find either that *substitutable* face-to-face contacts eventually materialize locally in response to their appearance, or that their own activities and contact requirements can be altered to take advantage of the opportunities offered by the local environment.

Secondly, *if* it is true that non-routine communications costs are inevitably magnified significantly at any location which is not a large metropolitan complex, and *if* economic criteria are the sole judgmental criteria employed, then it may be contended that most of those office units which are suitable for the poorly connected urban centres of high unemployment regions will have predominantly routine functions. (According to this line of reasoning, offices belonging to large multilocational organizations would be most appropriate, since those organizations can separate routine from non-routine operations more easily than their smaller counterparts.) If only routine-function offices are brought in, the impact on the regional labour market may be rather modest. This is so since offices with mainly routine functions normally have only a small component of highly salaried workers, and therefore the local employee-expenditure multipliers fostered by such offices will be abbreviated. However, even if the inhibiting role of costly face-to-face communications is accepted, the office-possibility picture for problem regions need not be entirely bleak. As Goddard (1975) has pointed out, research and development office units, with a goodly share of highly paid employees, are often reliant upon a limited set of familiar contacts that can be sustained via telecommunications plus widely spaced face-to-face meetings.

Thirdly, critics of office *relocation* policies often point to the numerous psychological, familial and social problems encountered by the individuals employed in office units that are to be partly or entirely decentralized. Individuals are subject to the uncertainties, anxieties and stress associated with deciding whether or not to move with their job. If a decision not to move is reached – whether because of a family's unwillingness to leave a familiar and emotionally secure physical environment and social network, or because of some other reason – then the often difficult task of finding a new position must be confronted. If a move is undertaken, and the individual is married, then an entire family must go through the throes of adjusting to a new place of residence, with the spouse's problem of finding a new, comparably paying job often proving to be particularly difficult (cf. Sidwell, 1974a, 1974b). These problems should not be minimized, even if they do not apply to all individuals,[12] especially in as much as each relocated worker means one less new employment role to be filled by the population of the receiving city or surrounding region. Therefore, it would appear that policy makers toying with office-oriented regional development schemes ought to give more consideration to the means for locationally influencing *new* units than to the measures necessary for attracting already existing units.

Finally, there are those who contend that any effort to reduce unemployment in the problem regions of advanced economies by emphasizing the creation of office-based job opportunities is ill-conceived since most of the unemployed in such regions are 'unsuitable' for the type of work involved. In other words, the resultant employment-role additions to local activity systems cannot be matched to the competencies of local population systems. The adherence to such a position by policy-makers can to some extent be a self-fulfilling prophecy since, as previously observed, the out-migration of young educated individuals so typical of problem regions is in some measure attributable to the scarcity of appropriate office employment roles. Such a position also ignores the possibility that the unemployed may acquire jobs as a result of the 'chains of opportunity' and multiplier effects spawned by new or relocated office units. Perhaps most importantly, a 'work-force unsuitability' position overlooks the potential for coordinating an office-oriented policy with long-range manpower training programmes, or the 'upgrading of human resources' (cf. Hansen, 1975).

Need for policy coordination

The way in which the process of city-system growth and development apparently operates in advanced economies means that the degree of success obtainable by any regional development strategy which emphasizes office activities is likely to depend on its ability to coordinate a variety of measures above and beyond manpower training programmes and related improvements in the quality of available education.

The large-scale placement of administrative functions, related business services and office activities in general in selected problem-region cities should normally demand some modification in long-distance interurban transportation routes and schedules. In model experiments for Sweden involving the hypothetical geographical allocation of 125 000 'contact-intensive' business and government office jobs, Törnqvist (1973) and Engström and Sahlberg (1973) have shown that when 'decentralization' is combined with an unaltered transportation system, it leads to increased rather than decreased regional differences in non-routine contact potential. That is, when problem-region cities and other decentralized locations obtain a greater share of new office activities than the large metropolitan complexes where those activities have traditionally concentrated, the large metropolitan complexes continue to have pronounced time and money advantages with respect to carrying out non-local face-to-face contacts. This is so because so many of the trips that now have to be made between centres of intermediate or smaller size can only occur if the time and travel costs of a detour via a large metropolitan complex are absorbed.[13] In order to prevent or remedy such circumstances, air or other travel services would have to be improved primarily between the cities receiving large doses of office activities, and secondarily between those locations and some large metropolitan complexes elsewhere in the country to which they are not presently linked by non-stop or direct flights. Once the major cities of one or more problem regions are made more accessible to one another at the same time as they are acquiring new or relocated office units – and perhaps some production units – the spontaneous appearance of new urban interdependencies and new spatial biases in the circulation of specialized information would be facilitated. If new interdependencies and spatial biases actually materialize, and if the model of city-system growth and development summarized in Figure 3.14 is at all representative of reality, these twin events should improve the long-term employment prospects of the selected problem-region cities by enhancing the probabilities for their benefiting in the future from implicit locational decisions and the intraregional and interregional diffusion of growth-inducing innovations.

In order further to insure the operation of job-creating feedbacks between selected cities in one or more high-unemployment regions, direct coordinating steps would have to be taken so that as many as possible of the office units appearing in those cities were functionally interdependent either with one another or with other new or already existing intraregional activity units of all types. In other words, the forging of intraregional urban interdependencies should not be left entirely to whatever voluntary results improved transportation services yield. This is vital, for if intraregional urban interdependencies are not intentionally encouraged while interurban travel services are simultaneously improved, the short-run multipliers and long-run employment payoffs following the birth and expansion of activities will leak out of the problem region to an unnecessary degree, mostly to large metropolitan complexes whose continued growth may not be desired. Or, if the two measures are not undertaken jointly, the high-unemployment region will continue to lack a truly functioning regional system of cities, and its largest urban units will remain in a 'colonial' relationship to one or more metropolitan complexes elsewhere in the national city-system (cf. p. 15, above, and Penouil, 1972).

Implicit in the suggested coordination of travel-service improvements and new interdependencies is the need for that coordination to occur in such a way that it involves only a small number of selected centres – preferably with populations ranging from 100000 to 500000. Concentration in cities of this size is probably necessary if the new and relocated office units attracted to high-unemployment regions are to have access to a minimally acceptable array of local external economies and contact opportunities. Because of the cost of starting up airline services, including possible subsidies, it is also clear that only a few centres can be given new jet connections and more frequent and better-timed flights on existing routes.[14]

Finally, if office-emphasizing regional development policies are to avoid being heedlessly counteracted, they probably ought to be coordinated with government policies affecting the location of new telecommunications developments. If investments in telecommunications infrastructure are left to evolve on their own, there is a great danger that costly innovations will be initially introduced in nationally dominant centres (cf. Clark, 1974) and that the specialized information advantages of those large metropolitan complexes will be increased, thereby reinforcing existing intraorganizational and interorganizational city-system interdependencies. This is very likely in some degree to occur at the expense of future employment growth in the problem-region cities where it is desired.

Boise revisited: a case example of the viability of high-level administrative functions in smaller metropolitan areas

Largely because of some of the same arguments that can be raised against office-emphasizing regional-development schemes, it is conventional wisdom that only large metropolitan complexes can sustain offices with high-level administrative functions. It is supposedly the case that lesser metropolitan units with populations of 100000 or more have contact conditions which are too 'poor' for offices whose highly salaried personnel must devote much of their time to coping with the great variety of problems and new opportunities spewed up by a constantly changing environment. Smaller metropolitan centres which are situated in high-unemployment or physically remote regions are often viewed as especially inappropriate for the high-level administrative units of large multilocational business organizations, which typically have a far-flung pattern of internal and interorganization contacts. In this context it may be instructive to examine conditions in Idaho's Boise City metropolitan area somewhat more closely.

It is to be recalled that Boise – with its extremely remote location within the US–Canadian city-system and modest population (112230 in 1970) – has a *per capita* index of non-local job control approaching that for the New York City metropolitan complex, thanks mainly to the locally present head offices of four large corporations (see p. 162, above). What factors have made it possible for the 'improperly' located headquarters of these four major corporations – as well as the chief offices of eight somewhat smaller multilocational businesses – both to manage the mostly successful rapid expansion of their activities and to coordinate their widespread operations in North America (Figures 3.9 and 3.10) and overseas?

(Aside from its foreign joint ventures, the Boise Cascade Corp. operates, among other things, sawmills and plywood and particle-board plants in the Philippines, Colombia, Costa Rica, and Singapore; pulp and paper mills in Guatemala and the Philippines; and corrugated container plants in Austria. During a relatively brief period in 1974–5, when the company already had major ongoing construction and engineering projects in Brazil, Panama, Paraguay, Bolivia, Ecuador, Guatemala, Costa Rica, Afghanistan, Bangladesh, Singapore, the Ivory Coast and the UK, the Morrison-Knudsen Co. Inc. obtained contracts enabling them to participate in new pipeline, highway and other ventures in, among other places, Iran, Benin (Dahomey) and the Netherlands.)[15]

For one thing, the physical environment and outdoors recreational facilities available to Boise have played a key role.[16] When mergers, acquisitions and internal expansion led to a burgeoning scale of total operations in the 1960s,[17] at least two of Boise's leading business organizations contemplated the relocation of their headquarters to much larger metropolitan complexes, such as Chicago, San Francisco–Oakland–San Jose or Portland. In light of the attachment held for Boise's physical amenities by management at the highest level, and because it was believed that those amenities could continue to be used to attract talented young personnel, relocation was rejected. At about the same time the major Boise corporations began to adopt measures which were clearly designed to compensate for the city's contact limitations. The Boise Cascade Corp., for example, became a pioneer among US business organizations in the establishment of an extensive video-telephone network in order to link together some of its major units that were spread across the nation. In addition, Boise Cascade instituted the practice of holding periodic seminars for managers in four or five cities simultaneously by pre-distributing up-to-date videotape reports from top officers and arranging for conference telephone hookups immediately after viewing. That same organization became a very heavy user of head-quarters-based computer facilities, both for the purposes of co-ordinating multilocational routine operations, such as wage and salary disbursal, and for more 'sophisticated' managerial purposes, such as the running of decision-scanning programmes. Likewise, Albertsons Inc. – considered to be one of the most efficiently run retailing organizations in the US – employs two very advanced computerized management information systems. These enable the company to make key merchandising, operating and expansion decisions for its retail stores. (These stores, unlike anything taken up by central-place theory, are principally concentrated in the considerably larger metropolitan complexes, of Los Angeles, San Francisco–Oakland–San Jose, Seattle–Tacoma, Denver, Portland and Salt Lake City.[18] However, more routine merchandising decisions are made at regional-division office units.

The functioning of major headquarters office units in Boise has also been made viable by the commercial airline services available to that geographically isolated metropolitan area. Early morning departures and convenient evening returns permit a full business day in the San Francisco–Oakland–San Jose metropolitan complex, which is one of the world's most important banking centres and a nerve centre for US–Asian business linkages. Early morning departures are also available to Chicago, and thence New York and other leading metropolitan complexes. Frequent flights occur to Seattle–Tacoma and Portland, the most physically proximate large metropolitan complexes, and Los Angeles is also relatively easily reached. In addition, Boise Cascade has acquired a fleet of small jet airplanes of its own.

Finally, most of the business services necessary to the operation of Boise's leading head offices are locally at hand. Only part of this is due to the availability of separately owned essential accounting, banking and legal services. (Two of Boises's other locally based multilocational businesses are banks, and there is a comparatively broad base for printing and legal services since the city is also occupied by the Idaho legislature and the headquarters of the state government's various agencies.)[19] The remainder is explained by the fact that some specialized services have been internalized. For example, the headquarters of Albertsons contains subunits for advertising, for the architectural design of supermarkets and other buildings, and for handling the legal side of industrial relations. Nevertheless, Boise corporations are dependent upon San Francisco for certain financial services, and Morrison-Knudsen purchases some tailor-made services in Cleveland, where it has a rather large unit specializing in the design and construction of industrial plants.

One case does not make a rule. The viability of the Boise City metropolitan area as a headquarters centre by no means proves that problem-region metropolitan areas with populations from 100000 to 500000 can always be reasonably expected to support a concentration of administrative functions of the very highest level. There are only so many headquarters of large multilocational business organizations (and government agencies) to go around. Moreover, communications requirements vary vastly from one business organization to another; so what may prove to be a satisfactory head-office location for one corporation may prove totally untenable for another.[20] All the same, it can be asserted that the Boise evidence indicates that lesser metropolitan units – whether or not situated in high-unemployment regions – possess the potential to house successfully other types of high-level administrative functions, such as divisional headquarters, units split off from organization-wide or divisional head offices, and research and development units. If Boise's experience is representative, there would have to be enough units to form a concentration, good air-travel connections would have to be available, and the organizations involved would have to invest heavily in telecommunications and computers and to internalize some business services. (Although the internalization of specialized services is presumably less of a problem for large-organization offices, it can be costly if the sub-units created are periodically confronted with slack periods.) This point of view is not only consistent with earlier arguments, but is also in keeping with the good headquarters-centre performance of several US metropolitan areas that have only recently approached or surpassed the population mark of 500000.

Other alternatives and issues

The choice of policy alternatives that may help to reduce or largely eliminate interregional inequalities of employment opportunity is obviously not entirely confined to either a continued emphasis on industrial production activities, or a more sectorally balanced approach that primarily stresses administrative functions, related business services and office activities in general. For the governments of economically advanced countries at least two other alternatives exist. Both are consistent with the interpretation of city-system growth and development summarized in Figure 3.14. Also, these alternatives need not be at odds with office-emphasizing regional development policies.

First, instead of focusing their efforts almost entirely on explicit locational decisions (i.e. on measures to influence the location and relocation of factories, offices and other job-providing units), policy-makers and regional-development planners could devote a large share of their energies to as yet highly neglected implicit locational decisions. If national and state (or provincial) governments were to accept the fact that there were job-creating or job-preserving implications attached to every one of their decisions to purchase a good or service, to award a contract, or to allocate funds to a project; and if it were realized that the enormous sums of money annually tied up in such decisions to a considerable extent work at cross-purposes with regional development policy objectives; then employment conditions in problem regions could be improved sizably by a coordinated screening and locational steering of such decisions. (In Great Britain some attempt has been made by the national government to structure its buying practices so as to favour the high-unemployment 'development areas' (Cameron, 1974). In West Germany certain problem areas have been given preferential treatment in the awarding of government contracts (Krumme, 1974). In both these cases, however, only one broad type of expenditure has been dealt with in a far from comprehensive manner.) Likewise, it is theoretically possible significantly to affect the job situation in high-unemployment regions if the private sector in general, and large multilocational organizations in particular, are induced to favour those regions when buying goods and services and when granting contracts or subcontracts. Incentives could take the form, for example, of tax benefits or subsidized price reductions, or disincentive penalties could be enforced.

The second alternative is based on the assumption that the interplay between spatial biases in the circulation of specialized information and the limited-search and uncertainty-reduction behaviour of organizations can be tampered with so as to produce more explicit and implicit locational decisions which generate or sustain employment opportunities in problem regions. This alternative would require that government and planning authorities establish an agency to subvert the limited-search syndrome by actively providing decision-making units with detailed opportunity- and cost-specific information on explicit and implicit locational options. The information supplied would be much more refined than that normally found in glossy promotional booklets and would in effect represent a public subsidization of search costs. The information would also be designed to reduce uncertainties about the viability of operating in 'backward', 'lagging' or 'depressed' regions. If effective with respect to implicit locational decisions, the information provided would help divert many employment multiplier effects away from large metropolitan complexes. Success on a wide scale with respect to both implicit and explicit locational decisions would presumably result in the creation of new self-perpetuating spatial biases in freely circulating specialized information which could have a long-term positive impact on problem-region employment.

Both the alternatives just described, as well as the earlier call for coordinating intraregional linkages and office clusters, suggest the need for a constant statistical monitoring of national and regional city-systems so as to identify the interdependence, employment and demographic conditions characterizing those systems at any particular point in time. In a perpetually changing world regional development policy strategies cannot be fixed, but instead should be capable of adjustment via a learning process. Thus, up-to-date city-system data on, for example, job-control linkages, the distribution of government spending, freight and communications flows, and migration are needed in order to establish policy priorities when striving to reduce interregional employment inequalities. If nothing else, a commitment to constant city-system monitoring should help eliminate some of the growth-centre and other planning blunders that arise from focusing on a single region or sector and ignoring the intricate process by which economic growth and employment multipliers are transmitted from one local labour market to another.

The spotlight thus far placed on reducing or largely eliminating interregional inequalities of employment opportunity should not obscure the existence of other regional problems and national settlement policy issues that are considered by some to be of equal or greater importance. Most of these competing issues deserve separate extensive treatment. Three of the most consequential of them can be briefly outlined in order to provide some perspective.

The energy issue

As an aftermath of the 1973–4 oil crisis, the question of energy consumption has frequently been given a central position in debates concerning economic and physical planning in general, and regional development in particular. It is possible to envisage a wide range of future energy-consumption scenarios, each of which might open very different alternatives for regional development policy formulation (cf. Wärneryd, 1975). With the passage of time economically advanced countries may find that technological advances permit a 'high-energy' society with continued increases in the *per capita* consumption of energy, *including transportation*. Or it may be decided to aim, as far as possible, at unaltered levels of *per capita* consumption of energy and transportation. Or conditions may dictate a 'low-energy' society where the *per capita* consumption of energy and transportation is reduced via price or rationing mechanisms. As Törnqvist (1975) has pointed out, the 'low-energy' scenario alone provides several different possibilities for the spatial organization of society. Substantially higher transportation costs could reduce both individual mobility and market areas, or the exploitation of scale economies, thereby encouraging some deconcentration of work-places and services. Considerably increased transport costs could also be used to reduce interurban interdependence and enhance locally contained multiplier effects by enabling the gradual replacement of extended production systems, or lengthy input-outputchains, by a more traditional and much less refined division of labour between activity units. In contrast, it may be determined that extremely costly transportation can be counteracted by retaining lengthy production systems and instead promoting the packing of activities and people in a limited number of large metropolitan complexes.

The intrametropolitan issue

With the vast bulk of the population of advanced economies dwelling in metropolitan areas (over 73 per cent in the case of the US), and with great spatial differences in employment levels, living standards, and social conditions existing within individual units – and especially within the larger metropolitan complexes – it may be contended that scarce resources ought to be channelled primarily toward the reduction of intrametropolitan inequalities, and only secondarily towards the diminishment of interregional inequalities (cf. Richardson, 1972). At the core of the intrametropolitan problem, in most instances, is the stark contrast between the central city – and perhaps some inner suburbs – on the one hand,[21] and the more prosperous suburbs and peripheral areas on the other hand. As is well known, the former areas normally have a disproportionate concentration of low-employment minority groups, aged and poor. As a result, local demands for welfare and public services are not easily satisfied, financed or administered. (These problems are often aggravated by the continual 'flight' of middle-class residents to suburban and peripheral housing and by the steady arrival of new unemployed migrants.) Furthermore, new and relocated service, office and industrial jobs have been accumulating in the outer suburbs and metropolitan fringes at the same time that the absolute total of employment opportunities has been falling off in the central city and other intrametropolitan poverty subareas. In other words, current trends are yielding a very high degree of mismatch between the activity and population subsystems of central cities (cf. p. 191, above), and also imposing higher average work-place accessibility costs on those poverty subarea inhabitants fortunate enough to be employed (cf. Deskins, 1973). All the same, an all too simple distinction is perhaps being made by those who contend that priority ought to be given to programmes designed to rectify intrametropolitan economic and social inequalities and to deal with related questions of intrametropolitan population distribution. In the context of precipitously declining rates of natural increase in the US and other advanced economies, *a growing number of metropolitan areas will, or already, find themselves in a no-growth or very slow-growth situation,* with their ability to cope with international problems especially sensitive to the allocation of employment opportunities within the national city-system as a whole (cf. Rust, 1975).

The regional sovereignty issue

In several economically advanced countries the issue of regional sovereignty is beginning to loom ever larger. A significant portion of the population in Scotland, Wales, the Canadian province of Québec, and the French provinces of Brittany and Corsica are clamouring for the right to maintain their distinctive language and cultural identity, and for the right to political and economic self-determination. It is worth noting that all the just named areas may be regarded as partially or totally 'backward', 'lagging' or 'depressed' regions. Hence quite plainly, if any of these areas were to acquire full independence or something closely resembling it, then their high-unemployment problems would become more of an internal matter than a question of interregional inequality.[22] In this connection, and in light of the socialist and politically radical orientation of many of the regional sovereignty movements, it is relevant that Hymer (1972) has proposed that the economic exploitation and geographical inequalities brought about by the actions of large multinational (or multilocational) corporations could be cancelled out by the formation of government institutions 'which organize many industries across one region'. Hymer's institutions would not only 'permit the centralization of capital, i.e. the coordination of many enterprises', under one roof, but also concentrate (*'all* levels of decision-making in one local' and thus provide the region with a full complement of skills and occupations.

The quality of life and service availability

General observations

The question regarding quality-of-life improvements in problem regions posed at the beginning of this chapter need not be given the same extended treatment as that just given the question of inter-regional inequalities of employment opportunity. Provided the definition here given to 'quality of life' is accepted, in a number of senses the quality-of-life question is an offshoot of the interregional employment inequality question. (In Chapter 1 it was stated that, at the very least, the 'quality of life' in a city or region refers to the accessibility of its inhabitants to employment alternatives, educational and medical facilities, essential public social services, a representative range of commercial and cultural services, and 'nature', or extensive recreational open spaces.)[23] To begin with, the question of quality-of-life improvements in problem regions is definitionally in some measure dependent upon a greater spatial equality of employment levels (or male and female labour-force participation rates), and geographically comparable spectrums of occupational opportunity. Furthermore, once more interregionally equitable employment conditions exist, many of the individuals in presently 'backward' or 'depressed' regions would presumably be in a better position to consume the public and private services which are so central to an improved quality of life (cf. Simmons, 1975). This would presumably result both from higher *per capita* disposable incomes and from the greater ability of local and state (provincial) governments to provide public services as a consequence of the increased tax revenues received from businesses and individuals. Note, however, that the provision of additional public (or private) services will not raise the quality of life of any particular individual in a problem region unless those new services fall within her perceived environment and preference structure.

More geographically comparable spectrums of occupational opportunity can also be linked to quality-of-life improvements in problem regions if it is allowed that job satisfaction, self-respect and place-of-residence stability are also important quality-of-life attributes. With an adequately representative array of employment opportunities available in a city or region, a greater percentage of the work force is likely to experience job satisfaction, and more individuals are apt to retain their self-respect by holding positions that are consistent with their training and talents. With lower levels of unemployment and a sufficiently diversified range of job opportunities, fewer families and individuals should be exposed to the hardships and psychological strains that arise from being pushed unwillingly into the interregional out-migration stream.

To the extent that accessibility to work-places and services are at the heart of quality-of-life conditions, it follows that quality-of-life improvements in problem regions most probably cannot occur without some planned modification of local or subregional public-transportation routes and schedules, plus some coordination of the operating hours of local or subregional businesses and services. Regardless of where individuals live, their ability freely to choose the activities in which they daily participate is restricted to a much greater extent than is generally realized by a variety of 'time-geographic' constraints and conflicts (Hägerstrand, 1970a, 1970b, 1972, 1975; Hägerstrand, Mårtensson, Lenntorp, Jenstav and Wallin, 1974; Lenntorp, 1975; Jenstav, 1975; Mårtensson, 1975; Pred, 1973c). It has already been noted that individuals are indivisible and thereby unable to participate in any pair of activities which have overlapping time requirements (cf. p. 28, above). In addition, even if an individual meets any competency or economic preconditions that may exist, he or she cannot take part in any two successive activities unless those activities are so located in space that the distance separating them can be covered in the time interval between the end of one and the beginning of the second. Put otherwise, every stop at a work-, consumption-, or leisure-activity 'station' (location) causes the time-space range of activity alternatives for the remainder of the day to shrink in proportion to the length of stay there. It is because of these and other constraints and conflicts that the quality of life of the young, the aged and the adult members of one-car families[24] are highly sensitive to both the routes and schedules of public transportation systems, and the operating hours of work-places and service outlets. Thus, for example, the introduction of more extensive and better-timed public transportation services between several closely located problem-region small cities can lead to quality-of-life improvements by broadening the activity-system base in which individuals can seek employment roles, and by easing the fulfilment of service thresholds. However, largely because of the difficulty of fulfilling service threshold conditions within reasonable time-distances (even with some modification of public transportation services and coordination of activity operating hours), it can prove rather costly to improve quality-of-life conditions substantially in any extensive sparsely populated areas that may occur in problem regions (cf. Weissglas, 1975).

Since time-geographic obstacles to improving quality-of-life conditions increase as the spatial packing of population and activities decreases, there are additional grounds for suggesting that interregional inequalities of employment opportunity be reduced by concentrating new and relocated administrative functions and other office activities in a small number of problem-region centres with populations of 100000–500000. A population of 100000 is often regarded as the minimum necessary for the existence of a local labour market that is both diversified and capable of providing a good measure of employment security in the face of constantly changing economic and technological conditions. A population of 100000 is also frequently considered necessary in order adequately to support a modernly equipped general hospital, a variety of specialized consumer services, and certain cultural facilities (e.g. a resident theatre). For most residents, cities in the 100000–500000 range should also normally have both less air and noise pollution and easier access to the open countryside and outdoor recreation than larger-scaled metropolitan complexes. Finally, there are some indications, based on US data, 'that large numbers of potentially mobile persons' in problem regions would prefer to move to nearby metropolitan areas of the size under discussion 'rather than stay at home or move to large metropolitan' complexes in other regions (Hansen, 1973, 1975; Sundqvist, 1975).

Future imponderables

The specific issue of bringing about quality-of-life improvements in the 'backward', 'lagging' and 'depressed' regions of advanced economies cannot be completely divorced from several more general and complex issues which are likely to be resolved in different ways in different countries. Only a few of these issues are captured in the following questions.

(1) If technological change enables real *per capita* income and leisure time to continue growing, how will the demand for manufactured

goods and non-essential services be affected *vis-à-vis* the demand for health care and public services?

(2)   How will increased longevity and falling birth rates affect the demand for services oriented toward the aged?

(3)   To what extent will the women's rights movement and increased female participation in the labour force affect the demand for access to child-care facilities? (In this connection it should be noted that female work-force participation rates are usually much lower in high unemployment regions than in large metropolitan complexes.) Will the need for child-care facilities be attenuated by a shorter workday for men and women? (A six-hour workday, for example, would permit parents to stagger their schedules so that one or the other of them was at home during most hours of the day.)

(4)   Will access to college-level adult educational facilities on a part- or full-time basis become ever more important as job competency requirements are altered by rapid technological change and as new leisure-time preferences emerge?

(5)   Will the high costs of supplying public services – as well as pensions and welfare payments – in combination with persistently high unemployment in problem regions and the core areas of large metropolitan complexes lead to public acceptance of the following proposition? A large share of the activity roles associated with the provision of care for children and the aged, health treatment, and other public services ought to be filled by young people compulsorily 'drafted' by the national government for a period of one or two years.

Quite clearly, if policy-makers and planners actually seek to up-grade quality-of-life conditions in problem regions they will have not only to come to grips with interregional inequalities of employment opportunity. They will also have to formulate strategies which are flexible enough to respond to the answers that begin to appear to the types of questions just stated.

Concluding remarks

There are no easy answers to the questions raised at the outset of this chapter. No easy answers are possible because – despite the materials presented in the previous chapter – the state of knowledge pertaining to the processes that generate metropolitan concentration and interregional economic and social inequalities ought be regarded as little more than primitive. No easy answers are possible because rapid change is the order of the day, because 'the stable state has been lost' (Schon, 1971), and because, consequently, planning institutions must become learning institutions and planning processes must involve learning feedback processes rather than the production of immutable regional development blueprints. Moreover, while empirically and conceptually founded suggestions of the type already made here may be in order, it should be kept in mind that political, social and cultural values and priorities vary considerably between economically advanced countries such as the US, Japan and Sweden. Therefore, it is quite unrealistic to proclaim universal regional development problem policy solutions that leave no room for the democratic expression of those values and priorities. All the same, on the basis of what has been said in this book, it may be appropriate to close by summarizing certain apparent realities that ought to be accepted by politicians and planners in all economically advanced countries if they are to develop strategies which will yield results that are consistent with their particular regional development or national settlement policy goals.

First, there are few, if any, circumstances where the employment and quality-of-life problems of 'backward', 'lagging' or 'depressed' regions in advanced economies can be ameliorated best by regional development policies which focus completely on the attraction or expansion of manufacturing establishments.

Secondly, except as a matter of luck, no regional planning or national settlement policy can be either goal-consistent or as successful as anticipated unless its formulation is preceded by studies establishing the particular structure of underlying growth-transmission interdependencies within the concerned regional and national city-systems. Unless the major self-reinforcing channels of inter-urban growth-transmission feedback are identified, they cannot be altered or manipulated. And, unless feedback channels are modified, planning authorities are very likely to preserve the status quo, their very actions preserving the 'is' inequality conditions fostered by economically dominant multilocational organizations rather than bringing about some new 'ought' equality conditions (cf. Olsson, 1974, 1975). Or, unless unverified and mistaken interurban growth transmission assumptions are cast aside, investment and resource allocations made by business and government organizations at specific places are apt to continue leading to sizable income and employment multipliers at other unanticipated places – perhaps even at places where the desired objective is dampened growth.

Thirdly, regional development policy-makers in advanced economies need to think in terms of the growth and development process
of the entire national system of cities, rather than confining their
attention to one or a few locations, regions or sectors. In this connection, it is especially important that the long-term feedbacks
created by spatial biases in the circulation and availability of specialized information be recognized and taken into account during policy
formulation.

Fourthly, given the high degree of interdependence typical of
'post-industrial' city-systems, regional development or national
settlement policy objectives cannot be met without some minimal
coordination of the explicit and *implicit* locational decision-making
of both private corporations and government organizations. This
means, among other things, that a completely *ad hoc* geographic
allocation of resources in association with legislation and executive
government action should be regarded as intolerable.

Finally and most importantly, if economically advanced capitalist
countries are to have seriously intended regional development or
national settlement policies, their policy-makers will have to face
up to the need to influence more directly the locational decision-
making of those self-interested multilocational business organizations
which directly or indirectly answer for a major share of all jobs, and
which are clearly the most important generators of interurban growth
transmission. 'Carrot' incentives for choosing problem regions and
permission obstacles to selecting large metropolitan complexes on
their own are insufficient to counteract many of the explicit and
implicit locational decisions that are contrary to policy goals (and,
that in addition, often produce public and personal diseconomies). If
serious, 'post-industrial' capitalist governments might well have to
make some difficult choices in order to obtain more direct influence
on where employment opportunities and related quality-of-life
improvements occur. These choices might include assuming partial
or total ownership of multilocational business organizations, ap-
pointing representatives to the management of such organizations,
or imposing stiff financial or tax penalties upon decisions involving
undesirable locations.[25] It is also probable that multilocational business organizations can be made more subject to influence on employment location and quality-of-life problems through some degree of
employee ownership and consumer representation on management
boards. If 'post-industrial' capitalist governments choose totally to
avoid the issue of influencing the locational behaviour of multiloca-

tional organizations, they may instead be forced by the accumulation of pressures to go into the business of acting as employer of last resort, through the operation of widely distributed job-guarantee offices.

Notes

Chapter 1 Basic problems and basic concepts (pp. 9–32)

(1) The decline of several large metropolitan complexes and the population growth of non-metropolitan counties in the US between 1970 and 1973 has been much publicized. However, roughly 73 per cent of the US population resided in metropolitan areas in 1973, and approximately 65 per cent of all 1970–3 US population growth occurred in metropolitan areas. Moreover, the counties with 10 or more per cent of their work force commuting to metropolitan areas accounted for about another 8 per cent of 1970–3 population growth, and were as a group the fastest growing counties in the country (Morrison, 1975). Finally, US non-metropolitan growth has to a considerable degree been associated with amenity-rich environments, but has hardly touched high unemployment regions such as Appalachia.

(2) The use of the term 'urban system' is intentionally refrained from owing to its inconsistent connotations. At times geographers and others utilize 'urban system' and 'system of cities' interchangeably. On other occasions the term is applied to individual cities, in which case the city is conceived as being comprised of various interacting and interdependent components.

(3) To the extent that the urban seats of power in small feudal and tribal states ruled over agricultural villages, it may be argued that the city and its subservient villages together composed a city-system. To the extent that agricultural villages had very few or no true urban functions, this position is refutable. Larger feudal states, of course, normally contained nascent systems of cities, i.e. two or more cities with some minimal degree of meaningful interaction and interdependence.

(4) The combination of the US and Canadian city-systems is also warranted by certain patterns of highly business-oriented air-passenger traffic. The volume of such traffic between Toronto and New

York is comparable to that between Toronto and Montréal, Canada's two largest metropolitan complexes. In addition, the flow of air passengers between Vancouver – Canada's third-ranking metropolitan complex – and Toronto and Montréal is comparable in size to that between Vancouver and the Los Angeles and San Francisco Bay Area metropolitan complexes. In fact Bourne (1975) has contended that: 'The Canadian urban system appears as a collection of highly regionalized subsystems, almost regional branch-plant economies, each one closely interrelated with neighboring American regions (in the west, Great Lakes, and Atlantic regions) . . .'

(5) Those previously unexposed to central-place theory are directed to Berry and Pred (1965) and Berry (1967) for a much more thorough introduction to the subject.

(6) For additional comments on the limits of Löschian central-place theory see Parr (1973b).

(7) Whenever the term information is employed in this book I, like Gould (1975), am referring to 'what we might legitimately call *real* information, the stuff acquired and used by human beings, as opposed to the binary-coded impulses of the electronic engineer that form a mislabelled area of theory' (i.e. information theory).

(8) In advanced economies rural-to-urban migration is now much less common than interurban migration simply because such a small portion of the total population resides in rural locations.

Chapter 2   Past growth: information circulation and channels of interdependence

(1) Given the physical expansion of individual urban complexes in advanced economies, especially since automobile ownership has become widespread, and given the frequent discrepancy between the spatial bounds of politically defined cities and the spatial bounds of functionally defined metropolitan units (which often include a great number of politically independent municipalities), it is normally quite difficult to achieve any measure of consistency when constructing urban population time series. In view of the growth and development concerns of this book, for any given date it is most meaningful to use population data based upon the functionally defined units of that time. Thus the reference to Metropolitan Economic Labour Areas, and the use of commuting-field and other functional criteria in Table 2.1.

(2)   Washington DC is arbitrarily excluded from the regional city-system rankings of Table 2.1 because its growth has derived largely from political rather than from strictly economic functions. The inclusion of Washington DC in the Northeastern regional system of cities would not significantly alter the long-term rank stability picture. The 1840 rank of Washington DC (including suburbs) would have been fifth, whereas its 1970 regional city-system rank would have been fourth.

(3)   The materials contained on pp. 39–84 are largely summarized from Pred (1973b). For further factual and methodological details and sources see that work and Pred (1971a, 1971b).

(4)   It is quite unlikely that the use of 1960 distances has led to any distortion in the potential values. This is so partly because of the relative stability of population centroids in almost all cases. In addition, any shift in the population gravity centre of a specific county between the mapped dates and 1960 could only alter its distances to other county centroids by a tiny percentage.

(5)   Place-by-place postal-receipt data do not exist for 1820. The correlation of 1822–40 receipt increases with 1820–40 population advances is permissible because the value of postage fees collected nationally in 1820 and 1822 was almost identical.

(6)   These figures should not suggest that all travel between New York and Philadelphia was undertaken by residents of the two places. However, each traveller, regardless of his city of residence or his ultimate destination, was a potential bearer of information to one or more New York or Philadelphia inhabitants.

(7)   See pp. 38–9, above.

(8)   The major goods involved are specified in Pred (1973b). Re-distributive shipments included either goods originating at one port and sent to a second to be reshipped out of the region, or goods originating outside the region and reshipped from one of the four ports to another.

(9)   This is somewhat misleading as to the extent of Philadelphia–Baltimore interdependence. See notes (c) and (f) in Table 2.5.

(10)   Here, and in the preceding discussion, the largest cities of the eastern Great Lakes and the Ohio and Upper Mississippi valleys are assigned to different regional city-systems because in 1840 there were still limited economic linkages between them. Today the two groups of cities may be regarded as members of a larger integrated regional system of cities.

(11)   The wholesaling-trading complex of pretelegraphic US cities

included four principal types of commercial activity: the coastal and interregional distribution of hinterland and local production; the hinterland and coastal redistribution of interregional and foreign imports; the foreign export of hinterland commodities; and the re-export of imported carrying-trade commodities. Although the whole-saling-trading complex as a whole dominated each urban economy, the relative importance of its four component functions varied over time and from city to city. Furthermore, almost all mercantile-city manufacturing activities (e.g. shipbuilding, printing, and the processing of sugar, tobacco, leather and other raw material imports) were either directly or indirectly linked to the wholesaling-trading functions of those places.

(12)   For an elaboration of this submodel see Pred (1973b), pp. 189–202.

(13)   Cf. earlier remarks (pp. 17–19) on the limitations of the hierarchical view of city-system interdependencies based on Christaller's central-place theory. In fairness, it should be stated that hierarchical-diffusion proponents (e.g. Robson, 1973) often allow for the simultaneous operation of neighbourhood effects.

(14)   By comparison, at no time between 1805 and 1840 did the population of these four major centres represent more than 4·9 per cent of the national total.

(15)   On the basis of some explicit, but simple probabilistic equations, this point is further developed in Pred (1973b, pp. 231–7). For other conceptual and empirical arguments against strictly hierarchical interpretations of interurban innovation diffusion see Sharp (1971); Brown and Cox (1971); and Cohen (1972).

(16)   The materials contained on pp. 85–92 and 94–7 are largely summarized from Pred (1966b). For further details and sources see that work and Pred (1965a, 1966a).

(17)   Unfortunately, data inconsistencies prevent the comparison of 1910 urban manufacturing figures with those for 1860 and 1890.

(18)   Owing to data inadequacies, these spatial distributional changes cannot be traced either back to 1860 or forward to 1910.

(19)   The few non-metropolitan counties of the Midwest that had neither absolute nor relative industrial reductions in their urban settlements during the 1870–1900 period were predominantly composed of cases where the virtual absence of manufacturing in 1870 distorted meagre absolute gains into impressive percentage increases. For example, seventeen of Iowa's eighteen 'non-conforming' counties had under 2·5 per cent of their respective 1900 populations employed

in manufacturing (Figure 2.14b), and in most of these instances the figure was actually well below 1·0 per cent.

(20) Cf. Myrdal (1957) on regional growth in the so-called 'dual' economies of developing nations.

(21) See pp. 30–1, above, for definitions of the italicized multiplier-effect types.

(22) This does not happen with *all* inventions or ideas, but, in fact, with only a small portion of them.

(23) That is, since non-threshold high-value-added industries are insensitive to transport costs and can serve extensive non-local as well as local markets, there are few, if any, economic limitations to the accumulation of adoptions at an initial or early adopting city – unless that city is not a large one and has a limited labour supply. Once such clustering occurs, success tends to breed success. 'Localization' economies become available, and new production technology innovations, often the result of competion, can spread locally before the initial product innovation has reached many other places.

(24) In these and other circumstances outlined below, market usurpation was not always equivalent to the total elimination of small-scale, small-city producers. Sometimes smaller manufacturers lost only part of their existing market area and continued to operate at a lower level of output. On other occasions, they held their own but failed to capture their share of increases in the local market that arose from population growth, purchasing power increments, or wider consumer acceptance of the products involved.

(25) The operation of external agglomeration economies is considered to have been of unique importance to the large-city concentration of US manufacturing prior to the First World War, and especially between 1860 and 1890. This is so since agglomeration diseconomies, such as high land costs and congestion, had not as yet reached oppressive levels.

Chapter 3   Present processes of change: multilocational organizations and the interurban transmission of growth

(1) The materials presented on pp. 99–181 to a considerable degree represent an elaboration and modification of ideas and data previously appearing in Pred (1973a, 1974a, 1974b, 1975a, 1975b, 1975c, 1976).

(2) Estimate based partly on figures appearing in Dun and Brad-

street Company (1974) and partly on data obtained from a survey of multilocational corporations and firms headquartered in selected metropolitan complexes of the western US.

(3)   Over the same period of time the foreign expansion of Philips and Unilever contributed to intraorganizational (and interorganizational) city-system interdependence in other countries as well as international linkages between those countries and the Netherlands.

(4)   If the Boeing Company's employment is subtracted from both the 1959 and 1974 Seattle–Tacoma totals, the resulting figures are 72 332 and 141 211. Thus, exclusive of the Boeing Company, the 1959–74 increase in employees controlled by multilocational business organizations headquartered in Seattle–Tacoma was no less than 95·2 per cent.

(5)   This observation should be tempered by the fact that metropolitan complexes in many other parts of the US had lower 1960–70 population growth rates than the western centres shown in Table 3.1.

(6)   Depending on the specific characteristics of a growing multilocational business organization, some office employment categories will expand more rapidly than others. In some instances office employment associated with market research, data processing, public relations or purchasing will increase most rapidly. In other instances the most rapid increases will fall to employment affiliated with planning, sales, research, personnel, legal, or yet other functions.

(7)   See Pred (1974b), especially pp. 5–6, for specific corporate examples.

(8)   Those unfamiliar with input-output analysis are referred to Isard (1960), pp. 309–74, and Richardson (1973a).

(9)   Occasionally, nationally functioning multilocational business organizations have only some of their components or divisions based on functional specialization, while other units or divisions are structured in geographically defined terms.

(10)   The group of 300 included the fifty largest organizations in each of the following categories: retailing, utilities, transportation, commercial banking, diversified financial and life insurance.

(11)   The fact that the New York metropolitan complex has lost a few major headquarters units in the last two years would seem to suggest that at some point the process described in Figure 3.1 may be countervailed by the diseconomies and negative features of the very largest metropolitan complexes. It is significant, however, that the units departing the New York complex without exception moved

to other relatively large metropolitan areas. During 1974–5, for example: Martin Marietta Corp. (a diversified manufacturing organization with close to 30000 employees) shifted its organization-wide head office to a Washington DC suburb; Cerro Corp. (a conglomerate with manufacturing emphasis and about 8000 employees) relocated its organization-wide headquarters to Chicago while leaving the highest offices of three of its divisions in New York; and Middle South Utilities (the fifteenth largest utility company in the US with well over 10000 employees) moved its organization-wide headquarters to New Orleans. In addition, tax and other considerations have caused numerous headquarters units to shift their location from the core of the New York metropolitan complex, Manhattan, to outer suburban locations in Connecticut and New Jersey.

(12) Even when contact-intensive employees are spatially proximate to each other in the same metropolitan complex, tightly packed individual schedules can raise a barrier (or what Hägerstrand (1970b; Pred, 1973c) would term a 'coupling constraint'), to their face-to-face meetings.

(13) The specialized information advantages of large metropolitan complexes can also be phrased in the language of that portion of Hägerstrand's 'time geography' framework that refers to the daily activity paths of individuals (Engström and Sahlberg, 1974; Törnqvist *et al.*, 1974).

(14) Polenske (1972, 1973) has supposedly demonstrated the methodological feasibility of carrying out input-output analyses that simultaneously deal with as many as forty areal units. However, her work was confined to freight flows, and thereby totally ignored intraorganizational and interorganizational service transactions over space. More significantly, of data-availability necessity, her basic areal unit was the individual US state and clusters of those states. From a city-system perspective this is highly inappropriate since many of the most important metropolitan complexes (e.g. New York, Chicago, Philadelphia and St Louis) span several states, while many populous states contain two or more metropolitan complexes with populations exceeding one million. For example, California contains the Los Angeles, San Francisco–Oakland–San Jose, and San Diego complexes, while Texas includes the Dallas–Fort Worth and Houston metropolitan complexes.

(15) The research reported on pp. 127–62 was undertaken with the aid of Larry Handle, to whom I would like to express my thanks.

(16) This was already suggested less clearly by Table 3.1, which

failed to distinguish between local, non-local US–Canadian, and foreign job control.

(17)   The gravity model states that interaction between two spatial units (I_{ij}) is determined by some variant of the following equation: $I_{ij} = kP_iP_j/D_{ijq}$, where P_i and P_j are the populations (or some other weighted measure) of the two units, D_{ij} is the distance separating units i and j, and k and q are empirically derived constants. Olsson (1965) is highly recommended to those previously unexposed to the gravity-model literature.

(18)   The exceptionally great relative importance of Honolulu's hinterland linkages is once more attributable to the traditional plantation-agriculture functions of its leading corporations and the metropolitan centre's time-zone and physical distances from the continental US.

(19)   The failure of the statement to hold for the Honolulu SMSA is quite understandable. See preceding note.

(20)   The direct transmission of growth to non-hinterland smaller towns and cities is not permitted here because it is presumed, in accord with Christaller-based diffusion hypotheses, that such urban places can only receive direct growth impulses from those metropolitan complexes within whose higher-order market area they are located.

(21)   See note (h) in Table 3.9 on the size-category assignment of the Phoenix SMSA.

(22)   Those unfamiliar with the methodology of trend surface mapping and analysis are directed to Chorley and Haggett (1965), King (1969) and Norcliffe (1969).

(23)   'Correspondent' banking ties occur when banks in one city carry accounts in the banks of another city, largely to facilitate interurban payments.

(24)   See pp. 30–1, above, for definitions of the italicized multiplier-effect types.

(25)   As employed in this model, 'services' may also refer to those functions performed by an administrative headquarters unit for other intraorganizational units.

(26)   The probabilistic aspects of this model are tentatively expressed as simple equations in Pred (1973a).

(27)   The new interurban interdependencies may be *intra*organizational, e.g. when a new production unit of necessity establishes linkages with an already existing sales or administrative unit located elsewhere. Or the new interdependencies may be *inter-*

organizational, e.g. when a new production or service unit has to obtain physical inputs or services from units located elsewhere within other organizations.
(28) Note, however, subsequent comments (pp. 188 ff.) on the frequently short life-span of 'trickled-down' factories.

Chapter 4 Future development options: office activities, services and the quality of life

(1) The use of migration stimulation as an alternative policy strategy for reducing interregional employment disparities is not discussed at length here. This alternative has at best yielded a very partial solution to regional unemployment problems and is no longer in extensive use anywhere. Induced migration schemes have been opposed in several European countries for being in conflict with democratic principles. In the 1930s the locational 'transference' of workers from Scotland and South Wales was generally met by 'resentment' or 'lack of enthusiasm'. Furthermore, from a strictly economic point of view, 'Moving workers to the work generally means pumping additional effective demand into a region that has an excess of it already' (Brown, 1972).
(2) In addition, in Great Britain, Sweden and elsewhere, employment has been bolstered in problem regions through the location and expansion of plants belonging to government-controlled industries.
(3) The 'development areas' consist of all of Scotland except for Edinburgh, Northern England, Merseyside, most of Wales, and a large part of the Southwest region.
(4) Very few industrial inventions actually become innovations, or enter into production.
(5) Evidence of the large scope of the 'trickling-down' effect has been complied for Great Britain (e.g. Keeble, 1971) and the US (e.g. Berry, 1973), as well as other advanced economies. It must be admitted that in the United Kingdom, at least, there is some question as to the relative closure vulnerability of 'trickled-down' branch plants. However, Keeble (1975) observes, with 'considerable caution', that imperfect 1945–65 data point to 'higher closure rates for [plant] moves to Development Area' problem regions than for moves to other regions.
(6) The likelihood of future out-migration is compounded by

the fact that the high-unemployment regions of advanced economies usually have comparatively high rates of natural increase.

(7)   Another 37 per cent of the total was to be dispersed to the 'intermediate areas', where moderate unemployment problems are characteristic. These areas include Edinburgh; the Northwest, Yorkshire and Humberside regions; the northern coast of Wales; and parts of the Southwest.

(8)   See note 7, above.

(9)   'The Swedish authorities obtained some limited experience . . . from [government] service relocations which took place in the early 1960s. The National Fishery Board had been established in Gothenburg [Göteborg] rather than in Stockholm. The headquarters of the National Defence Industries (Corporation) was moved in 1965 from Stockholm to Eskilstuna, one hundred miles to the west. In addition, the Central Statistics Bureau had set up a data preparation unit in Örebro, about 150 miles west of the capital city' (Thorngren, 1973).

(10)   A universal comparison is not possible between office- and factory-job creation costs, among other reasons because plants vary greatly in capital intensity. In addition, whether offices or plants are involved, the costs of relocation are likely to be very different from the costs for founding completely new units.

(11)   Habitual face-to-face contacts may persist, despite alternatives which are closer in terms of time and cost, either because limited search fails to identify those alternatives, or because decision-making authority continues to be exerted by a head-office or higher-level administrative unit located elsewhere which does not choose to alter existing relationships.

(12)   Some individuals and families may look forward to relocation due, for example, to the promise of a better climate or other physical amenities, or the possibility of resuming severed social or family ties.

(13)   In addition, poor scheduling may prohibit the completion of a meeting or trip within a single day and thereby add the costs of an overnight stay.

(14)   It should also be apparent that a scattered pattern of *interdependent* office activities would be synonymous with a very high total cost of non-local face-to-face contacts for the problem region as a whole.

(15)   By 1974, Morrison-Knudsen at one time or another had been responsible for major projects in sixty-six foreign countries and every

state of the US – including such landmarks as Hoover Dam and the the San Francisco–Oakland Bay Bridge.

(16) Boise, sheltered on two sides by a mile-high ridge, derived its name from the French *boisé* (wooded). This was in reference to its tree-lined river, which provided a welcome relief to early settlers who had just crossed the desolate Snake River plains.

(17) In 1957 the Boise Cascade Corp. was still a small non-diversified lumber company with operations confined to the US Pacific Northwest. Basically via vigorous merger activity the corporation had branched out into thirty-three product areas by the early 1970s. These included doors, cabinets and other building materials; sectionalized manufactured houses; paper and paper products; and office supply, equipment and furniture distribution. The only real setback suffered by Boise Cascade during this interlude resulted from a highly questionable and almost financially catastrophic venture into the development of recreation communities in locations spread from New Hampshire to Hawaii (Boschen, 1974).

(18) See Table 3.8 for populations.

(19) The size of Idaho's state government is small by US standards, since the state as a whole only has about 750 000 inhabitants.

(20) Note, however, that while aware of the importance of communications factors to office unit operations, very few multilocational organizations 'have any detailed knowledge about their existing contact patterns' and costs (Goddard, 1975).

(21) In large 'multinuclear' metropolitan complexes this category may also include a number of older and smaller central cities that were once physically independent, but which have been engulfed since the coming of the automobile.

(22) However, the unemployment difficulties of an independent Scotland, Wales, Brittany or Corsica could well become a matter of concern for Common Market economic-planning authorities in Brussels.

(23) As should be evident from the next paragraph, this minimal definition of 'quality of life' can be extended to encompass a variety of non-material components, including the political role which the individual is allowed to play.

(24) Even in the state of California, where automobile ownership rates are probably the highest in the world, a substantial portion of the adult population is without daytime personal access to a car. As recently as 1971, 41 per cent of those participating in the labour force of the San Francisco Bay Area had no access to a car for commuting

purposes, often because a single car had to be shared with a spouse. (25)   These alternatives are complicated by the fact that multilocational business organizations are often multinational in character. Therefore, efforts to influence more directly their locational decision-making could result in the transferral or creation of employment opportunities in other countries. Also, a system of penalties could cause domestic multilocational business organizations to eliminate altogether some job-promoting locational decisions.

References

English-language works

Aguilar, F. (1967), *Scanning the Business Environment.* Macmillan, New York.

Alonso, W. and Medrich, E. (1972), 'Spontaneous growth centers in twentieth century American urbanization', in N. M. Hansen (Ed.), *Growth Centers in Regional Economic Development*, pp. 229–65. The Free Press, New York.

Ansoff, H. I. (1965), *Corporate Strategy.* McGraw-Hill, New York.

Armstrong, R. B. (1972), *The Office Industry: Patterns of Growth and Location.* The MIT Press, Cambridge, Mass.

Artle, R. (1965), *The Structure of the Stockholm Economy.* Cornell University Press, Ithaca.

Bannister, G. (1975), 'Population change in southern Ontario', *Annals of the Association of American Geographers,* **65**, 177–88.

Beaujeu-Garnier, J. (1974), 'Toward a new equilibrium in France?', *Annals of the Association of American Geographers,* **64**, 113–25.

Bergsman, J., Greenston, P. and Healy, R. (1972), 'The agglomeration process in urban growth', *Urban Studies,* **9**, 263–88.

Berry, B. J. L. (1961), 'City size distribution and economic development', *Economic Development and Cultural Change,* **9**, 573–87.

Berry, B. J. L. (1964), 'Cities as systems within systems of cities', *Papers of the Regional Science Association,* **13**, 147–63.

Berry, B. J. L. (1967), *The Geography of Market Centers and Retail Distribution.* Prentice-Hall Inc., Englewood Cliffs, NJ.

Berry, B. J. L. (1968), *Theories of Urban Location.* Association of American Geographers, Washington DC.

Berry, B. J. L. (1969), 'Relationships between regional economic development and the urban system: The case of Chile', *Tijdschrift voor Econ. en Soc. Geografie,* **60**, 283–307.

Berry, B. J. L. (1972), 'Hierarchical diffusion: The basis of development filtering and spread in a system of cities', in N. M.

Hansen (Ed.), *Growth Centers in Regional Economic Development*, pp. 108–38. The Free Press, New York.

Berry, B. J. L. (1973), *Growth Centers in the American Urban System*. 2 vols., Ballinger Publishing Co., Cambridge, Mass.

Berry, B. J. L. and Horton, F. E. (1970), *Geographic Perspectives on Urban Systems*. Prentice-Hall Inc., Englewood Cliffs, N. J.

Berry, B. J. L. and Pred, A. R. (1965), *Central Place Studies: A Bibliography of Theory and Applications*. 2nd ed., Regional Science Research Institute, Philadelphia.

Beyers, W. B. (1974), 'On geographical properties of growth center linkage systems', *Economic Geography*, **50**, 203–18.

Blainey, G. (1966), *The Tyranny of Distance: How Distance Shaped Australia's History*. Sun Books, Melbourne.

Blair, J. M. (1972), *Economic Concentration: Structure, Behavior and Public Policy*. Harcourt Brace Jovanovich, Inc., New York.

Blau, P. M. (1972), Interdependence and hierarchy in organizations, *Social Science Research*, **1**, 1–24.

Borchert, J. R. (1967), 'American metropolitan evolution', *Geographical Review*, **57**, 301–32.

Borchert, J. R. (1972), 'America's changing metropolitan regions', *Annals of the Association of American Geographers*, **62**, 352–73.

Boschen, H. L. (1974), *Corporate Power and the Mismarketing of Urban Development: Boise Cascade Recreation Communities*. Praeger, New York.

Boudeville, J. R. (1966), *Problems of Regional Economic Planning*, The University Press, Edinburgh.

Bourne, L. (1974), 'Forecasting urban systems: Research design, alternative methodologies and urbanization trends with Canadian examples', *Regional Studies*, **8**, 197–210.

Bourne, L. (1975), *Urban Systems: Strategies for Regulation – A Comparison of Policies in Britain, Sweden, Australia and Canada*. Oxford University Press, London.

Bourne, L. and Gad, G. (1972), 'Urbanization and urban growth in Ontario and Canada: An overview', in L. Bourne and R. D. Mackinnon (Eds.), *Urban Systems Development in Canada: Selected Papers*, pp. 35–49. University of Toronto Press, Toronto.

Britton, J. N. H. (1974), 'Environmental adaptation of industrial plants: Service linkages, locational environment and organization', in F. E. I. Hamilton (Ed.), *Spatial Perspectives on Industrial Organization and Decision-Making*, pp. 363–90. John Wiley, New York.

Brown, A. (1972), *The Framework of Regional Economics in Great Britain*. Cambridge University Press, Cambridge, Eng.

Brown, L. A. (1975), 'The market and infrastructure context of adoption: A spatial perspective on the diffusion of innovation', *Economic Geography*, **51**, 185–216.

Brown, L. A. and Cox, K. R. (1971), 'Empirical regularities in the diffusion of innovation', *Annals of the Association of American Geographers*, **3**, 157–61.

Buckley, W. (1967), *Sociology and Modern Systems Theory*. Prentice-Hall Inc., Englewood Cliffs, NJ.

Burnley, I. (Ed.) (1974), *Urbanization in Australia: The Post-War Experience*. Cambridge University Press, Cambridge, Eng.

Burrows, E. M. (1973), 'Office Employment and the regional problem', *Regional Studies*, **9**, 17–29.

Cameron, G. C. (1974), 'Regional economic policy in the United Kingdom', in N. M. Hansen (Ed.), *Regional Policy and Regional Economic Development*, pp. 65–102. Ballinger Publishing Co., Cambridge, Mass.

Cameron, G. C. and Evans, A. W. (1973), 'The British conurbation centres', *Regional Studies*, **7**, 47–55.

Chandler, A. D., Jr. (1962), *Strategy and Structure*. The MIT Press, Cambridge, Mass.

Chandler, A. D., Jr. and Redlich, F. (1961), 'Recent developments in American business administration and their conceptualization', *Business History Review*, Spring, 103–28.

Chapman, K. (1974), 'Corporate systems in the United Kingdom petro-chemical industry', *Annals of the Association of American Geographers*, **64**, 126–37.

Child, J. (1973a), 'Parkinson's Progress: Accounting for the number of specialists in organizations', *Administrative Science Quarterly*, **18**, 328–48.

Child, J. (1973b), 'Predicting and understanding organization structure', *Administrative Science Quarterly*, **18**, 168–85.

Chisholm, M. (1974), 'Regional policies for the 1970s', *Geographical Journal*, **140**, 215–44.

Chisholm, M. and Oeppen, J. (1973), *The Changing Pattern of Employment: Regional Specialisation and Industrial Location in Britain*. Croom Helm, London.

Chorley, R. J. and Haggett, P. (1965), 'Trend surface mapping in geographical research', *Transactions of the Institute of British Geographers*, **37**, 47–67.

Christaller, W. (1966), *Central Places in Southern Germany*. Prentice-Hall Inc., Englewood Cliffs, NJ. Originally published in 1933 as *Die Zentralenen Orte in Süddeutschland*.

Clark, D. (1974), 'Technology, diffusion, and time-space convergence: The example of STD telephone', *Area*, **6**, 181–4.

Cohen, Y. S. (1972), *Diffusion of an Innovation in an Urban System: The Spread of Planned Shopping Centers in the United States: 1949–1968*. Department of Geography Research Paper No. 140, University of Chicago.

Cyert, R. M. and March, J. G. (1963), *A Behavioral Theory of the Firm*. Prentice-Hall Inc., Englewood Cliffs, NJ.

Daniels, P. W. (1975), *Office Location: An Urban and Regional Study*. G. Bell and Sons Ltd, London.

Darwent, D. F. (1969), 'Growth poles and growth centers in regional planning – A review', *Environment and Planning*, **1**, 5–32.

Davies, J. B. (1972), 'Behaviour of the Ontario–Quebec urban system by size distribution', in L. Bourne and R. D. Mackinnon (Eds.) *Urban Systems Development in Canada: Selected Papers*, pp. 35–49. University of Toronto Press, Toronto.

Deskins, D. R. (1973), 'Residence-workplace interaction vectors for the Detroit Metropolitan Area: 1953 to 1965', in M. Albaum (Ed.), *Geography and Contemporary Issues*, pp. 157–74. John Wiley, New York.

Deutsch, K. W. (1961), 'On social communication and the metropolis', *Daedalus*, 99–110.

Dicken, P. (1971) 'Some aspects of the decision making behavior of business organizations', *Economic Geography*, **47**, 426–37.

Dun and Bradstreet Company (1960–66, 1974), *Million Dollar Directory*. New York.

Duncan, B. and Leiberson, S. (1970), *Metropolis and Region Revisited*. Sage Publications, Los Angeles.

Duncan, O. D. Scott, W. R. Leiberson, S., Duncan, B. and Winsborough, H. H. (1960), *Metropolis and Region*. The Johns Hopkins Press, Baltimore.

Dunn, E. S. (1970), 'A flow network image of urban structures', *Urban Studies*, **7**, 239–58.

Earickson, R. A. (1972), 'The "lead firm" concept: An analysis of theoretical elements', *Tijdschrift voor Econ. en Soc. Geografie*, **63**, 426–37.

Earickson, R. A. (1974), 'The regional impact of growth firms: The case of Boeing, 1963–1968', *Land Economies*, **50**, 127–36.

Earickson, R. A. (1975), 'The spatial pattern of income generation in lead firm, growth area linkage systems', *Economic Geography*, **51**, 17–26.

EFTA Economic Development Committee (1974), *National Settlement Strategies: A Framework for Regional Development*. Secretariat of the European Free Trade Association, Geneva.

Engström, M.–G. and Sahlberg, B. (1973), *Travel Demand, Transport Systems and Regional Development: Models in Coordinated Planning*. Lund Studies in Geography, Series B, **39**.

Feller, I. (1975), 'Invention, diffusion and industrial location', in L. Collins and D. F. Walker (Eds.), *The Dynamics of Manufacturing Activity*, pp. 83–107.

Firn, J. R. (1974), *External Control and Regional Development: The Case of Scotland*. Department of Social and Economic Research, University of Glasgow.

Galbraith, J. K. (1973), *Economics and the Public Purpose*. Houghton Mifflin, Boston.

Gilmour, J. M. (1974), 'External economies of scale, interindustry linkages and decision making in manufacturing', in F. E. I. Hamilton (Ed.), *Spatial Perspectives on Industrial Organization and Decision-making*, pp. 335–62. John Wiley, New York.

Goddard, J. B. (1973a), 'Office employment, urban development and regional policy', in M. J. Bannon (Ed.), *Office Location and Regional Development*, pp. 21–36. An Foras Forbartha, Dublin.

Goddard, J. B. (1973b), *Office Linkages and Location: A Study of Communications and Spatial Patterns in Central London*. Pergamon Press, Oxford.

Goddard, J. B. (1975), *Office Location in Urban and Regional Development*. Oxford University Press, London.

Goddard, J. B. and Morris, D. (1975), *The Communications Factor in Office Decentralization*. Pergamon Press, Oxford.

Goodwin, W. (1965), 'The management center in the United States', *Geographical Review*, **55**, 1–16.

Gould, P. (1975), 'Acquiring spatial information', *Economic Geography*, **51**, 87–99.

Hägerstrand, T. (1965), 'Aspects of the spatial structure of social communication and the diffusion of information', *Papers of the Regional Science Association*, **16**, 27–42.

Hägerstrand, T. (1967), *Innovation Diffusion as a Spatial Process* (with postscript by A. R. Pred). Originally published in 1953 as

Innovationsförloppet ur korologisk synpunkt. C. W. K. Gleerup, Lund.

Hägerstrand, T. (1970b), 'What about people in regional science?', *Papers of the Regional Science Association*, **24**, 7–21.

Hale, C. W. (1972), 'Employment spread effects in Appalachia and the South', *Growth and Change*, **3**, 10–14.

Hall, P. (1971), 'Spatial structure of metropolitan England and Wales', in M. Chisholm and G. Manners (Eds.), *Spatial Policy Problems of the British Economy*, pp. 96–125. Cambridge University Press, Cambridge, Eng.

Hansen, N. M. (1971), *Intermediate-Size Cities as Growth Centers*. Praeger, New York.

Hansen, N. M. (1973), *Location Preferences, Migration, and Regional Growth: A Study of the South and Southwestern United States*. Praeger, New York.

Hansen, N. M. (Ed.) (1974), *Public and Regional Economic Development: The Experience of Nine Western Countries*. Ballinger Publishing Co., Cambridge, Mass.

Hansen, N. M. (1975a), 'An evaluation of growth-center theory and practice', *Environment and Planning*, **7**, 361–9.

Hansen, N. M. (1975b), 'Urban hierarchy, region and public policy', *Économie appliquée*, **28**, 165–83.

Harris, C. D. (1954), 'The market as a factor in the localization of industry in the United States', *Annals of the Association of American Geographers*, **44**, 315–48.

Harvey, D. (1973), *Social Justice and the City*. Johns Hopkins Press, Baltimore.

Hermansen, T. (1972), 'Development poles and development centers in national and regional development – elements of a theoretical framework', in A. R. Kuklinski (Ed.), *Growth Poles and Regional Policies*, pp. 1–67. Mouton, The Hague.

Huang, J.-C. and Gould, P. (1974), 'Diffusion in an urban hierarchy: The case of Rotary Clubs', *Economic Geography*, **50**, 333–40.

Hudson, J. C. (1969), 'Diffusion in a central place system', *Geographical Analysis*, **1**, 59–75.

Hudson, J. C. (1970), *Geographical Diffusion Theory*. Northwestern University Studies in Geography, **19**.

Hymer, S. (1972), 'The multinational corporation and the law of uneven development', in J. N. Bhagwati (Ed.), *Economics and the World Order: From the 1970s to the 1990s*, pp. 113–40. The Macmillan Co., London.

Isard, W. (1960), *Methods of Regional Analysis.* The MIT Press, Cambridge, Mass.

Isard, W. and Langford, T. W. (1971), *Regional Input-Output Study: Recollections and Diverse Notes on the Philadelphia Experience.* The MIT Press, Cambridge, Mass.

Janelle, D. G. (1969), 'Spatial reorganization: A model and concept', *Annals of the Association of American Geographers*, **59**, 348–64.

Jansen, A. V. M. (1970), 'The value of the growth pole theory for economic geography', *Tijdschrift voor Econ. en Soc. Geografie*, **61**, 67–76.

Jefferson, M. (1939), 'The law of the primate city', *Geographical Review*, **29**, 226–32.

Kabaya, R. (1971), *Development of Poor Regions: General Considerations and the Case of Japan.* Working Paper 159, Institute of Urban and Regional Development, University of California, Berkeley.

Katz, E. (1957), 'The two-step flow of communications: An up-to-date report on an hypothesis', *Public Opinion Quarterly*, **21**, 61–78.

Keeble, D. E. (1971), 'Employment mobility in Britain', in M. Chisholm and G. Manners (Eds.), *Spatial Policy Problems of the British Economy*, pp. 24–68. Cambridge University Press, Cambridge, Eng.

Keeble, D. E. (1975), 'Industrial mobility: In which industries has plant location changed most? – a comment', *Regional Studies*, **9**, 297–99.

King, L. J. (1969), *Statistical Analysis in Geography.* Prentice-Hall Inc., Englewood Cliffs, NJ.

Kongstad, P. (1974), 'Growth poles and urbanization: A critique of Perroux and Friedmann', *Antipode*, **6**, 114–21.

Krumme, G. (1970a), 'Comments on interregional subcontracting patterns and bilateral feedbacks', *Journal of Regional Science*, **10**, 237–42.

Krumme, G. (1970b), 'The interregional corporation and the region: A case study of Siemens growth characteristics and response patterns in Munich, West Germany', *Tijdschrift voor Econ. en Soc. Geografie*, **61**, 318–33.

Krumme, G. (1974), 'Regional policies in West Germany', in N. M. Hansen (Ed.), *Regional Policy and Economic Development*, pp. 103–35. Ballinger Publishing Co., Cambridge, Mass.

Krumme G. and Hayter, R. (1975), 'Implications of corporate strategies and product cycle adjustments for regional employment changes', in L. Collins and D. F. Walker (Eds.), *The Dynamics of Manufacturing Activity*, pp. 325–56. John Wiley, New York.

Lampard, E. R. (1955), 'The history of cities in the economically advanced areas', *Economic Development and Cultural Change*, 3, 81–136.

Lampard, E. R. (1968), 'The evolving system of cities in the United States: Urbanization and economic development', in H. S. Perloff and L. Wingo (Eds.), *Issues in Urban Economies*, pp. 81–139.

Lasuén, J. R. (1969), 'On growth poles', *Urban Studies*, 6, 137–61.

Lasuén, J. R. (1971), 'Multi-regional economic development: An open-system approach', in T. Hägerstrand and A. R. Kuklinski (Eds.), *Information Systems for Regional Development – A Seminar*, pp. 169–211. *Lund Studies in Geography*, Series B, 37.

Lasuén, J. R. (1973), 'Urbanization and development – The temporal interaction between geographical and sectoral clusters', *Urban Studies*, 10, 163–88.

Lever, W. (1974), 'Manufacturing linkages and the search for suppliers and markets', in F. E. I. Hamilton (Ed.), *Spatial Perspectives on Industrial Organization and Decision-making*, pp. 309–33. John Wiley, New York.

Logan, M. I. (1970), 'The process of regional development and its implications for planning', *Journal of the Geographical Association of Nigeria*, 3, 109–20.

Lonsdale, R. E. (1972), 'Manufacturing decentralization: The discouraging record in Australia', *Land Economics*, 48, 321–28.

Lorsch, J. W. and Allen III, S. A. (1973), *Managing Diversity and Interdependence: An Organizational Study of Multidivisional Firms*. Harvard University Graduate School of Business Administration, Division of Research, Boston.

Lösch, A. (1954), *The Economics of Location*. Yale University Press, New Haven.

Lukermann, F. (1966), 'Empirical expressions of nodality and hierarchy in a circulation manifold', *East Lakes Geographer*, 2, 17–44.

Madden, C. H. (1956), 'On some indications of stability in the growth of cities in the United States', *Economic Development and Cultural Change*, 4, 236–52.

Manners, G. (1974), 'The office in metropolis: An opportunity for shaping metropolitan America', *Economic Geography*, 50, 93–110.

Meier, R. L. (1962), *A Communications Theory of Urban Growth*. The MIT Press, Cambridge, Mass.

Mera, K. (1975), 'A multiple layer theory of national urban systems', in H. Swain and R. D. Mackinnon (Eds.), *Issues in the Management of Urban Systems*, pp. 134–54. International Institute for Applied Systems Analysis, Schloss Laxenburg, Austria.

Mønstad, M. (1974), 'François Perroux's theory of "growth pole" and "development pole": A critique', *Antipode*, **6**, 106–13.

Morrill, R. L. and Pitts, F. R. (1967), 'Marriage, migration and the mean information field', *Annals of the Association of American Geographers*, **57**, 401–22.

Morrison, P. A. (1975), *The Current Demographic Context of National Growth and Development*. The Rand Corporation, Santa Monica, Calif.

Moseley, M. J. (1973a), 'The impact of growth centres in rural regions – I: An analysis of spatial "patterns" in Brittany', *Regional Studies*, **7**, 57–75.

Moseley, M. J. (1973b), 'The impact of growth centres in rural regions – II: An analysis of spatial "flows" in East Anglia', *Regional Studies*, **7**, 77–94.

Moseley, M. J. and Townroe, P. M. (1973), 'Linkage adjustment following industrial movement', *Tijdschrift voor Econ. en Soc. Geografie*, **64**, 137–44.

Myrdal, G. (1957), *Economic Theory and Under-Developed Regions*. Gerald Duckworth and Co. Ltd, London.

Norcliffe, G. B. (1969), 'On the use and limitations of trend surface models', *Canadian Geographer*, **13**, 338–48.

North, D. J. (1973), *The Process of Locational Change in Different Manufacturing Organizations*. Occasional Papers No. 23, Department of Geography, University College, London.

Olsson, G. (1965), *Distance and Human Interaction*. Regional Science Research Institute, Philadelphia.

Olsson, G. (1974), 'Servitude and inequality in spatial planning: Ideology and methodology in conflict', *Antipode*, **6**, 16–21.

Olsson, G. (1975), *Birds in Egg*. Michigan Geographical Publication No. 15, University of Michigan, Ann Arbor.

Palm, R. and Pred, A. R. (1974), *A Time-Geographic Perspective on Problems of Inequality for Women*, Working Paper No. 236, Institute of Urban and Regional Development, University of California, Berkeley.

Parr, J. B. (1973a), 'Growth poles, regional development, and central place theory', *Papers of the Regional Science Association*, **31**, 173–212.

Parr, J. B. (1973b), 'Structure and size in the urban system of Lösch', *Economic Geography*, **49**, 185–212.

Pedersen, P. O. (1970), 'Innovation diffusion within and between national urban systems', *Geographical Analysis*, **2**, 203–54.

Penouil, M. (1969), 'An appraisal of regional development policy in the Aquitaine Region', in E. A. G. Robinson (Ed.), *Backward Areas in Advanced Economies*, pp. 62–112. Macmillan, London.

Penouil, M. (1972), 'Growth poles in underdeveloped regions and countries', in A. Kuklinski and R. Petrella (Eds.), *Growth Poles and Regional Policies*, pp. 119–43. Mouton, The Hague.

Perroux, F. (1950), 'Economic space: Theory and applications', *Quarterly Journal of Economics*, **64**, 89–104.

Phillips, B. D. (1972), 'A note on the spatial distribution of unemployment by occupation in 1968', *Journal of Regional Science*, **12**, 295–98.

Polenske, K. R. (1972), 'The implementation of a multiregional input-output model for the United States', in A. Brody and A. P. Carter (Eds.), *Input-Output Techniques*, pp. 171–89. North Holland Publishing Co., Amsterdam.

Polenske, K. R. (1973), 'An analysis of United States commodity freight shipments', in G. G. Judge and T. Takamaya (Eds.), *Studies in Economic Planning over Space and Time*, pp. 163–79. North Holland Publishing Co., Amsterdam.

Pondy, L. R. (1969), 'Effects of size, complexity and ownership on administrative intensity', *Administrative Science Quarterly*, **14**, 47–61.

Pred, A. R. (1962), *The External Relations of Cities during 'Industrial Revolution'*. Department of Geography Research Paper No. 76, University of Chicago.

Pred, A. R. (1965a), 'Industrialization, initial advantage, and American metropolitan growth', *Geographical Review*, **55**, 158–85.

Pred, A. R. (1965b), 'The concentration of high-value-added manufacturing', *Economic Geography*, **41**, 108–32.

Pred, A. R. (1966a), 'Some locational relationships between industrial inventions, industrial innovations and urban growth', *East Lakes Geographer*, **2**, 45–70.

Pred, A. R. (1966b), *The Spatial Dynamics of US Urban-Industrial Growth, 1800–1914: Interpretive and Theoretical Essays*. The MIT Press, Cambridge, Mass.

Pred, A. R. (1971a), 'Large-city interdependence and the preelectronic diffusion of innovations in the US, *Geographical Analysis*, 3, 165–81.

Pred, A. R. (1971b), 'Urban systems development and the long-distance flow of information through preelectronic US newspapers', *Economic Geography*, 47, 498–524.

Pred, A. R. (1973a), 'The growth and development of systems of cities in advanced economies', in A. R. Pred and G. E. Törnqvist, *Systems of Cities and Information Flows: Two Essays*, pp. 1–82. *Lund Studies in Geography*, Series B, 38.

Pred, A. R. (1973b), *Urban Growth and the Circulation of Information: The United States System of Cities, 1790–1840*. Harvard University Press, Cambridge, Mass.

Pred, A. R. (1973c), 'Urbanisation, domestic planning problems and Swedish geographic research', *Progress in Geography*, 5, 1–76.

Pred, A. R. (1974a), 'Industry, information and city-system interdependencies', in F. E. I. Hamilton (Ed.), *Spatial Perspectives on Industrial Organization and Decision-making*, pp. 105–39. John Wiley, New York.

Pred, A. R. (1974b), *Major Job-Providing Organizations and Systems of Cities*. Association of American Geographers, Commission on College Geography Resource Paper No. 27. Washington DC.

Pred, A. R. (1975a), 'Diffusion, organizational spatial structure, and city-system development', *Economic Geography*, 51, 252–68.

Pred, A. R. (1975b), 'Growth transmission within the Australian system of cities: General observations and study recommendations', *Cities Commission Occasional Paper No. 3*, pp. 30–55. Australian Government Publishing Service, Canberra.

Pred, A. R. (1975c), 'On the spatial structure of organizations and the complexity of metropolitan interdepencence', *Papers of the Regional Science Association*, 35, 115–42.

Pred, A. R. (1976), 'The interurban transmission of growth in advanced economies: Empirical findings versus regional-planning assumptions', *Regional Studies*, 10, 151–71.

Prud'Homme, R. (1974), 'Regional economic policy in France', in N. M. Hansen (Ed.), *Regional Policy and Regional Economic Development*, pp. 33–63. Ballinger Publishing Co., Cambridge, Mass.

Pyle, G. F. (1969), 'The diffusion of cholera in the United States in the nineteenth century', *Geographical Analysis*, 1, 59–75.

Rhodes, J. and Kan, A. (1971), *Office Dispersal and Regional Policy*. Cambridge University Press, Cambridge, Eng.

Richardson, H. W. (1972), 'Optimality in city size, systems of cities and urban policy: A sceptic's view', *Urban Studies*, **9**, 29–48.

Richardson, H. W. (1973a), *Input-output and Regional Economics*. John Wiley, New York.

Richardson, H. W. (1973b), *Regional Growth Theory*. John Wiley, New York.

Robinson, E. A. G. (Ed.) (1969), *Backward Areas in Advanced Countries*. Macmillan Co., London.

Robson, B. T. (1973), *Urban Growth: An Approach*. Methuen and Co., London.

Rogers, E. M. and Shoemaker, F. F. (1971), *The Communication of Innovations: A Cross-Cultural Approach*. The Free Press, New York.

Rushing, W. A. (1967), 'The effects of industry size and division of labor on administration', *Administrative Science Quarterly*, **12**, 273–95.

Rust, E. (1975), *No Growth: Impacts on Metropolitan Areas*. D. C. Heath, Lexington, Mass.

Salt, J. (1967), 'The impact of the Ford and Vauxhall plants on employment on Merseyside, 1962–65', *Tijdschrift voor Econ. en Soc. Geografie*, **58**, 255–63.

Schon, D. A. (1967), *Technology and Change: The New Heraclitus*. Dell Publishing Co., New York.

Schon, D. A. (1971), *Beyond the Stable State*. Random House, New York.

Semple, R. K. (1973), 'Recent trends in the spatial concentration of corporate headquarters', *Economic Geography*, **49**, 309–18.

Sharp, V. L. (1971), 'The 1970 postal strikes: Diffusion with a behavioral twist', *Proceedings of the Association of American Geographers*, **3**, 157–61.

Sidwell, E. (1974a), *The Attitudes of Firms and Local Authorities to Office Centralisation and Office Development*. Discussion Paper No. 53, Graduate Geography Department, London School of Economics and Political Science.

Sidwell, E. (1974b), *The Problem for Employees in Office Dispersal: A Methodology*. Discussion Paper No. 48, Graduate Geography Department, London School of Economics and Political Science.

Simmons, J. W. (1974a), *Canada as an Urban System: A Conceptual Framework*. Research Paper No. 62, Centre for Urban and Community Studies, University of Toronto.

Simmons, J. W. (1974b), *The Growth of the Canadian Urban System*.

Research Paper No. 65, Centre for Urban and Community Studies, University of Toronto.

Simmons, J. W. (1975), *Canada: Choices in a National Urban Strategy*. Research Paper No. 70, Centre for Urban and Community Studies, University of Toronto.

Smailes, A. E. (1957), *The Geography of Towns*. Hutchinson, London.

Smith, D. M. (1971), *Industrial Location: An Economic Geographical Analysis*. John Wiley, New York.

Steed, G. P. F. (1971), 'Changing processes of corporate environment relations', *Area*, 3, 207–11.

Steele, D. B. (1969), 'Regional multipliers in Great Britain', *Oxford Economic Papers*, 21, 268–92.

Stephens, F. H. (1975), 'The Hardman report: A critique', *Regional Studies*, 9, 111–16.

Stewart, R. (1967), *Managers and Their Jobs*. Macmillan, London.

Stilwell, F. J. B. (1974), 'Economic factors and the growth of cities', in I. H. Burnley (Ed.), *Urbanization in Australia: The Post-War Experience*, pp. 9–43. The University Press, Cambridge, Eng.

Sundqvist, J. L. (1975), *Dispersing Population: What America Can Learn from Europe*. Brookings Institution, Washington DC.

Thompson, D. (1974), 'Spatial interaction data', *Annals of the Association of American Geographers*, 64, 560–75.

Thompson, W. R. (1965), *A Preface to Urban Economics*. Johns Hopkins Press, Baltimore.

Thorngren, B. (1970), 'How do contact systems affect regional development?', *Environment and Planning*, 2, 409–27.

Thorngren, B. (1973), 'Communications studies for government office dispersal in Sweden', in M. J. Bannon (Ed.), *Office Location and Regional Development*, pp. 47–58. An Foras Forbartha, Dublin.

Toby, J. (1973), 'Regional development and government office relocation in the Netherlands', in M. J. Bannon (Ed.) *Office Location and Regional Development*, pp. 37–46. An Foras Forbartha, Dublin.

Todd, D. (1973), *The Development Pole Concept and its Application to Regional Analysis: An Appraisal of the Art*. Discussion Paper No. 47, Graduate Geography Department, London School of Economics and Political Science.

Todd, D. (1974), 'An appraisal of the development pole concept in regional analysis', *Environment and Planning*, 6, 291–306.

Törnqvist, G. E. (1970), *Contact Systems and Regional Development*. *Lund Studies in Geography*, Series B, **35**.

Törnqvist, G. E. (1973), 'Contact requirements and travel facilities: Contact models of Sweden and regional development alternatives in the future', in A. R. Pred and G. E. Törnqvist, *Systems of Cities and Information Flows: Two Essays*, pp. 83–121. *Lund Studies in Geography*, Series B, **38**.

Törnqvist G. E. (1975), 'Spatial organization of activity spheres', in H. Swain and R. D. Mackinnon (Eds.), *Issues in the Management of Urban Systems*, pp. 226–65. International Institute for Applied Systems Analysis, Schloss Laxenburg, Austria.

Vance, J. E. (1970), *The Merchant's World: The Geography of Wholesaling*. Prentice-Hall Inc., Englewood Cliffs, NJ.

Vapnarsky, C. A. (1969), 'On rank size distributions of cities: An ecological approach', *Economic Development and Cultural Change*, **17**, 584–95.

von Böventer, E. (1973), 'City size systems: Theoretical issues, empirical regularities and planning guides', *Urban Studies*, **10**, 145–62.

Walker, D. F. (1975), 'Governmental influence on manufacturing location: Canadian experience with special reference to the Atlantic Provinces', *Regional Studies*, **9**, 203–17.

Wärneryd, O. (1968), *Interdependence in Urban Systems*. Regionkonsult Aktiebolag, Göteborg.

Weissglas, G. (1975), *Studies on Service Problems in the Sparsely Populated Areas in Northern Sweden*. Geographical Reports, No. 5, University of Umeå.

Westaway, J. (1974a), 'Contact potential and the occupational structure of the British urban system, 1961–1966: An empirical study', *Regional Studies*, **8**, 57–73.

Westaway, J. (1974b), 'The spatial hierarchy of business organizations and its implications for the British urban system', *Regional Studies*, **8**, 145–55.

Whebell, C. F. J. (1969), 'Corridors: A theory of urban systems', *Annals of the Association of American Geographers*, **59**, 1–26.

White, H. C. (1970), *Chains of Opportunity: System Models of Mobility in Organizations*. Harvard University Press, Cambridge, Mass.

Williams, B. R. and Scott, W. D. (1970), *Investment Proposals and Decisions*. George Allen and Unwin, London.

Williamson, O. E. (1970), *Corporate Control and Business Behavior:*

An Inquiry into the Effects of Organization Form on Enterprise Behavior. Prentice-Hall Inc., Englewood Cliffs, NJ.

Wilmoth, D. (1974), 'Communications in the urban system', *Journal of the Proceedings of the Ecological Society of Australia*, **8**, 211–30.

Wingo, L. (1973), 'The quality of life: Toward a micro-economic definition', *Urban Studies*, **10**, 3–18.

Yannopoulos, G. (1973), 'The impact of office relocation on the local economy of the reception areas', in M. J. Bannon (Ed.), *Office Location and Regional Development*, pp. 59–71. An Foras Forbartha, Dublin.

Zaltman, G., Duncan, R. and Holbek, J. (1973), *Innovations and Organizations*. John Wiley, New York.

Zelinsky, W. (1971), 'The hypothesis of the mobility transition', *Geographical Review*, **61**, 219–49.

Zipf, G. K. (1941), *National Unity and Disunity*. Principia Press, Bloomington, Ind.

Foreign-language works
*indicates English summary included

*Ahnström, L. (1973), *Styrande och ledande verksamhet i Västeuropa- en ekonomisk-geografisk studie*. Ekonomiska Forskningsinstitut vid Handelshögskolan i Stockholm, Stockholm.

Bylund, H. and Ek, T. (1974), 'Regionala beroendeförhållanden– en studie av näringslivet i Malmö A-region', in Statens offentliga utredningar (SOU) 1974:3, *Produktionskostnader och regionala produktionssystem*, pp. 489–520. Allmänna Förlaget, Stockholm.

*Claval, P. (1973), 'Le système urbain et les réseaux d'information', *Revue Géographique de Montréal*, **27**, 5–15.

Engström, M.-G. (1974), 'Förändringar i den regionala arbetsfördelningen', in ERU (Expertgrupp för regional utredningsverksamhet), *Samhällsutvecklingen i storstäderna*, pp. 129–90. Arbetsmarknadsdepartementet (Ministry of Labour), Stockholm.

Engström, M.-G. and Sahlberg, B. W. (1974), 'Kommunikationer och regional utveckling – nuvarande och framtida utvecklingslinjer', in Statens offentliga utredningar (SOU) 1974:3, *Produktionskostnader och produktionssystem*, pp. 253–323. Allmänna Förlaget, Stockholm.

Erson, O. (1974), 'Skellefteå regionen – företag och marknader', in Statens offentliga utredningar (SOU) 1974:3, *Produktionskost-*

nader och regional produktionssystem, pp. 553–78. Allmänna Förlaget, Stockholm.

ERU (Expertgrupp för regional utredningsverksamhet) (1974), *Samhällsutvecklingen i storstäderna*. Arbetsmarknadsdepartementet (Ministry of Labour), Stockholm.

Fredriksson, C. and Lindmark, L. (1974), 'Lokala underleveranser i Skellefteå A-region', in Statens offentliga utredningar (SOU) 1974:3, *Produktionskostnader och regionala produktionssystem*, pp. 527–52. Allmänna Förlaget, Stockholm.

*Godlund, S. (1972), *Näringsliv och styrcentra, produktutveckling och trygghet*. Meddelanden från Göteborgs Universitets Geografiska institutioner, Series B, No. 25.

Godlund, S., Nordström, L., Godlund, K. and Lorentzon, S. (1973), *Örebro kommun: Utvecklingsmöjligheter och handlingsprogram för en bättre struktur*. Regionkonsult Aktiebolag, Göteborg.

Hägerstrand, T. (1970a), 'Tidsanvändning och omgivningsstruktur', in Statens offentliga utredningar (SOU) 1970:14, *Urbaniseringen i Sverige – En geografisk samhällsanalys*, pp. 4:1 – 4:146. Allmänna Förlaget, Stockholm.

Hägerstrand, T. (1972), 'Tätortsgrupper som regionsamhällen: Tillgången till förvärvsarbete och tjänster utanför de större städerna', in ERU (Expertgruppen för regional utredningsverksamhet), *Regioner att leva i*, pp. 141–73. Allmänna Förlaget, Stockholm.

Hägerstrand, T. (1975), 'Tidsgeografisk beskrivning: Syfte och postulat', *Svensk Geografisk Årsbok*, **50**, 86–94.

Hägerstrand, T., Ellegård, K. and Lenntorp, B. (1975), *Två framtidsbilder av verksamhetsformer och resebehov*. Kulturgeografiska Institutionen, Lunds Universitet, Lund.

Hägerstrand, T., Mårtensson, S, Lenntorp, B., Jenstav, M. and Wallin, E. (1974), 'Ortssystem och levnadsvillkor', in Statens offentliga utredningar (SOU) 1974:2, *Ortsbundna levnadsvillkor*, pp. 219–333. Allmänna Förlaget, Stockholm.

Herlitz, C. (1974), 'Falun-Borlänge – en komponent i det nationella produktionssystemet', in Statens offentliga utredningar (SOU) 1974:3, *Produktionskostnader och regionala produktionssystem*, pp. 459–88. Allmänna Förlaget, Stockholm.

*Jansen, A. C. M. (1972), 'Enkele aspekter van het ruimtelijk gedrag van grote industriele concerns in Nederland, 1950–1971', *Tijdschrift voor Econ. en Soc. Geografie*, **63**, 411–25.

Jenstav, M. (1975), 'Samtidighetskonflikter vid uttag av persontid', *Svensk Geografisk Årsbok*, **50**, 136–47.

Lenntorp, B. (1975), 'Grupperingar och arrangemang av odelbara enheter', *Svensk Geografisk Årsbok*, **50**, 95–113.

Mårtensson, S. (1975), 'Primärgrupp, sekundärgrupp och förbrukningen av persontid', *Svensk Geografisk Årsbok*, **50**, 126–35.

Nordström, L. (1968), *Organisationer i rummet*. Kulturgeografiska Institutionen vid Göteborgs Universitet, Göteborg.

*Nordström, L. (1971), *Rumsliga förändringar och ekonomisk utveckling*. Regionkonsult Aktiebolag, Göteborg.

Nordström, L. (1974), 'Mellanregionala beroende – maktens regionala koncentration', in Statens offentliga utredningar (SOU) 1974:3, *Produktionskostnader och regionala produktionssystem*, pp. 345–69. Allmänna Förlaget, Stockholm.

Pedersen, P. O. (1971), 'Vaekscentrer og byssystemer', *Økonomi og Politik*, 141–67.

Perroux, F. (1955), 'Note sur la notion de pôle de croissance,' *Économie Appliquée*, **8**, 307–20.

*Persson, C. (1974), *Kontaktarbete och framtida lokaliseringsförändringar*. C. W. K. Gleerup, Lund.

Pottier, P. (1963), 'Axes de communication et théorie de développement', *Revue Économique*, **14**, 70–128.

*Törnqvist, G. E. and research associates (1975), 'Lokalisering i det efterindustriella samhället – studier av kontakter och transporter', *Svensk Geografisk Årsbok*, **50**, 34–85.

Wallin, E. (1974), 'Yrkeskarriär och stabilitet i bosättningen', in Statens offentliga utredningar (SOU) 1974:2, *Ortsbundna levnadsvillkor*, pp. 298–322. Allmänna Förlaget, Stockholm.

Wärneryd, O. (1975), 'Boende och sysselsättning – ett scenario inom kulturgeografin', *Svensk Geografisk Årsbok*, **50**, 7–12.

Index